The Least Dangerous Branch?

The Least Dangerous Branch?

Consequences of Judicial Activism

Stephen P. Powers and Stanley Rothman

*Under the auspices of the Center for the Study of Social and
Political Change, Smith College*

 PRAEGER

Westport, Connecticut
London

Library of Congress Cataloging-in-Publication Data

Powers, Stephen, 1961–
   The least dangerous branch? : consequences of judicial activism / Stephen P. Powers
and Stanley Rothman.
      p. cm.
   "Under the auspices of the Center for the Study of Social and Political Change, Smith College."
   Includes bibliographical references and index.
   ISBN 0–275–97536–3 (alk. paper)—ISBN 0–275–97537–1 (pbk. : alk. paper)
      1. Courts—United States.   2. Political questions and judicial power—United States.   3.
United States.   Supreme Court   I. Rothman, Stanley, 1927–   II.   Smith College. Center for
the Study of Social and Political Change.   III. Title.
   KF5130.P69 2002
   347.73′1—dc21   2002025311

British Library Cataloguing in Publication Data is available.

Library of Congress Catalog Card Number: 2002025311
ISBN: 0–275–97536–3 hc   0–275–97537–1 pb

First published in 2002

Praeger Publishers, 88 Post Road West, Westport, CT 06881
An imprint of Greenwood Publishing Group, Inc.
www.praeger.com

Printed in the United States of America

The paper used in this book complies with the
Permanent Paper Standard issued by the National
Information Standards Organization (Z39.48–1984).

10   9   8   7   6   5   4   3   2   1

Stephen P. Powers: To family, friends, and especially Caitlin, Hannah, and Bev

Stanley Rothman: To Ellie

Contents

Preface

In 1962 Alexander Bickel called the U.S. Supreme Court the least dangerous branch because of the inevitable limitations it accepted as part of its mandate. Bickel's analysis no longer holds. The Court has taken on an increasingly large role in influencing American public policy.

This book assesses the impact of judicial intervention in the areas of busing, affirmative action, prisons, mental health policy, law enforcement, and voting rights. It also explores the consequences of judicial activism for broader social, political, and legal trends in the United States.

This study is sponsored by the Center for the Study of Social and Political Change, directed by Stanley Rothman, and has been supported with grants from the Olin Foundation, the Sarah Scaife Foundation, and the Earhart Foundation. We wish to thank all those who read and commented on the manuscript, especially R. Shep Melnick of Boston College. We also wish to acknowledge the following individuals for reviewing various chapters of the manuscript: Lisa Budzynski, Leonard Leo, Roger Clegg, Kent Scheidegger, Algert Agricola, Jr., Ronald Rychlak, and Greg Coleman. Their comments and criticisms were very helpful. We wish to thank Janice Mason for just about everything.

Introduction: Hamilton, Bickel, Democracy, and the Courts

This book synthesizes a significant amount of legal scholarship and empirical study of some of the most controversial social and political issues that confronted Americans in the latter half of the twentieth century. It is a most telling commentary on modern judicial power that controversial court rulings have played an important role in informing the American public about issues such as desegregation and busing, affirmative action, voting rights, prison reform, rights of the accused, and deinstitutionalization of the mentally ill. In some respects this is a positive development. By clarifying the status of various rights claims, the Supreme Court has contributed to America's awareness of, and policies to address, troublesome social and political problems. Yet there is another side to our judicial edification. Only in the past fifty years has the Court been so systematically involved with social, economic, and political questions central to the nation's order and well-being, and this suggests a potential imbalance in our national institutions. Today's courts are "activist" courts.

Since John Marshall established the precedent for judicial review in *Marbury v. Madison* (1803), the Supreme Court has exercised this power to interpret the meaning of the Constitution. When we speak of "judicial activism," we must be careful not to confuse it with the power of judicial review itself. The fact that the judiciary interprets the Constitution and other laws in one way or another is not in itself indicative of judicial activism at all. What the Supreme Court and the lower federal judiciary have been engaged in during the past fifty years is the systematic application of jurisdictional principles derived from the Constitution (and in many cases these derivations have been matters of intense controversy) to the reform of public institutions. To provide specific examples from the areas we will be evaluating, the federal judiciary has intervened to alter the operation of public schools, colleges, and universities, corporations, correctional facilities, police departments, mental health facilities, and electoral districts.

In the areas we examine, the courts seem to conform to one of the following general patterns. In the cases of prison litigation, mental health reform, rights of the accused, and busing, a court finds an institution or number of institutions in violation of a particular Bill of Rights provision—frequently in a class-action lawsuit. It strikes down the practice or law deemed to be violative of the right, providing a legal rationale in the ruling. The court proposes a remedy, or set of minimal standards, intended to correct the violation within the institution. The remedy is then applied at an institutional level (that is, well beyond the confines of the original case) and becomes an accepted remedy, or perhaps the only acceptable remedy, to the perceived violation. The remedy is either upheld on appeal to the Supreme Court, or the Supreme Court creates its own remedy or standards in order to provide guidance to the lower courts. This process attracts enough attention to provide a useful precedent for other courts, and the ruling gains notoriety in and out of the legal system. The number of cases raising similar issues begins to mushroom. The federal courts begin to impose similar mandates on institutions similarly situated throughout the entire nation.

The second type of activism, exemplified in the affirmative-action and voting rights areas, involves a reinterpretation of statutory law that amounts to a substantial alteration of the intent of Congress in enacting the law. Rather than discovering and adhering to the legislature's intent at the time of enactment, the judiciary redirects implementation and enforcement of the law according to a reconstructed meaning of the statute. This is most clearly exemplified by *Griggs v. Duke Power Co.* (1971), which shifted the emphasis of the Civil Rights Act toward proportional representation in employment, and by *Allen v. State Board of Elections* (1969) and *Thornburg v. Gingles* (1986), which shifted the Voting Rights Act toward proportional representation in redistricting. Thus we might say that when courts impose a remedy or set of remedies or standards, mixing a large measure of legislative (policy-making) and/or executive (enforcement) power into the process of interpreting law, they are being more activist. That is what we are referring to when we talk about judicial activism in this book. The Supreme Court's decision in the 2000 presidential election seems an entirely different type of decision. Overruling a state supreme court decision by interpreting the meaning of the equal protection clause in ways that we may agree or disagree with does not neatly conform to either of the two patterns we have observed in our study. That is not to say that it could not be considered an activist ruling, only that it seems quite different from the cases we have examined. Moreover, it is undoubtedly too soon to assess the consequences of such a decision for the political system, which is what we are interested in doing here.

At the nation's founding Alexander Hamilton (perhaps the strongest advocate of a powerful and independent judiciary) was quite sanguine about the judiciary's integral, yet circumscribed and relatively modest, role in the American constitutional order. It was, after all, the intention of the framers to create a limited government that could be popularly controlled and at the same time be capable of controlling itself. As part of this plan for government, the judiciary would provide a check on the legislature (and in some cases the executive) through its exercise of judicial review. In Hamilton's words, the Court would stand as "an intermediate body between the people and the legislature, in order, among other things, to keep the latter within the limits assigned to their authority" (Hamilton, Madison, and Jay, 1961, 78).

Given the historical legacy of the abuses of monarchy and parliamentary government, the framers were understandably convinced that other institutions were more likely to aggrandize power than the courts they were establishing. Hamilton apparently regarded the judiciary as the least dangerous branch and depicted it as such in *Federalist* 78:

Whoever attentively considers the different departments of power must perceive, that in a government in which they are separated from each other, the judiciary, from the nature of its functions, will always be the least dangerous to the political rights of the constitution; because it will be least in a capacity to annoy or injure them. The executive not only dispenses the honors, but holds the sword of the community. The legislature not only commands the purse, but prescribes the rules by which the duties and rights of every citizen are to be regulated. The judiciary on the contrary has no influence over either the sword or the purse, no direction either of the strength or of the wealth of the society; and must ultimately depend upon the aid of the executive arm even for the efficacy of its judgments. (Hamilton, Madison, and Jay, 1961, 78)

Despite Hamilton's characterization, the Supreme Court was to become a controversial and powerful institution within a few decades of its establishment. Except during a few brief periods of crisis, as the nation grew in wealth and power, so too did the prestige and influence of the Supreme Court (Lasser, 1988; Schwartz, 1993).

In a general sense much of the growth of judicial power is attributable to the historical transformation of America into a modern welfare state. Though it seems trite to say so at the beginning of the twenty-first century, none of the framers could possibly have envisioned the truly awesome power and complexity of American society full grown from its seed in European culture and commerce.

A strong scholarly tradition extending from Hamilton himself argues that the judiciary remains comparatively weak in a comparatively weak American state. Our contention is that while this line of thinking contains important truths, because it takes into account important institutional and political limitations on the judiciary, it underestimates the strategic advantages accruing to modern courts because they function in a heavily bureaucratic policy-making environment. Much like the vast growth in federal regulation with which it is intimately entangled, the expansion of judicial power has been a gradually developing phenomenon, a seemingly endless procession of small steps, leading over time to a tremendous aggregation of authority. The courts have extended their reach into so many areas and the jagged trail of legal precedent has become so voluminous and complex that it is virtually inconceivable that it could be in any way discarded without threatening prolonged disruption of the political system or even systemic failure. This long-term trend is partly attributable to the inherent power Hamilton and the illustrious practitioner John Marshall secured for the judiciary. It is also partly due to unforeseen historical circumstances. Before turning to the more intriguing question of how judicial power has expanded, we should first take stock of some of the arguments that emphasize the continued weakness of the judiciary.

As we have already suggested, Hamilton himself seems to have regarded the judiciary as "beyond comparison the weakest of the three departments of power." He cited Montesquieu's observation that the relative power of the judiciary is "next to nothing" (Hamilton, Madison, and Jay, 1961, 78). Assessing judicial power in the twentieth century, in 1957 Robert Dahl concluded that the Supreme Court was not a very powerful institution (Dahl, 1957). The Court continued to be dependent upon the executive branch for implementation of its decisions and remained in a merely reactive position to Congress and the state legislatures. Even when it did act against legislatures, it could only do so to uphold a higher constitutional principle. It never functioned as a "council of revision," an institution that was contemplated, but did not survive the deliberations of the Constitutional Convention. A council of revision would have been a more purely policy-making adjunct to the legislative branch, continually "revising" legislation. Perhaps most important, according to Dahl, the Court was always susceptible to massive resistance when it strayed too far from majority will.

Similarly, Alexander Bickel argued brilliantly, even in the wake of the Supreme Court's controversial and historic *Brown* desegregation decision, that the judiciary remained the "least dangerous branch," as Hamilton had depicted it. In *The Least Dangerous Branch* (1962) Bickel assures us that judicial review is a legitimate and integral part of the American political order, and he sets out to define the scope of its appropriate exercise. Bickel begins with the jurisprudence of John Marshall and with the question of whether the courts, rather than the president or Congress, should decide upon the constitutionality of a statute. Bickel argues that there is no clear authorization of judicial review in the Constitution but that the intent of the framers suggests that the power is legitimate. The principal problem, and it is a purely political one, is that when the Supreme Court strikes down a federal or state law, it acts contrary to the will of elected officials. This is the "counter-majoritarian difficulty" inherent in judicial power (Bickel, 1962:16–17).

Bickel's own formulation of the Court's appropriate role, the thesis of his book, is that its unique function is to judge on the basis of principle. Legislatures and the president are not sufficiently insulated from political pressure to make difficult principled decisions. Courts are not perfectly suited to this task either, but Bickel argues that they are better. "Judges have, or should have, the leisure, the training, and the insulation to follow the ways of the scholar in pursuing the ends of government. . . . Their insulation and the marvelous mystery of time give courts the capacity to appeal to men's better natures, to call forth their aspirations, which may have been forgotten in the moment's hue and cry" (Bickel, 1962:25–26). The judiciary is designed to be insulated enough from public opinion and political expediency to rule on the basis of principle, constrained by application to cases and controversies, yet not so constrained as to be prevented from rising above the case and invoking and enforcing general principles. General principles are absolute in the sense that they may not give way to expedient considerations in various cases; however, they may have internal flexibility that allows for varying implementation by courts, legislative bodies, or executive agencies (Bickel, 1962:59).

Of course, the Court still runs up against the charge of being an antidemocratic institution, but if the principles are consistent enough with what majority opinion considers to be fair rules of play, even where a majority may lose a political battle to a minority, the Court will survive and the principle will stand. The Court is an instrument of moral education and stands at the fore in an ongoing colloquy about rights and fair play in society. Between the lines Bickel imbues the democratic political process (with the judiciary acting as the most insulated "republican" institution within that overall system) with a sense of moral progress that is, if not inevitable, at least attainable through reason and its application in law. Law and the continuity that the Supreme Court imparts to the political process resolve the tension that principles versus politics generate. Nevertheless, says Bickel, the Court functions best by avoiding the political fray often enough to make judgments based on general principles rather than policy preferences. A number of institutional mechanisms facilitate this type of jurisprudence.

Bickel argues that the Court's reliance on the "passive virtues" is what allows it to exercise the power of judicial review against majoritarian forces without sacrificing institutional legitimacy. The doctrines of "standing, case and controversy, ripeness and political questions" are the Court's means of deflecting political pressures that would lead to an activist, politicized judiciary. In essence these passive virtues available to the Court allow it to exercise judicial review judiciously, with a concern for its institutional uniqueness and legitimacy. That is why the Court remains (in 1962) a highly regarded institution, in spite of controversial rulings (Bickel, 1962:197). "The means exist and are in vigorous use for providing a wide-ranging and effective rule of principle, while at the same time eschewing full dominion and affording the necessary leeway to expedient accommodation" (Bickel, 1962:200).

Finally, Bickel turns to the segregation cases (*Brown* and its progeny) to illustrate the thesis that the Court can effectively guide by principle without establishing universal constraints on the policy process. Although Bickel's theory is clearly one that advocates a good dose of judicial restraint, it is hard to believe, especially after forty years more of judicial activism, that it is still applicable. Critics of an activist judiciary charge that the passive virtues, in which Bickel places so much faith, have been ignored by the courts. The "rules of principle" themselves appear to multiply confusingly and expediently.

Bickel's characterization of the Supreme Court as a countermajoritarian institution is itself problematic. It reflects an ambivalence inherent in American judicial power that has existed since the Constitutional Convention and has never been resolved. We attribute this ambivalence primarily to Hamilton's ideas and the pragmatic approach of Marshall, though we credit several other intellectual forces on the Court with carrying the tradition into the twentieth century and greatly expand-

ing upon it. As Bickel carefully points out, the Court is a countermajoritarian institution in process, yet because it lacks any wholly independent means of
implementing its rulings, the Court is potentially extremely vulnerable, even to the
point of impotence, in the face of majoritarian resistance. Thus the Court must remain responsive to democratic pressures, though it need not be overwhelmed by
them in the business of interpreting the Constitution.

As a political institution functioning in a democratic society, however, any court
is obliged to weather the consequences of its decisions. It is for this reason that
Bickel discovers and cannot expunge the dualistic mandate plaguing the judiciary.
As Laura Kalman notes:

[W]ithin pages of introducing that epigram [countermajoritarian], Bickel came around to
the pluralist view that judicial review *was* democratic. Instead of following Marshall or the
Federalist, however, he justified judicial review by proclaiming it the Court's role to pro-
nounce and guard public values in principled fashion and to build consensus around them.
On some occasions, such as *Brown* . . . the Court did need to inject "itself decisively into the
political process." Such occasions were "relatively few," the Court must bank its prestige
for them, and having acted, it must "foster assent, and compliance through consent." Bickel
applauded *Brown* II and the "all deliberate speed" formula precisely because it represented
such an attempt. For even on the rare occasions the Court appropriately intervened in the political process, its law could not ultimately prevail "if it ran counter to deeply felt popular
needs or convictions, or even if it was opposed by a determined and substantial minority and
received with indifference by the rest of the country. This, in the end, is how and why judicial review is consistent with the theory and practice of political democracy." (Kalman,
1996:40)

Looking back on Bickel's relatively modest prescriptions for the appropriate role
of the Supreme Court in modern politics, one wonders what could have changed so
radically since 1962 to bring about the pervasive involvement of the courts in
late-twentieth-century government. Looking forward, it seems nearly a foregone
conclusion that the courts will continue to exercise an even more pervasive influence on American society in the twenty-first century than they have in the twentieth. Regardless of causes advanced, the die appears to be cast in favor of judicial
activism.

In defense of legal realism, which we discuss in chapter 1, advocates of contemporary judicial practice point out that absent judicial interventions, the political
process would be even more vulnerable to overbearing majorities. Jesse Choper
argues that the Supreme Court remains weak in spite of its review power because
countermajoritarian rulings are likely to face intense resistance and the court loses
prestige the more it runs against political tides. Yet he contends that judicial review remains a necessary component of an imperfect democratic system. If "judicial review were nonexistent for popularly frustrated minorities, the fight, already
lost in the legislative halls, would have only one remaining battleground—the
streets . . . the alternatives to judicial review for individual constitutional rights are
either disobedience of the law or discontented acceptance" (Choper, 1980:128).
Thus episodic discontent with the Supreme Court is a sign of systemic good health

provided the judges do not go too far for too long. In the interim, far from hindering the political system, the Court provides further possibilities for democratic learning.

In defense of judicial activism, Ronald Dworkin argues that the Supreme Court should not abandon broader principles of justice to uphold static, historically bounded views of the Constitution. Pivotal constitutional provisions are necessarily abstract to allow for a certain fluidity of jurisprudence. In fact, says Dworkin, conservatives advocating judicial restraint are the revisionists. "They argue that the apparently abstract clauses of free speech and due process and liberty and equality should be treated only as coded messages or shorthand statements of very concrete, detailed historical agreements" (Dworkin, 1993:128). It is the indefinite meaning of the Constitution itself that forces judges to accept responsibility for interpreting and applying it.

This is no esoteric academic argument. Rather, it is one that was wholeheartedly embraced by William Brennan, perhaps the leading intellectual force on the Court in the Warren/Burger era. Nevertheless, Dworkin's and Brennan's thinking, though it has tended to predominate, merely begs the more fundamental question whether it makes sense or not to root the Constitution historically. If not, taking it to the extreme, why bother with a Constitution at all? If so, how abstract are the meanings of particularly problematic phrases? As Antonin Scalia has asked, where beyond the text can judges look for answers without overstepping their authority? Scalia is perhaps the most devoted textualist on the Supreme Court, yet his jurisprudence is not without its activist moments (Rosen, 1997). Jeffrey Rosen has called Scalia to task for his "uncanny ability to reach the result that happens to coincide with his own preferences in case after case." Rosen charges that Scalia himself has strayed from "originalism" to "conserve traditional moral values against legal and cultural change" (Rosen, 1997:34).

Despite the value of theoretical arguments pointing out the inherent complexity of the judiciary's task in interpreting the Constitution and its institutional precariousness, most observers agree that the courts have vastly expanded their role in the American political system, that the executive and legislative branches have sometimes grudgingly, sometimes enthusiastically acquiesced in this expansion, and that the public for the most part has also accepted it. There has been a sea change in the public philosophy with regard to judicial governance. In a very real sense we are today watched over by the bevy of Platonic guardians that Judge Learned Hand warned against, and this is now considered legitimate by a plurality, if not a majority, of constitutional "experts" (Gunther, 1994).

Strictly speaking, in expounding rights enshrined in the Constitution, the judiciary was not expected to produce controversy and political division. With a few important exceptions, the expectation and the historical reality until the Warren era were quite the contrary. The judiciary was established to resolve contentious issues in law by applying widely accepted understandings of constitutional provisions to particular cases. When the court did stray into more novel interpretation, it met fierce political opposition. There is opposition today, but the judiciary has largely succeeded in expanding its interpretive authority to include a broad power to apply Bill of Rights guarantees to all levels of government and administration. This is what is fundamentally different about the modern activist judiciary. Until the early 1950s the courts seldom intervened in the formulation and implementation of public policy. Since that time judicial activism has been characterized by the ongoing interpretation, application, and expansion of Bill of Rights guarantees, dramatically impacting state and federal legislation and the operation of executive institutions at federal, state, and local levels.

Far from embodying a unifying and consensus-building institution, for nearly fifty years the courts have foreclosed public debate on many divisive issues through their pronouncements. Controversy, not consensus, has been the hallmark of modern jurisprudence. In many cases the courts have further polarized those with opposing views in a way that perhaps invites and invigorates Madison's most feared enemy of freedom—the evil of faction.

Hence our work reevaluates Hamilton's assertion, upon which Bickel crafted his influential book, in the form of a question. Can the judiciary still be considered "the least dangerous branch"? Moreover, if judicial activism poses certain risks, then what are they? Are some forms of judicial intervention more dangerous and costly than others? Would other institutions be capable of reform if it were not for an activist judiciary?

Like most other areas of government activity, judicial intervention is not wholly good or wholly destructive when it is viewed in terms of the causes advanced. In part because it is judged more by the consequences of its doctrinal pronouncements than fidelity to the letter of the Constitution, the judiciary has retained much of its institutional legitimacy in the American polity. As James Q. Wilson astutely observes:

The court is a vitally important forum in which individuals can assert fundamental rights and seek appropriate remedies, even (especially!) against administrative agencies. The courts began the process of school desegregation, put a stop to some bestial practices in prisons and mental hospitals, and have enabled thousands of people to get benefits to which they were entitled or ended abuses they were suffering. Without courts and lawyers skilled at using them some of these conditions might be far more common today. But like all human institutions, courts are not universal problem solvers competent to manage any difficulty or resolve any dispute. There are certain things courts are good at and some things they are not so good at. (Wilson, 1989:290)

More enthusiastic proponents of judicial activism argue that as the American state expanded its authority, courts simply needed to retain a proportionate influence over the growing responsibilities of legislative and administrative institutions. The judiciary's growth in power was necessary to ensure that it could continue to safeguard individual rights and protect interest groups and the public in an increasingly complex and insular bureaucratic policy-making environment.

Stephen Breyer has argued that lower federal court judges have simply filled an institutional void. He emphasizes that the lower federal judiciary has become more active in administrative law only in response to Congress passing the Administrative Procedure Act and various amendments. Congress authorized greater judicial involvement in order to curtail "excessive agency freedom" (Breyer, 1982:378). Thus the growth of court power within the bureaucracy has resulted from legislative responses to continuous expansion of the administrative responsibilities of the state during the twentieth century.

Undertaking an empirical analysis of pivotal district-court decisions, including ones on busing, housing, and mental health, Phillip Cooper argues that not enough empirical evidence has yet been marshaled to justify the ideological claims of either liberals or conservatives about expanding judicial power. Cooper is more concerned with judicial decision making itself, and his research demonstrates that a fuller assessment of the consequences of judicial input into controversial policy-making areas is needed (Cooper, 1988).

Indeed, there is a strong case for what we can describe as the "institutional-growth–judicial-response" explanation for increased judicial activism. Congress itself has directed the courts to intervene in many new areas of governmental regulation, often preferring an intensified and ongoing judicial review of statutory and administrative provisions to its own oversight. No longer is Congress content to grant the kind of discretion to regulatory agencies that they had in the New Deal era; and the courts, frequently more so than Congress, have become an important forum for competing interests to fight pitched battles. In his study of environmental regulation and the courts R. Shep Melnick argues persuasively that courts have had a profound impact upon the regulatory process, transforming environmental policy making into a polycentric rather than a bipolar process (Melnick, 1983:17). From their more decentralized position within the federal government, the courts have become equilibrators of competing societal interests, using their own discretion in applying general rules to particular cases.

Judicial activism has generated an explosion in litigation, which in and of itself has become a problem for the courts. This immediately suggests that intervention, whether it brings about desirable institutional reforms or not, comes at a cost. Moreover, if political compromise is less likely to come from a court battle than from floor debates and committee hearings, then at least some of the polarization evident in the larger political system can be attributed to court decisions that settle public policy disputes in terms of political rights. Such an approach is generally more rigid than are legislative outcomes. Thus costs must be evaluated on at least two levels: a policy-making or microlevel that is specific to the area in which the court is ruling and also a systemic level, taking into account costs to the larger political system in which courts have been operating.

Of course, it would be wrong to lay too much blame at the judiciary's doorstep. Legislative institutions have often failed to live up to the responsibilities of representative governance, and the courts are an important check against unbridled executive discretion as well as legislative aggrandizement. Some observers and judges themselves argue that this is precisely why the courts have intervened so extensively. Yet the assumption of institutional failure still begs the question of why the courts choose to act. As Ronald Kahn rightly observes, "[To] assume that the Supreme Court in general, or the Warren Court in particular, accepts in their entirety the political malfunction principles of the *Carolene Products* footnote . . . is to oversimplify the basis of Court decision making and to disregard the effect of complex external factors, such as the dialogue between the Court and the interpretive community, on doctrinal change" (Kahn, 1994:60). The *Carolene Products* footnote provided a crucial modus operandi for the Warren Court by calling for special protections for "discrete and insular minorities." Kahn argues persuasively that changes in the jurisprudence of the federal judiciary are necessarily linked to "major ideational changes within social science and legal theory in pre– and post–World War II America" (Kahn, 1994:66).

The first part of this book will explain how such important changes in American jurisprudence came about and why judicial activism has become an all-but-irreversible trend. We could easily leave our analysis at that. Many books have attempted to describe and explain even small pieces of this large and complex legal-historical puzzle, so our approach will of necessity be highly selective, with an eye toward what we are most interested in understanding, namely, what it is that the judiciary has achieved in a number of important areas of public policy. When and why has the judiciary chosen to act? What are the impacts or the consequences of judicial rulings? What new institutional relationships have arisen as a result? Who has benefited from judicial involvement? Who has lost out? What might have happened if, in the many areas of social controversy that they have confronted, the courts followed Felix Frankfurter's advice and, through one means or another, decided not to decide? These themes will make up the second (and much larger) portion of our book.

In raising these questions and admittedly casting a critical eye over the judiciary's work, our wish is to avoid what Mark Tushnet has described with reference to analysis of the Warren Court as compiling a mere "scorecard toting up decisions the analyst likes and dislikes" (Tushnet, 1993:1). On the contrary, we wish to evaluate the Court's record in terms of societal benefits and opportunity costs rather than to make normative or legalistic judgments about particular cases and social/political controversies. We may hold certain views about the rightness or wrongness of many aspects of judicial policymaking, but our goal is to suspend these judgments, at least until we have taken into consideration the state of knowledge concerning the impact the courts have had.

Similarly, we may agree or disagree with judicial reasoning or even wholesale trends in judge-made law, but for the purposes of our investigation we accept as historical facts the various decisions around which controversies in civil rights, civil liberties, and criminal procedure have arisen. At least with respect to assessing judicial impact, this is the beginning of our analysis, not the end. We intend to look beyond the decisions to the policy outcome of important adjudicated social and political controversies.

In most, if not all, areas into which we will delve, the evidence is not altogether clear. Some areas are better understood than others. What we can investigate, beyond the relatively incomplete picture we can provide from impact studies and the like (and it is one of our principal methods of measuring what the courts have done), is the activity or inactivity of other governmental and nongovernmental actors before, during, and after judicial intervention. What was the state of affairs prior to judicial intervention? How did the actors involved respond to the courts' efforts—antagonistically, indifferently, cooperatively? Did these relationships change over time? Did the courts contribute to a greater responsiveness, fairness, and inclusiveness in addressing controversial issues? Answering these questions will give us an impression of whether the courts helped or made matters worse in the policy-making process. Finally, we can assess in more general terms what impact the courts have had upon the larger political system as their more specific institutional interventions have produced systemic changes in the political system. We expect to find a hodgepodge.

The areas we have chosen are all controversial, but more important, over the past forty or fifty years they have comprised the great bulk of the courts' work. They are some of the most important and frequently litigated issues before the courts and are therefore of central importance to us in determining the capacity of courts to govern. To the extent that we can shed light on this question, we believe that we make a contribution to an important debate.

Chapter 1

Hamilton's Wager and the Rise of Judicial Activism

FUNDAMENTAL LAW AND POLITICAL CHANGE

In attempting to explain how the courts came to occupy a central and at times controversial role in the American state in the later twentieth century, one could simply argue that the organizational imperatives of a reformed American political system dictated that the courts step in. The courts were forced to act because of external pressures originating in the larger society and impacting the political system as a whole. Issues came before the courts as a matter of course, because other political institutions, either through action or inaction, had failed to resolve or had even exacerbated serious social and political problems. The courts were simply applying constitutional provisions to new circumstances. That is one argument.

There is no doubt that judicial activism has paralleled and is inextricably connected with the growth of American state power in the twentieth century. The state is more intimately intertwined in the daily lives of American citizens than at any other point in history, and the courts have played an active part in this. As the modern welfare state emerged, it was unlikely that the courts would remain on the sidelines. Increasingly complex and numerous cases ran their course through the appeals process. When they reached the circuit courts and ultimately the Supreme Court, authoritative pronouncements were, if not inevitable, highly probable. Why did decisions that the Supreme Court and increasingly the lower federal courts rendered tend to favor more frequent judicial involvement in the political system?

Before attempting to answer that question, we should emphasize that Hamilton and others perceived a great advantage in establishing a supreme court. A supreme court would apply principles of justice interpreted from the Constitution more uniformly in an emerging judicial system prone to substantial fragmentation and decentralization. Hamilton intended the Supreme Court to be a centralizing institution from the start:

If there are such things as political axioms, the propriety of the judicial power of a government being co-extensive with its legislative, may be ranked among the number. The mere necessity of uniformity in the interpretation of the national laws, decides the question. Thirteen independent courts of final jurisdiction over the same causes, arising upon the same laws, is a hydra in government, from which nothing but contradiction and confusion can proceed. (Hamilton, Madison, and Jay, 1961, 80)

In defending the Constitution, the Supreme Court would be able to counteract the centrifugal tendencies of the fragmented state and lower federal judiciaries.

The ambiguity of Hamilton's vision for the appropriate role of the Court becomes evident when he contemplates the nature of its substantive work. Hamilton defended the Court's independence by arguing that judges would primarily rule on the letter of the law and would refrain from pronouncements as to its spirit. Yet Hamilton essentially conceded that once the independent power to interpret the law was granted, there was no immediate mechanism to prevent judges from doing exactly this. There were important internal and external constraints, and there was the ultimate wrath of the legislature and the people, but these would be deterrent forces, not internal institutional or legal guarantees against abuse. Hamilton believed that the independence of the judges in interpreting the laws was of paramount importance. He wrote, "A constitution is in fact, and must be, regarded by the judges as a fundamental law. It therefore belongs to them to ascertain its meaning as well as the meaning of any particular act proceeding from the legislative body" (Hamilton, Madison, and Jay, 1961, 78). But what would happen if the Court could not decide what the Constitution meant? What if considerable dissensus as to the nature and scope of various constitutional provisions arose? How would these issues be resolved? Would the courts help, or should they stand aside? Or, in the process of interpreting the law, would they possibly even deepen these political divisions?

Having granted them the power to interpret the law, Hamilton concedes in *Federalist* 81 that mistakes and abuses are quite possible:

Particular misconstructions and contraventions of the will of the legislature may now and then happen; but they can never be so extensive as to amount to an inconvenience, or in any sensible degree to affect the order of the political system. This may be inferred with certainty from the general nature of the judicial power; from the objects to which it relates; from the manner in which it is exercised; from its comparative weakness; and from its total incapacity to support its usurpations by force. (Hamilton, Madison, and Jay, 1961, 81)

There was a certain risk in coupling the power of review with judicial independence, but it was a risk that Hamilton believed was both manageable and necessary to counter the greater threat of legislative aggrandizement. The most notable Antifederalist to argue that the risk was unacceptable was Robert Yates, writing as Brutus:

We have seen, that they will be authorized to give the constitution a construction according to its spirit and reason, and not to confine themselves to its letter . . . as the general government acquires power and jurisdiction, by the liberal construction which the judges may give the constitution, will those of the states lose its rights, until they become so trifling and unimportant, as not to be worth having? (Brutus XII)

Brutus is most concerned about the potential for the judiciary to centralize government, not that it would become more powerful than the legislature itself. In many instances where the federal courts have intervened in the reform of social policy, this is exactly what has happened. As we shall learn from our case studies in this book, the courts have indeed acted as a centralizing institution in American politics, diminishing the authority and autonomy of state, local, and nongovernmental institutions.

The Antifederalists generally desired a more localized regulation of domestic affairs than the Federalists. As many observers emphasize in studying early American political culture, protecting liberty was a paramount concern of the American people. Discussing the Puritan influence on New England culture, politics, and criminal justice, Edgar McManus cautions that modern state regulation had no parallel in local social and political regulation in the seventeenth and early eighteenth centuries:

Long before their fall from grace, New Englanders had a commitment to liberty more compelling than the official morality. Even the most zealous holy watchers prized personal freedom too highly to become conscious instruments of an overreaching state. Like the pious minister who informed on his son, they spied more to save the sinner than to exalt the state. . . . The cost to privacy was high, but there were also benefits in the form of safe streets and personal security. . . . Perhaps even more important, official law enforcers did not pose a threat to liberty. Local accountability and rotation in office made it unlikely that their police powers would be abused. . . . Power subject to such constraints was naturally geared to moderation, giving New Englanders the happy paradox of a society where life, liberty, and property were equally protected. (McManus, 1993:71–72)

McManus emphasizes that the spirit of ordered liberty was embedded within and safeguarded by the local community in late-eighteenth-century America.

It was this freedom that the Antifederalists fought hard to preserve. Hamilton could not easily dismiss the charge that the proposed judiciary would help to centralize government and threaten to undermine local self-government and cherished freedoms. He responds to Brutus's claim in *Federalist* 81, where he states that while the courts might try to usurp local authority through an expansive interpretation of federal power under the Constitution, that tendency ran counter to the "general theory of a limited constitution" deeply ingrained in American political culture (Bailyn, 1967). Hamilton argued that the Supreme Court was no more powerful in its sphere than any state court:

[T]here is not a syllable in the plan under consideration, which directly empowers the national courts to construe the laws according to the spirit of the constitution, or which gives them any greater latitude in this respect, than may be claimed by the courts of every state. I admit, however, that the constitution ought to be the standard of construction for the laws, and that wherever there is an evident opposition, the laws ought to give place to the constitution. But this doctrine is not deducible from any circumstance peculiar to the plan of the convention, but from the general theory of a limited constitution; and as far as it is true, is equally applicable to most, if not all the state governments. (Hamilton, Madison, and Jay, 1961, 81)

Thus Hamilton recognized the potential vices of an ambitious judiciary but wagered that institutional, professional, and, above all, cultural constraints would be sufficient to check them.

The Judicial Dilemma: Judicial Review and the Constitution

There is little question that Hamilton placed considerable faith in the common law and in "common sense" to temper ambitious legal interpretation by judges (Hamilton, Madison, and Jay, 1961, 78).

To avoid an arbitrary discretion in the courts, it is indispensable that they should be bound down by strict rules and precedents, which serve to define and point out their duty in every particular case that comes before them; and it will readily be conceived from the variety of controversies which grow out of the folly and wickedness of mankind, that the records of those precedents must unavoidably swell to a very considerable bulk, and must demand long and laborious study to acquire a competent knowledge of them. (Hamilton, Madison, and Jay, 1961, 78)

Stare decisis (literally meaning to stand by that which is decided) would be the great professional restraint that the tradition of adjudication of the common law would instill in those who rose to the highest offices of the judiciary. Courts would be obliged to follow precedent-setting rulings in similar cases.

Yet this reliance on *stare decisis* and the common law turns out to be a remedy to the problem of historical change that carries with it a certain risk. Adjudication involves the management of an unavoidable conflict between steadfast adherence to fundamental law (a principle central to constitutional government) and the desire for expediency in responding to changing historical circumstances, a more Machiavellian impulse. In a penetrating analysis of modern executive power, *Taming the Prince*, Harvey Mansfield (1989) argues that in spite of the ambivalent nature of executive power, the oscillation between strong and weak executive authority allows for its continued legitimacy in the American political system. The president can be both Machiavellian prince and errand boy of the legislature, depending upon the ingenuity of the statesman and external pressures on the institution. Mansfield's theory seems to have its judicial analog, couched in the doctrine of *stare decisis*.

As Karl Llewellyn once observed, "[T]he doctrine of precedent . . . is two-headed. It is Janus-faced . . . there is one doctrine for getting rid of precedents deemed troublesome and one doctrine for making use of precedents that seem helpful. . . . An ignorant, an unskillful judge will find it hard to use: the past will bind him. But the skillful judge—he whom we would make free—is thus made free. He has the knife in hand; and he can free himself" (quoted in Wardle, 1987:219). Acting in his own independent sphere, the judge himself has his Machiavellian moments, opportunities to wield power at critical occasions of ambiguity and tension among constitutional, legislative, executive, or popular mandates.

Throughout American history judges have wrestled with this inherent tension between a static and fluid interpretation of the law. On a theoretical level the difficulty stems from a more general conflict between republican ideals and the exigencies attendant to the passage of time and changing circumstance, identified by J.G.A. Pocock in *The Machiavellian Moment* (1975). A voluminous literature documents the various successive points in American history at which the judiciary has shifted political ground in order to adjust to external social and political pressures.[1]

In the course of generating an immense body of common law over the past two hundred years, the American courts have not acted unilaterally to satisfy their own political ends. They have frequently been drawn into the policy-making arena by the direct invitation or acquiescence of Congress and the president. Carrying on the American common-law tradition provides a tremendous resource for the augmentation of judicial power, and liberals and conservatives alike have relied upon it episodically, usually either in the service of or to resist social and political reforms. The great virtue of the common law is that it allows for systemic accommodation without precipitating crisis; its vice is that over time it tends to do violence to the Constitution, that is, if we gravitate toward a conception of it as unchanging, fundamental law. The gradual accretion of rules and precedents in any given area of the common law can diminish the pristine quality of fundamental law, slowly eroding the assumptions that flow from previously accepted interpretations of constitutional provisions. *Stare decisis* has thus proved a blessing and a curse. Paradoxically, it is both the primary mechanism of judicial restraint and a potential wellspring of judicial activism.

While we can sense a certain risk to constitutionalism in the common-law tradition because it is a source of flexibility in the law and especially in the application of rights, its incremental nature is a critical safeguard. Common-law changes have generally followed in the wake of shifting societal values, proceeding at a glacial-enough pace to allow the necessary time for institutional adjustment in support of the innovations. The common law has tended to reflect rather than shape society's understanding of rights. The contemporary volatility of rights appears to be less a consequence of the historical evolution of the common law and more likely a result of the American experiment with constitutional and statutory interpretation.

John Marshall and Judicial Review

John Marshall, probably the best-known and leading intellectual influence on the Supreme Court, clearly shared Hamilton's view that the courts should be vested with the power of judicial review:

Marshall shared Hamilton's legalistic conception of constitutional structure as a hierarchy of laws which placed judgment and judicial authority firmly at the center of liberal politics . . . yet the legal and jurisprudential history of the new American republic determined that the legitimacy of this authority could not depend on claims of "superior" legal or moral knowledge. . . . Marshall reflected James Wilson's vision of judicial review as an institution carrying forward the jurisprudential claims of the Revolution's challenge to hierarchic common law theories of epistemology and politics. (Stimson, 1990:141)

In cases such as *Marbury v. Madison* (1803) and *McCulloch v. Maryland* (1819), Marshall put Hamilton's plan into practice, declaring the Supreme Court's power to decide independently upon the constitutionality of a statute.

Marshall had already proudly and unequivocally defended judicial review at the Virginia Constitutional Convention: "If they [the government] were to make a law not warranted by any of the powers enumerated, it would be considered by the judges as an infringement of the Constitution which they are to guard. They would consider such a law as coming under their jurisdiction. They would declare it void" (Gerber, 1995:103). Marshall's great contribution to this somewhat Machiavellian undercurrent of American law was in institutionalizing the independence of the judiciary, establishing the power of the courts to protect the Constitution and at the same time enabling them to generate a distinct common law through their daily operations.

Hamilton planted and Marshall nourished the seed that allowed the judiciary to evolve into a much different institution than most of the framers would have envisioned. Americanizing the common law was only the first step in the growth of judicial power. The institutionalization of judicial review in the nineteenth century, which established the rule of precedent and a selective incorporation of English common law, was a precondition for the legal community's later acceptance of the expansion of judicial power through substantive due process (that is, imparting substantive meaning to the due process clause). In and of itself, nineteenth-century jurisprudence was a relatively modest innovation. As Hamilton had wagered, until at least the late nineteenth century, the courts indeed remained the least dangerous branch.

THE TRANSFORMATION OF AMERICAN CONSTITUTIONAL LAW

The potential power of judicial review was not widely comprehended until the early twentieth century. In *The Rise of Modern Judicial Review* (1986) Christopher Wolfe provides an incisive account of the most important periods of the judiciary's transformation into a more purely political institution. Wolfe argues that from the Constitutional Convention until the Civil War the courts exercised power with an understanding of the nature and limits of judicial review inherited from the framers of the Constitution. In the second, post–Civil War era the judiciary became more active as it adopted a substantive due process jurisprudence based on natural law and property rights and struck down many state economic regulations. In the third era, after the "constitutional revolution" of the New Deal, the judiciary shifted to a jurisprudence of restraint, deferring to legislative bodies in social and economic regulation. Finally, from the 1950s to the 1970s, the Warren and Burger Courts articulated an expansive egalitarian jurisprudence nationalizing an array of civil rights and liberties.

Traditional Judicial Review

Since *Marbury v. Madison* (1803) the Supreme Court has exercised the authority to decide on the constitutionality of particular legislation. Yet for the first century of American national government the sphere of judicial review remained quite narrow:

Judicial review "won out" in early American history after genuine struggles, but the form in which it won was critical to its success. In a different form, it is likely that it would not have survived. The form it took was "moderate" judicial review, and the major qualifying components it incorporated were inherent limits of judicial power, legislative deference, and the political questions doctrine. (Wolfe, 1986:101)

The Court's business was not to decide what laws were best for the nation, but to rule only in cases where a law seemed clearly to conflict with constitutional provisions. The appropriate forum for deciding these issues was in the course of resolving particular "cases and controversies," as the Constitution directs. Moreover, judicial review was "not to be exercised in a 'doubtful case'. In cases in which they had doubts about the proper interpretation of the Constitution, judges would defer to legislative opinions of constitutionality" (Wolfe, 1986:104). The degree of deference here is determined after substantial investigation into the intent of the legislature in enacting the statute and the intent of the framers in including a particular principle in the Constitution. Even by these moderate standards the substantive interpretation of the Fourteenth Amendment of the Constitution, now a common undertaking of the Supreme Court, would be considered an abuse of judicial power. To understand how this became possible in the twentieth century, we must look to the Court's shifting jurisprudence in the late nineteenth century.

The Court's unwillingness to infuse any substantive political doctrine into the due process clause of the Fourteenth Amendment until the beginning of the twentieth century (*Lochner v. New York*, 1905) is indicative of self-imposed limitations on the exercise of judicial power. Generally, the Court adhered to the view taken by Alexander Hamilton in 1787: "[N]o man shall be disenfranchised or deprived of any right, but by 'due process of law', or the judgment of his peers. The words 'due process of law' have a precise technical import, and are only applicable to the process and proceedings of the courts of justice; they can never be referred to an act of legislature" (Hickok and McDowell, 1993:93). In short, due process in the nineteenth century was viewed as a procedural guarantee of the courts against arbitrary deprivations of liberty only. No substantive meaning was applicable, nor was due process considered a vague guarantee against state and private institutions to be infused with meaning by the courts. Consonant with this understanding, even as pressures mounted in the legal profession to overturn state and federal legislation affecting economic regulations, the court by and large deferred to legislative institutions. From the *Slaughterhouse Cases* (1872), where the Court initially rejected any protection of economic interests under the Fourteenth Amendment, to *Munn v. Illinois* (1876), the Supreme Court occasionally held that the government could legitimately regulate industries, for example, if they were deemed to be "affected with a public interest." Although the Court noted that state and federal regulatory power could be abused, the majority opinion conceded in *Munn* that "the people must resort to the polls, not to the courts" in such cases. Clearly, this period of due process interpretation was characterized by a deference to the deliberations of legislative bodies. The Court did reserve some jurisdiction to decide cases "relating to matters in which the public has no interest," in principle claiming authority to grapple with laws involving the most arbitrary or capricious infringements of economic liberty, but these cases were exceptional (94 U.S. 113, 126, 134 [1876]). Justice Stephen Field's dissenting view in the *Slaughterhouse Cases*, that liberty of contract should be elevated to the status of a right and should be defended by the judiciary, would not gain any credence until progressive reformers challenged nineteenth-century American political economy in the late 1800s.

Economic Substantive Due Process

It was thus during the Progressive Era that the Supreme Court first departed from the moderate exercise of judicial review. From the 1890s to the New Deal the Supreme Court abandoned its deference to the legislature in cases of economic regulation, striking down dozens of state laws for violating the due process clause. In striking down a state law regulating the hours a baker could work in *Lochner v. New York* (1905), the Court declared that the "mere assertion that the subject relates, though but in a remote degree, to the public health does not necessarily render the enactment valid. The act must have a more direct relation, as a means to an end, and the end itself must be appropriate and legitimate, before an act can be held to be valid which interferes with the general right of an individual to be free in his person and in his power to contract in relation to his own labor" (198 U.S. 45, 58 [1905]). The Court thus shifted from what had been in practice a highly deferential standard of review to a much stricter scrutiny of economic regulation. The substantive political doctrine upheld an extremely individualistic view of the relationship between persons contracting for labor in society. Following this precedent, the courts would strike down virtually any regulations that might restrict the freedom to enter into employment contracts.

The Court's Challenge to Congressional Power to Regulate Commerce

At the same time that courts were striking down state economic regulations under the "liberty-of-contract" doctrine, the Supreme Court also began shifting away from the conception of regulation of commerce as a plenary power of Congress.

This interpretation of an unfettered congressional power to regulate commerce had been established by Justice Marshall's ruling in *Gibbons v. Ogden* (1824), and the precedent prevailed until the late 1800s. At that time the Court moved toward a more restrictive definition of the commerce power, based on whether it determined that "intrastate" activity was or was not substantially related to "interstate" commerce. For example, in cases such as *United States v. E.C. Knight Co.* (1895) and *Hammer v. Dagenhart* (1918), the Court ruled that manufacturing was not sufficiently linked to interstate commerce to warrant a presumption of constitutionality for statutes regulating various aspects of manufacture. Thus interpretation of the commerce power by the courts from the late 1800s to the New Deal was not only coterminous with economic substantive due process but was essentially analogous to it. The Court diverged sharply from Marshall's jurisprudence in *Gibbons*, which, in effect, had conceded that Congress possessed broad power to define commerce and regulate it as it saw fit. Instead, the Court began to substantively define commerce power and strike down legislation regulating "intrastate" activities that it determined had only indirect impact on interstate commerce.

Following Franklin Roosevelt's court-packing plan and the reorientation of the Supreme Court in favor of the New Deal, the Court reverted to the deference to Congress established in *Gibbons*. In *National Labor Relations Board v. Jones and Laughlin Steel Corporation* (1937) the Court invalidated *E.C. Knight*. In this case the Court argued that Congress could regulate labor in the steel industry because labor disputes could disrupt the "stream" of interstate commerce. This was so even though the defendants argued that the steel industry was a manufacturing enterprise and therefore was not subject to regulation pursuant to the *E.C. Knight* precedent. In *United States v. Darby* (1941) the Supreme Court overruled *Hammer* and upheld the Fair Labor Standards Act of 1938 that regulated child labor. Manufacturing was held to be sufficiently related to interstate commerce to justify regulation.

For the most part the Court continues to adhere to the New Deal view of the commerce clause as granting a plenary power to Congress. The one notable exception came in 1976 in *National League of Cities v. Usery*. In *Usery* Justice William Rehnquist argued that the Tenth Amendment protected the states from federal intrusion that would substantially impinge on their sovereignty in "areas of traditional governmental functions," in this case the autonomous regulation of state employees. The Court overturned this ruling in *Garcia v. San Antonio Metropolitan Transit Authority* (1985), arguing that Congress had a legitimate authority under the commerce clause to regulate state employees under the Fair Labor Standards Act, and that Rehnquist's attempt to establish a standard for differentiating among appropriately state and federal regulatory responsibilities was an exercise in substantive due process and unworkable. Justice Harry Blackmun argued that the states' participation in both houses in Congress was a sufficient safeguard against undue burdens imposed on the states by legislation enacted under the commerce clause. In short, in modern commerce clause jurisprudence, as is evidenced by acceptance of the Civil Rights Act in *Heart of Atlanta Motel Inc. v. United States* (1964), the courts have not made any significant attempts since the 1930s to impose limits on federal regulation adopted under the authority of the commerce clause.

Politically, the significance of the *Lochner* period of economic substantive due process and the Supreme Court's challenge to congressional regulation of commerce was its extension of judicial power to cast a protective net supportive of capitalist interests at a time when they were coming under attack by Populists and Progressives (Fish, 1973:17). Its significance in American legal history is that it reflected a determination by the Supreme Court to use the power of judicial review to serve political ends. Moreover, if the legal profession and the courts could develop a defensible rationale for reading substantive political doctrine into the due process clause of the Fourteenth Amendment, the *Lochner* and anti-commerce-power precedents could also be employed as an instrument of progressive judicial activism. As American political culture changed in the wake of the industrial revolution, and especially in the midst of the Great Depression, the Court came under overwhelming pressure to allow state regulation of the economy.

The Rise of Legal Realism

The legal profession itself proved decisive in bringing this change about. Important changes in legal and political culture were preconditions for the rise of an activist judiciary. They provided the key ideas and innovations establishing and legitimating modern judicial power. The progressive Wilsonian view of regarding the Constitution not as a historically bounded document but rather as something like an organic and evolving manifestation of the general will facilitated acceptance of greater judicial activism even with respect to constitutional questions. The rise of legal realism at the turn of the century, reflected in the thinking of progressive jurists such as Louis Brandeis, Benjamin Cardozo, Oliver Wendell Holmes, Roscoe Pound, Karl Llewellyn, and Jerome Frank, granted legitimacy to a more humane jurisprudence that could transcend what was perceived as an "essentially unjust status quo" (Jacobsohn, 1986:25).

The hallmark of the legal-realist reform approach was its disregard for common-law jurisprudence in favor of extralegal information relevant to the case. Louis Brandeis, arguing before the Court in the famous case *Muller v. Oregon* (1908), is widely credited with introducing statistics and social science information as a legitimate basis for legal argument (Johnson, 1981; Fetner, 1982:26). The so-called Brandeis brief became a model for progressive litigation. Faith in a jurisprudence that takes into account social and historical realities rather than abstract general principles was also essential in the thinking of Oliver Wendell Holmes (though Holmes proceeded cautiously and skeptically within the common-law tradition):

The life of the law has not been logic: it has been experience. The felt necessities of the time, the prevalent moral and political theories, intuitions of public policy, avowed or unconscious, even the prejudices which judges share with their fellow men, have had a good deal more to do than the syllogism in determining the rules by which men should be governed. (Holmes, 1993:9)

These and other prominent jurists had a profound impact on the future of the legal profession (Horwitz, 1992:193, 200–201). Their call for extralegal information, linked to their desire for more broad-based legal reform, presaged a decline in common-law adjudication as it was employed in the nineteenth century. From then on, legal formalism receded in the wake of a growing mass of modern data and so-cial-scientific argument.

John Johnson has shown that common-law cases declined precipitously, begin-ning in the late 1800s, from 40 percent of Supreme Court caseload in 1875 to less than 10 percent in the 1960s. Supreme Court caseload shifted to predominantly statutory- and constitutional-construction cases—exactly the type of cases that would rely much more heavily upon "extralegal information" of the type that Brandeis, other legal realists, and their progeny furnished (Johnson, 1981:52–53). David O'Brien has presented data indicating that particularly after 1941, when the legal realists were firmly established on the New Deal Court, individual rather than court-drafted opinions increased substantially. Prior to that time court-ren-dered opinions averaged in the 80 to 90 percent range. Since the 1940s that per-centage has declined from 60 percent to as low as 40 percent. Accordingly, individual opinions have risen from less than 20 percent in the 1930s to as high as 60 percent during the Burger Court era (O'Brien, 1999:101, table 4.3).

If one takes these developments into account, it is understandable that in the course of interpreting the meaning of statutes or the Constitution, judges would be more likely to render novel decisions that broke free of existing precedent. Whereas the common law had been the vehicle for episodic judicial innovation in the nineteenth century, statutory and constitutional interpretation became the more common means in the twentieth century. Thus the activist jurisprudence of the past three decades is a direct descendant of the type of adjudication that had begun to be practiced at the turn of the century. Yet although the courts became quite activist in the 1960s and 1970s, they had remained curiously reticent throughout the New Deal. What accounts for the difference?

No doubt Franklin Roosevelt's assault on the Supreme Court provided a crucial political catalyst reorienting twentieth-century constitutional interpretation (Schwartz, 1993:234). Economic substantive due process and limits on Con-gress's power to regulate commerce were swept away as the New Deal gained mo-mentum. These changes were the result of both ideological shifts of the Supreme Court and majoritarian pressures for reform that eventually overwhelmed the Lochner Court's rearguard action. In short, the New Deal gave reform-minded lawyers and judges the political climate they had been awaiting—progressive gov-ernment and burgeoning economic and social regulation.

The New Deal Court and Judicial Deference

The Supreme Court's eventual acceptance of the need for a strengthened administrative state made the policies of the New Deal era possible:

For nearly 50 years, the Court tried, on a case-by-case basis, to decide which particular industries could be regulated and which could not. In 1934, it gave up the fruitless attempt at an impossible distinction, and declared in *Nebbia v. New York* that there was no specific class of businesses affected with a public interest, but that the states were free to "adopt whatever economic policy may reasonably be deemed to promote public welfare." (Reagan, 1987:40)

In the *Lochner* era (from 1905 to *Nebbia* in 1934) an activist Court had defended the rights of private-sector contract against state intrusion. The New Deal Court now reversed course, limiting judicial review to a "reasonableness" standard that amounted to almost no scrutiny of state regulation at all. This was precisely the simple and minimal standard Oliver Wendell Holmes had advocated in dissenting from *Lochner*. In this sphere of government activity the courts thus allowed for considerable expansion of legislative control of the economy.

Court rulings legitimated the expansion of the public sector in the constitutional order at both state and federal levels. In the early 1930s the Supreme Court first granted formidable regulatory powers to the states. *Nebbia v. New York* (1934) and *West Coast Hotel Co. v. Parrish* (1937) signaled the end of the *Lochner* "freedom-of-contract" era by granting the states broad regulatory power over industry. Unless a state law was proven to be arbitrary and capricious, it was presumed constitutional. By contrast, the Supreme Court initially struck down a number of Roosevelt's New Deal programs. The *Schechter Poultry Corp. v. United States* (1935) decision halted Roosevelt's National Recovery Administration (NRA) on the grounds that it was an unconstitutional delegation of legislative power to the president; and in *United States v. Butler* (1936) the Supreme Court struck down Roosevelt's Agricultural Adjustment Administration (AAA) on the grounds that it would provide too broad a grant of power to the federal government in preserving the general welfare. However, after Roosevelt's campaign against the Court, it suddenly reversed course in *National Labor Relations Board v. Jones and Laughlin Steel Corporation* (1937). These cases were the foundation of a whole series of decisions in support of the New Deal. They sanctioned the expansion of regulatory power at both national and state levels.

The *Carolene Products* Exception and the Bill of Rights

In the area of social and economic regulation the courts accepted a highly deferential and restraintist role, although in the *United States v. Carolene Products Co.* (1938) decision Justice Harlan Fiske Stone had charted a new course for future judicial activism.[2] While the Court abandoned any serious scrutiny of economic regulation with respect to the Bill of Rights via the due process clause, the judiciary reserved the power to protect rights of "discrete and insular minorities" from legislative acts. The so-called famous footnote in the *Carolene Products* case left certain legislation open to more "searching review" by the high court. Justice Stone wrote:

There may be a narrower scope for operation of the presumption of constitutionality when legislation appears on its face to be within a specific prohibition of the Constitution, such as those of the first ten Amendments, which are deemed equally specific when held to be embraced within the 14th. . . .

It is unnecessary to consider now whether legislation which restricts those political processes which can ordinarily be expected to bring about repeal of undesirable legislation, is to be subjected to more exacting judicial scrutiny under the prohibitions of the 14th Amendment than are most other types of legislation. . . . On restriction upon the right to vote . . . on restraints upon the dissemination of information . . . on interferences with political organizations . . . and as to prohibition of peaceable assembly. . . .

Nor need we enquire whether similar considerations enter into the review of statutes directed at particular religious . . . or national . . . or racial minorities . . . whether prejudice against discrete and insular minorities may be a special condition, which tends seriously to curtail the operation of those political processes ordinarily to be relied upon to protect minorities, and which call for a correspondingly more searching judicial inquiry. (304 U.S. 144, 153, n. 4)

Martin Shapiro has described the aftermath of the *Carolene Products* decision as reserving a "preferred position" for economically underprivileged groups while leaving business and the wealthy with virtually no constitutional protection. Shapiro remarks that the "constitutional rationale for providing this preferred position for political and civil rights over economic rights is less important than its ideological function . . . to transfer its patronage from a Republican to a Democratic clientele" (Shapiro, 1978:190–91). In effect, this amounted to a double standard in the interpretation of the due process clause—a double standard imposed by the Supreme Court that helped to preserve the New Deal coalition.

Redirecting its scope of review after 1938, the federal judiciary gradually expanded its authority over the states in civil rights and civil liberties by incorporating Bill of Rights guarantees under the protection of the Fourteenth Amendment. The Warren and Burger Courts largely completed this process, in effect establishing the independent authority of the Court to define due process and equal protection in terms of more contemporary societal values:

The *Brown* decision ushered in an era of Supreme Court activism under Chief Justice Earl Warren that introduced unprecedented change in American politics and law. In a series of important decisions, the Warren Court rewrote the laws governing political redistricting, civil rights, criminal justice, federalism, and the First Amendment. The exercise of judicial power under the Constitution was transformed, as the Court became a powerful engine for the reform of social and political institutions. That judicial transformation continued under Warren's successor, Warren Burger. . . . The judicial activism of the Burger Court may not have been as vibrant, but it continued the legacy of judicial policy-making inherited from Burger's predecessor. (Hickok and McDowell, 1993:202)

The Supreme Court decides what laws require only a simple reasonableness standard (meaning that the presumption of constitutionality favors the statute) and what laws will be held to a higher level of scrutiny and are required to demonstrate a compelling state interest (meaning that the presumption is that the law probably violates the rights of the individual or group before the Court).

The more aggressively individualistic objectives of the 1960s and 1970s legal-reform advocates did not coincide as closely with majoritarian politics as did those of the early legal realists. By that time the forces of reform were pushing beyond majoritarian political limits, particularly in civil rights and civil liberties cases. With the *Brown* ruling in 1954 the legal profession began to champion the cause of fundamental rights precisely because it perceived that democratic institutions would not protect the "discrete and insular minorities" that Justice Stone had referred to in the *Carolene Products* case. The courts went much further than this during the 1960s and 1970s, actually "discovering" implicit rights as well as expansively interpreting existing ones.

Discovering New Rights: Privacy and Abortion

Certainly one of the most controversial of the Supreme Court's decisions in the Warren/Burger era was the abortion ruling. The establishment of a right of privacy in *Griswold v. Connecticut* (1965) demarcated a "zone of privacy . . . [s]urrounding the marriage relationship" (381 U.S. 479, 485). Extending the *Griswold* precedent of personal autonomy, the Court proceeded in *Roe v. Wade* (1973) to find abortion rights to be "fundamental," though not "absolute." The right would be weighed against the "reasonable and appropriate . . . State . . . interest" in the "health of the mother or that of potential human life" (410 U.S. 113, 159). Justice Rehnquist dissented. Rejecting the majority's claim that abortion constituted a fundamental right of privacy, Rehnquist argued that the "test traditionally applied in the area of social and economic legislation is whether or not a law such as that challenged has a rational relation to a state objective" (410 U.S. 113, 174). Therefore, the Court had no business overruling abortion statutes. Yet in 1973 the majority of the justices had already shifted away from New Deal deference to legislative institutions where Bill of Rights claims were advanced. The Supreme Court was expanding the application of fundamental rights to areas that were not explicitly referenced in the Constitution.

By the early 1990s the political winds had once again shifted. With the appointment of more conservative justices Anthony Kennedy, David Souter, Antonin Scalia, and Clarence Thomas to the Court, by the time *Planned Parenthood of Southeastern Pennsylvania v. Casey* (1992) came before the Court, many expected that *Roe* would be overturned. On the contrary, a majority clung to the *stare decisis* doctrine and concerns for the institutional legitimacy of the Court, narrowing the *Roe* decision but refusing to overturn it. The Court's opinion stated that after "considering the fundamental constitutional questions resolved by *Roe*, principles of institutional integrity, and the rule of *stare decisis*, we are led to conclude this: the essential holding of *Roe v. Wade* should be retained and once again reaffirmed"

(505 U.S. 833, 845–46). Further, a "decision to overrule *Roe*'s essential holding under the existing circumstances would address error, if error there was, at the cost of both profound and unnecessary damage to the Court's legitimacy, and the Nation's commitment to the rule of law" (505 U.S. 833, 869).

Justices Rehnquist, Byron White, Scalia, and Thomas, concurring in part and dissenting in part, argued that "in terming this right fundamental, the Court in *Roe* read the earlier opinions upon which it based its decision much too broadly. Unlike marriage, procreation and contraception, abortion 'involves the purposeful termination of potential life' " (505 U.S. 833, 952). Joined by Justices Thomas and White, Justice Scalia argued that the issue before the Court was whether an unborn child constituted a human life or was only "potentially human" and that in *Roe* the Court had substituted "personal predilection" for "reasoned judgment" in forming any definition of the unborn child. As the dissenting opinion emphasized, there is no way to resolve the question "as a legal matter; it is in fact a value judgment" (505 U.S. 833, 982). Absent any historical justification for abortion rights, any specific mention of abortion in the Constitution, or even any "reasoned judgment" by the Court, Scalia could find no reason for applying strict scrutiny in *Roe*.

The abortion issue presents the deciding moment for the Court between an activist and restraintist jurisprudence, and at present the Court stands by its initial ruling in *Roe v. Wade*. Not surprisingly, the abortion cases have brought intense criticism upon the courts, perhaps more than any other issue since slavery and *Dred Scott* or freedom of contract and *Lochner*. The Court's division in adjudicating the abortion issue reflects the pressures of intense societal conflict. It is a critically important case, demonstrating the extent of some judges' commitment to the principle of *stare decisis* and the limitation it places upon more conservative justices.

The abortion issue highlights a crucial fact of modern judicial activism. Since the Warren era both liberal and conservative jurists have created intense political controversy and conflict. They have failed to resolve issues because in superimposing the veil of rights and remedial law over sociopolitical and institutional policy controversies, they have frequently short-circuited the regular channels of democratic governance and reform. Conservative ideology, insofar as it has genuinely embraced judicial restraint, may have helped; but with a wide array of rights in flux, both liberal and conservative political reformers desire to harness judicial activism in favor of their cause. The courts are very susceptible to these political forces. They are powerful institutions, but they are also politically vulnerable.

Contemporary Ideological Cleavage in the Judiciary

With the growth of conservative sentiment that began in the late 1960s, the courts clearly demonstrated their susceptibility to ideological cleavages in the larger political system. Political scientist R. Shep Melnick observes that "[o]ver the past two decades the federal judiciary has mirrored the political system as a whole in an important way: it is seriously divided internally" (Melnick, 1994:35). One of the consequences of this ideological cleavage is that the "absence of clear directives from the Supreme Court vests substantial discretion in the lower courts, which decide the vast majority of cases on the meaning of particular federal laws" (Melnick, 1994:38). Lower federal courts have become battlegrounds between liberal Carter and Clinton appointees and conservative Reagan and Bush jurists.

The contemporary courts are thus reminiscent of Hamilton's "hydra head" in government, a development that Hamilton believed that the Supreme Court would help prevent. Divisions on the Supreme Court itself and the partisan, ideological split in the lower federal courts reflect deep divisions in the legal community and in American society about the nature and application of constitutional rights to modern social and political controversies. Traditionally, constitutional rights have not been created at dramatic intervals by judicial will. They have evolved in the common law and then perhaps been encoded by constitutional amendments or by the unanimous decision of the Supreme Court. The other aspect of modern judicial review that sets it apart from earlier jurisprudence lies in the discovery and application of appropriate remedies. The long list of specific administrative remedies in prison-reform litigation exemplifies a distinct break with past judicial deference to the expertise of administrative agencies.

Advocates of judicial restraint have had an important influence on judicial philosophy among more conservative jurists, but recognizing the potential for political reform from within the federal judiciary, several conservative writers have argued that to adopt a jurisprudence of "original intent" or a greater reliance on *stare decisis* would hinder the courts in thwarting previous liberal activism (Bandow, 1987:277–78). Essentially mirroring liberal substantive due process adherents, some conservatives argue that rather than confining themselves under strict constructionist jurisprudence, the courts should redirect substantive due process again to protect property interests and individual rights from government intervention.

Yet even with a new bloc of conservative justices on the Supreme Court, conservatives have been disappointed in their expectations for reform. As one analyst of the Rehnquist Court has observed, "If, in fact, the Rehnquist era previously had begun to take on a recognizable identity, notions of a coherent majority, veering to the far Right of the political spectrum, proved to be premature and unreliable. Instead, a moderately directed conservative coalition has emerged, pledged to no abiding ideological agenda that can be regarded as overweening" (Friedelbaum, 1994:145).

A keystone of the jurisprudence of the more conservative justices is a strong commitment to the doctrine of *stare decisis*. This principle has restrained them from overturning the rulings of their liberal predecessors (the *Casey* abortion ruling being the most notable example), paradoxically casting a protective veil over the substantive due process jurisprudence of the Warren and Burger Courts. As Antonin Scalia has commented:

[A]s bad as some feel judicial "activism" has gotten without substantive due process in the economic field, absent that memento of judicial humility it might have gotten even worse. . . . [T]his issue presents the moment of truth for many conservatives who have been criticizing the courts in recent years. They must decide whether they really believe, as they have been saying, that the courts are doing too much, or whether they are actually nursing only the less principled grievance that the courts have not been doing what they want. (Scalia, 1987:35)

As we pointed out in the introduction, more recently Justice Scalia has been accused of falling victim to his own ideological preferences in some cases (Rosen, 1997:26–36). Confounding conservative hopes for a more traditional jurisprudence, Clinton's appointments to the Supreme Court brought the Court back to within one vote of a liberal majority on many controversial issues.

JUDICIAL ACTIVISM IN ADMINISTRATIVE LAW

With the Supreme Court helping to pave the way for the development of the modern welfare state, the lower courts gradually took the appropriate cues from Congress and began carving out a significant role in overseeing the activity of newly created federal regulatory agencies. For much of the New Deal the judiciary's role in administrative law was confined to simple procedural details, leaving much of the business of economic regulation to the discretion of various executive agencies.

In a 1982 work entitled *Regulation and Its Reform*, Stephen Breyer, who later became a Supreme Court justice, summarized the growth of administrative law as follows:

Modern American administrative law grew out of the government's efforts to regulate private economic activity in the last part of the nineteenth century. Its original objective was to control government incursions upon private liberty and property interests by relying upon the judiciary to confine agency powers to those granted by the legislature. Thus, judges would scrutinize agency decisions to make certain they conformed to the agency's legislative mandate. The agency was required to follow procedures that would prevent it from straying beyond the bounds of the statute and that would help judges determine whether in a particular case it had done so.

Using these standards, judges overturned many agency actions until the New Deal. At that time the judiciary, while using the same standards in principle, began in practice to show far greater deference to agencies. The agencies were left with few checks on their discretion, except the check of "professional discipline." (Breyer, 1982:378)

At the turn of the century the federal courts followed the activist lead of the Supreme Court, carefully scrutinizing the few administrative agencies in existence to ensure that they were doing no more than the legislature directed. After the New Deal, as the executive branch of the federal government grew in power in its attempts to rectify what were increasingly perceived as the failures of laissez-faire economic organization, the judiciary tended to defer almost blindly to the agencies under a permissive "reasonableness" standard of review.

Beginning in the early 1960s, however, administrative law became more of a wellspring of judicial activism, strengthening the judiciary's institutional power

relative to the executive branch. With the rise of public interest litigation a growing segment of the legal profession began to challenge executive decision making
at all levels. A unifying presumption of these advocates was that economic inequalities created unavoidable infringements of individual rights and collective
rights of groups or, as in the area of environmental pollution, even led to widespread risks to the public.

During the 1960s, responding more favorably to the new public law litigation,
the federal courts began to employ what is referred to as the "hard-look" standard
of review. In many cases a harder look resulted in prolonged and intensive judicial
involvement in administrative law and policy. Rather than relying on a traditional
jurisprudence based on the "fair disposition of the controversy upon the record as
made by the parties," courts began to exercise a "power of 'independent' investigation." In the context of the ongoing reform of governmental institutions in the
1960s and 1970s, the deference previously granted by the courts to executive agencies became less and less acceptable to the legal profession.

Thus, as James Landis characterized it, judge-made administrative law repre-
sents an "effort to find an answer to those inadequacies [of modern economic orga-
nization] by some other method than merely increasing executive power" (Landis,
1987:6–7). To put it somewhat differently, since the 1960s and 1970s the courts and
the legal community have more frequently approached administrative law with the
suspicion that government agencies have been co-opted to some degree by the industries they were intended to regulate. They thus have been more likely to heighten
the level of scrutiny with the intention of spurring agencies into regulatory action,
rather than to inhibit or set limits on their execution of legislative mandates.

In administrative law, then, we see the courts opening avenues of reform to allow for more democratic and egalitarian forces to penetrate bureaucratic policy
making. Among other things, the courts broadened standing requirements and encouraged more elaborate notice and comment procedures to "democratize" the administrative process. In so doing the courts eventually created a network of
constituencies and their representatives that have come to expect a certain level of
protection or service from the courts.

Congress, rather than the executive branch, has been the primary institutional
ally of the federal judiciary in bringing about this change. Congress has enhanced
the federal courts' oversight of administrative agencies and has encouraged them
to make sure that the laws are indeed faithfully executed. To a considerable degree,
the meaning of these laws is interpreted as the courts see fit. Congressional committees are much more likely to question agencies than decisions of the federal
courts. That is the trade-off. Congress delegates authority to the courts, and they in
turn assume more responsibility in the day-to-day operations of government
(Gambitta, May, and Foster, 1981:13).

The Administrative Procedure Act

Since the turn of the century the federal courts have overseen the agency
rulemaking process. As one analyst notes:

No institution of government has been as persistent in its oversight of rulemaking for a longer period of time as the federal judiciary. Before Congress concerned itself in any meaningful way with the rulemaking process it set in motion, the courts were reviewing its results
and determining whether they were lawful instruments of governmental authority. Decades
before any president sought to oversee the rulemaking that occurred in departments and
agencies, judges were remaking the process of rulemaking and reformulating the substance
of rules through decisions in individual cases. The courts remain extremely important
overseers of rulemaking. (Kerwin, 1994:250)

Passage of the Administrative Procedure Act (APA) in 1946 sought to open up the
courts even more to review of rulemaking by prodding them to adopt a more liberal
standing doctrine. More liberal standing requirements meant that plaintiffs, especially public interest advocates, found it easier to bring cases before the courts.
With its requirements for agency "notice and comment" procedures, fairness, and
opportunity for parties to give evidence and testimony, the APA formally sanctioned and significantly expanded the role of the courts in the regulatory process.

As Stephen Breyer described it, the "act imposed certain procedural constraints
upon federal administrative bodies—whether located in the executive branch or in
independent agencies. Its basic object was to achieve 'fairness' rather than 'control.' It forms the basis of current federal administrative law" (Breyer, 1982:378).
Reflecting the rather ubiquitous deference to administrative agencies of the New
Deal era, the APA was not designed to open up the rulemaking process to general
appraisal by all interested and not-so-interested parties. Rather,

the APA authorized agencies to promulgate general rules after simply offering advance notice of new rules in the *Federal Register* and then allowing time for the public to submit
comments, criticisms, or suggestions through the mail. The APA then directed that when
the validity of a rule did come before a court, it should be upheld unless deemed "arbitrary
and capricious," while individualized orders should be judged by the more demanding standard that they be "supported by substantial evidence" (Rabkin, 1989:18)

Thus the presumption was generally in favor of the agency, which was granted
considerable discretion in promulgating rules.

In the 1960s, as public interest advocates and the courts began to perceive too
comfortable an association between various agencies and regulated industries, the
courts essentially independently transformed the meaning of the APA by adopting
a "hard-look" standard of review. The public's eroding confidence in the executive
branch and the intention of Congress to reassert its authority over public policy areas both old and new came after the judiciary's own housecleaning efforts, not before. By the 1970s the courts had already substantially altered the application of
the APA by subjecting agencies to more intense scrutiny. As political scientist R.
Shep Melnick explains it, the federal courts "increasingly have read the Administrative Procedures Act and other federal statutes to guarantee a wide variety of
groups the right to participate directly in agency deliberations as well as to bring
their complaints to court. . . . Second, in reviewing the reasonableness of agency
action under the Administrative Procedures Act, the courts have increased the bur-

den on the agencies to explain the rationale for their decisions and to demonstrate that they have considered other policy options" (Melnick, 1983:10–11). This has a profound impact on agencies in the sense that in their rulemaking efforts they must be continually prepared to justify their activities before the courts. The courts thus have become the forum in which interest groups exercise enormous influence over public policy (Kerwin, 1994). Congress and the federal judiciary have continued to actively encourage this participation through a number of important procedural reforms initiated in the past several decades.

Standing Requirements

It was not until the 1960s, with the "revolution in standing," that the federal courts began to engage more frequently in substantive review of agency decisions and rulemaking (McCraw, 1981:284). In a series of cases decided in the mid-1960s the federal courts held that various associations, such as environmental interest groups, could be granted standing in court in order to facilitate judicial review of administrative procedures. For example, in *Office of Communication of the United Church of Christ v. FCC* (1966) the District of Columbia Circuit Court stated that "such community organizations as civic associations, professional societies, unions, churches, and educational institutions or associations might well be helpful to the Commission and therefore have standing" (359 F.2d 994, 1005 [D.C. Cir. 1966]).

In another case, *Scenic Hudson Preservation Conference v. FPC* (1965), the Court of Appeals for the Second Circuit ruled that, pursuant to statutory authorization, various groups joining in a class-action lawsuit against a Federal Power Commission decision were entitled to a hearing as an "aggrieved party" (354 F.2d 608, 616 [2d Cir. 1965]). While the Burger Court remained reluctant to expand traditional standing requirements, Congress began passing more and more legislation inviting litigants to file class-action lawsuits. In turn, the lower federal courts granted them standing as aggrieved parties.

A number of social regulation statutes, especially environmental legislation, have lowered standing requirements to encourage citizen participation. One of the most important results of the new legislative directives is the rise of the "common-question class-action" lawsuit. As one author observes, "[C]ases usually do not start large, but they often end that way. To cite but one example from health and safety litigation, once a hazardous substance has been identified and successfully attacked in a first case involving high levels of exposure, subsequent suits involving lower levels of exposure and more people follow almost automatically" (Huber, 1988:137). One of the more unfortunate consequences of this litigation for the private sector is that it has nearly eliminated private insurance for handlers of hazardous materials and landfill operators. The ultimate impact has been to drastically curtail the provision of vital services to the public. In a similar vein, pharmaceutical companies faced with liability for vaccines they produce have increasingly opted out of the vaccine market for lack of adequate insurance coverage. Class-action lawsuits have dramatically impacted the relationship between producers or service providers and consumers.

As we have previously implied, underlying the revolution in standing was a dramatic shift in the relations of federal government institutions in the 1960s and 1970s. From the presidencies of Franklin Roosevelt to Lyndon Johnson the New Deal coalition had essentially accepted, even encouraged, presidential and executive-agency dominance in the national political system. By the end of Johnson's administration, largely as a result of the Vietnam War and the South's resistance to the civil rights movement, the presidency came under attack from both liberals and conservatives. Later, Watergate helped substantiate the claims of those who believed that too much power now resided in the office of the presidency.

Prior to this momentous transition in American political culture, to which the legal profession was a contributing party, Congress and the courts had remained relatively deferential to executive agencies in the administration of federal programs. As Congress became more active, undergoing a transformation of its own with the demise of the seniority system and the proliferation of subcommittees, legislation and federal expenditures increased dramatically. At the same time, the legal profession evidenced a growing discomfort with administrative expertise. "For legal scholars who 'had looked to the administrative process with such exalted expectations,' the performance of the post–New Deal agencies was 'a particularly bitter experience' " (Chase, 1982:149).

With the emergence of new social policies in the 1960s and 1970s and the resulting federal intervention in state-level and private social and economic activity, the role of the judiciary shifted toward an alliance with Congress and a less deferential review of executive-agency decision making. Congressional ascendancy in the 1970s resulted in "a huge body of entitlement law for the courts to interpret. Just as importantly, Congress promoted litigation by protecting the budget and the independence of the Legal Services Corporation, by expanding the circumstances in which courts can award attorneys' fees, and by making it easier for plaintiffs to get into court" (Melnick, 1989:213). Put simply, Congress succeeded in establishing an activist role for the courts (and they were predisposed to assume a more active role), wresting a considerable amount of control of the bureaucracy from the White House. Since then the courts have been reluctant to function as the handmaiden of either Congress or the bureaucracy. Instead, they have become a formidable policy-making institution in their own right (Gambitta, May, and Foster, 1981). The end result has been a quiet revolution in the operation of the federal government.

Statutory Interpretation

Another more basic distinction that influences the likelihood of activist decision making by judges is whether cases raise constitutional questions or merely issues of statutory interpretation. Whereas many judges might tend to restrain their pronouncements in the former cases, decisions in cases of statutory interpretation do not trigger the same degree of restraint. "Judges concerned to avoid the excesses that are believed to have characterized the Supreme Court of the 1930s and 1960s may still embark on ambitious ventures of judicial reform in the name of statutory construction" (Horowitz, 1977:13). Judicial oversight of administrative law provides the forum in which statutory interpretation takes place. The courts have in many cases interpreted statutes more broadly than the agencies and have forced more stringent regulations (Melnick, 1983). The Court's broad reading of Title VII of the Civil Rights Act, allowing for inclusion of race as a factor in university admissions in *Regents of the University of California v. Bakke* (1978) and voluntary affirmative action in *United Steelworkers v. Weber* (1978) are good examples of this type of creative interpretation (Nalbandian, 1989:43). The legislation was indisputably intended to prohibit any race-conscious distinctions, but the courts changed all that, as we shall see in our assessment of the courts' role in the affirmative-action controversy.

The Public Interest Lobby

Within the past three decades public interest groups have played a major role in the expansion of the judiciary's policy-making authority:

When the Court attempts to forge major changes, its rulings galvanize special-interest groups. *Brown* sent a signal to groups like the NAACP and the ACLU to use the judicial process to achieve what they could not through the political process. The school prayer and abortion decisions, likewise, fragmented the Court's public. Polarized by the Court's decisions and often divided over its authority to decide major issues of public policy, special-interest groups fuel political struggles at all levels of government. (O'Brien, 1986:300)

Liberal legislation on health, safety, and environmental regulations was especially tailored to allow the public interest groups access to agency rulemaking and standard setting and to relax standing requirements for these groups, giving them much broader access to the judiciary as plaintiffs for the people. Greatly encouraged by the success of the National Association for the Advancement of Colored People (NAACP) in civil rights litigation, numerous other activist groups plunged into the litigation game. "The disabled, welfare rights activists, consumer advocates, environmentalists, and pro-choice groups all saw the advantages of presenting their positions in terms of rights and of using litigation as a central (but seldom exclusive) element of their political strategy" (Melnick, 1994:27). The class-action lawsuit has become a favorite means of challenging private parties or executive agencies, whichever happens to be the violator of the public interest in the case.

The courts themselves have sometimes facilitated this participation. "In one decision, an attorney's fee was awarded even though the plaintiff's lawyer had agreed to represent him without charge. The court said the award would encourage lawyers to represent public interest clients without fees in the hope that a fee will be awarded" (Horowitz, 1977:11). The basis for attorney's-fee awards originates in the Supreme Court's interpretation of Title II of the Civil Rights Act, which authorized allocation of attorneys' fees to private attorneys in class-action lawsuits. As political scientists Karen O'Connor and Lee Epstein note, in *Newman v. Piggie Park Enterprises, Inc.* (1968) the Court concluded that "those who sued on behalf of others and not simply as individuals could recover the cost of their attorneys' fees from the private party found guilty of discrimination prohibited by the act." The impact on interest-group participation in class-action lawsuits was dramatic. "[F]ollowing *Newman* through 1974, more than 50 new groups were created to litigate on behalf of the public interest . . . most interpreted the decision to apply to all areas of public interest law. Buttressing this assumption was the fact that Congress was beginning to include specific authorizations providing for attorneys' fees recovery in most major pieces of legislation of interest to existing groups" (O'Connor and Epstein, 1985:240–41).

The public interest lobby plays a crucial role in furthering the aims of its constituents in the federal courts:

Lawyers working for organizations such as the NAACP Legal Defense Fund, the Natural Resource Defense Council, the American Civil Liberties Union, the Food Research and Action Center, the National Association for Retarded Citizens, and the Legal Services Corporation are sophisticated repeat players with long-range litigational strategies. Since they are often the party initiating litigation, they have the opportunity to engage in forum shopping to argue before the most sympathetic judges. (Melnick, 1994:40)

Professional public law litigants have advantages in court that would be unavailable to the average citizen making an isolated claim. Forum shopping by public interest advocates has mitigated the more conservative influence of Reagan and Bush appointees during the past two decades. At the same time, since the late 1970s conservative public interest groups have adopted litigation strategies similar to those of their liberal counterparts (Epstein, 1985; Caldeira and Wright, 1995:60–61).

Empowered by the class-action lawsuit, interest groups have introduced a unique bias to the practice of administrative law.

Their substantive foci—conservation, consumer interests, environmental safety, children, the poor—differ, but they share a common characteristic: all depend on fund-raising for a substantial part of their operating expenses. That commonality provides a limitation on class litigation not expressed in the rule itself. For example, many groups may have a general interest in conservation, but only those who have achieved the organizational level of the Sierra Club or the Environmental Defense Fund will be regular class representatives. . . . The interest group is therefore transformed into a social group. (Yeazell, 1987:263)

The opening up of the administrative process through class-action litigation has empowered new special interests rather than the public. "The apparently open invitation for all interest groups to join in class litigation in fact narrows to the subset of interest groups that have also achieved organization and solvency" (Yeazell, 1987:263). The largest and most successful organizations, concerned with their relevant policy areas, then "represent" a constituency of interested parties that is much narrower than the broader society.

It is in this respect that the public interest lobby has gained tremendous influence over public policy in relation to executive agencies. Public law litigation grants them access to the courts and a harder look at the policies in contention. Because of the potential advantages that a more activist judiciary affords to interest groups, public interest lawyers consider the reforms of the 1960s and 1970s to be a successful advancement of public participation in the administrative process. While this may be true to an extent, the new politics of judicial activism has created new stresses on the political system and unintended consequences for public policy as well.

The remaining chapters of this book attempt to assess the impact of the judiciary on some of the most controversial public policy issues from the 1960s to the present. Undoubtedly the courts will continue to adjudicate controversial policy in America for some time to come. In advancing remedies and reinterpreting laws they have profoundly changed a number of public institutions and have affected millions of Americans in the process. For this reason we think it important to consider how effectively courts are governing and to what end.

NOTES

1. Barry Cushman (1998) argues persuasively that New Deal Court shifts resulted from an internal transformation of the Court's commerce clause jurisprudence, not external political pressures. According to Cushman, the crucial shift on the high court came with the judicial appointments of "progressive" president Herbert Hoover. New Deal jurisprudence did not so much reflect a deference to Roosevelt's electoral victory in 1936 as it did the attainment of a critical mass of progressive legal thought. This in turn led to the Supreme Court's acceptance of more active state regulation of economic activity.

2. The *Carolene Products* footnote did not prove to be a frequently cited precedent. Its significance was much broader and less specific than a legal rule. Rather, it demarcated a shift in the Supreme Court's jurisprudence in the direction of protecting groups and interests that were considered to be disadvantaged by the very majoritarian politics that normally provided avenues for political participation and social justice. Lucas Powe (2000:487–88) has noted that footnote 4 is perhaps best seen as a set of unifying principles on which the Court could base its efforts at protecting political minorities.

Chapter 2

Brown, Busing, and the Consequences of Desegregation

BROWN AND THE LEGACY OF JUDICIAL INTERVENTION

St. Louis, Missouri, is home to the nation's largest busing experiment designed to achieve racial integration of its schools. As an article in the *Economist* pointed out in 1994, the city's black mayor, Freeman Bosley, strongly opposed the court-ordered desegregation plan. Bosley believes that the plan "has harmed the children it was meant to help. Studies suggest that black children schooled in the suburbs fare, on average, no better academically than blacks at the city schools, and those at the city's magnet schools do better than any other blacks. Meanwhile, the mayor says, busing has sapped city neighborhoods by undermining local schools. That, in turn, has accelerated urban decay" ("Off the Buses," 1994:30). One of the more protracted, complex, and controversial court-initiated policies, busing to achieve racial integration in the nation's public schools reveals some important problems and limitations of judicial activism.

In this chapter we summarize the pivotal cases that brought about the widespread adoption of busing as a means of desegregating public schools, as well as those that began to limit its scope. We then evaluate some of the evidence amassed by social scientists of the consequences of court-ordered busing for the courts, black and white students, and the larger society then and now. In spite of intense controversy and innovations creating more "voluntary" methods of school desegregation, busing has been the most prevalent means of achieving racial balance in school districts (Rossell and Armor, 1996:281). Beginning in the early 1990s, when hundreds of school districts remained under judicial decree (Rosen, 1995:24), Supreme Court decisions established guidelines for gradually dismantling these desegregation plans. The federal courts seemed to be conceding that desegregation had run its course and had largely been overtaken by social and demographic forces that minimized its impact.

In *Hard Judicial Choices* Phillip Cooper underscores the central irony of the federal judiciary's involvement in desegregation, observing that the courts have been "the focus of some of the greatest praise ever accorded the judiciary and also much of the harshest criticism. The opinion in *Brown v. Board of Education* declaring segregation unconstitutional has been lauded as a second Emancipation Proclamation, yet the later rulings attempting to enforce the mandate to eliminate segregated schools 'root and branch' have made the federal courts at all levels targets of vituperation" (Cooper, 1988:85). How did the *Brown* decision, regarded by many people as the quintessential example of the Supreme Court's assertion of moral authority in interpreting the American Constitution, lead to such prolonged conflict and controversy?

Brown v. Board of Education of Topeka, Kansas (1954) is widely regarded as the point of origin for the judicial activism of the Warren Court. Certainly *Brown* signaled that the Supreme Court was willing to risk national controversy, if necessary, to advance a fundamental rights jurisprudence that extended equal educational opportunity to discrete and insular minorities. The Supreme Court's argument was based in part on social science evidence suggesting that black students were psychologically injured by segregation. But at root the decision was a moral judgment that racial segregation in education was simply wrong and could not be tolerated under the American creed of liberty and equality of opportunity for all citizens. As the Supreme Court acknowledged, "[T]hese days, it is doubtful that any child may reasonably be expected to succeed in life if he is denied the opportunity of an education. Such an opportunity, where the state has undertaken to provide it, is a right which must be made available to all on equal terms" (347 U.S. 483, 493).

Thus, the *Brown* decision rejected the "separate-but-equal" doctrine of *Plessy v. Ferguson* (1896), "struck down school segregation and destroyed the legal foundation that had supported the Jim Crow that had become the dominant feature in southern life" (Schwartz, 1986:46). In the *Brown* opinion, speaking for the majority, Chief Justice Earl Warren invoked the authority of the self-esteem theory in articulating the psychologically damaging impact of segregation on black students:

To separate [black students] from others of similar age and qualifications solely because of their race generates a feeling of inferiority as to their status in the community that may affect their hearts and minds in a way unlikely ever to be undone. . . . Whatever may have been the extent of psychological knowledge at the time of *Plessy v. Ferguson*, this finding is amply supported by modern authority. . . . Separate educational facilities are inherently unequal. (347 U.S. 483, 486; 74 S. Ct. 686, 689)

The *Brown* case declares that segregation of any kind is inherently debilitating, and as Thomas Sowell has argued in *Civil Rights: Rhetoric or Reality?*, desegregation to achieve equality of result in education was inherent (if implicit) in the logic of the decision:

If it was the separation that made schools inferior, thereby violating the Fourteenth Amendment, then only "integrated" schools could provide "equality" in education. . . . Compul-
sory busing orders were upheld by the Supreme Court even in states that had never assigned
students by race and which even had legal prohibitions against racial assignments long before *Brown v. Board*. (Sowell, 1984:65–69)

Despite the assertion that black schools were unequal to white schools, there was
growing evidence that this historical reality was changing by the early 1960s.

Most segregated schools were inferior simply because historically, racial
discrimination deprived them of adequate educational resources and staff and
equal opportunities for graduating black students joining the labor force. In a
discussion of the impact of government policy on the economic status of
blacks, James Heckman notes that under the "separate-but-equal" doctrine
black schools were grossly inferior to white schools. "Black schools met for
fewer days per year . . . 97 days for blacks, 143 days for whites in 1929–1930.
Classroom size was bigger, teacher salaries were lower, and per pupil expenditures were lower in black schools." Yet in spite of these obstacles, Heckman
notes, black schools were beginning to reach approximate parity with white
schools "around the time of the 1954 *Brown v. Topeka Board of Education* decision" (Heckman, 1989:74).

One of the most controversial findings of James Coleman and colleagues' famous and controversial 1966 report *Equality of Educational Opportunity* was that
educational resources for blacks and whites were roughly equivalent in the 1960s
(Coleman et al., 1966). Thomas Sowell's research is widely noted for pointing out
that a number of all-black schools were also known for high academic achievement before the push for school integration (Sowell, 1984:83). Gradually and unevenly, black educational opportunities were improving throughout the 1940s and
1950s. That separate schools for blacks were inherently unequal was a notion advanced by advocates of school desegregation, and the idea was codified into law
by the Warren Court, but the basis for that conclusion may have been, as Sowell
contends, more rhetoric than reality.

Clearly at the time of the *Brown* decision, and today, there are many good reasons to work toward more fully integrated public schools, but this does not mean,
as a matter of course, that segregated schools were, or remain, inherently inferior.
Declaring segregated schools violative of constitutional guarantees of equal protection was justified simply on the grounds that they were products of a system of
legally sanctioned racial oppression.

The Supreme Court went further, relying on some very preliminary social science evidence of the psychological impairment of segregated black students, and
this eventually influenced the nature of remedies in desegregation cases in the direction of proportional representation (Powers, Rothman, and Rothman, 1990).
Initially a tertiary argument defended by some educators and social scientists, the
notion that social interaction of black and white students itself would raise black
self-esteem became more commonplace as more and more studies tended to show
only marginal improvement in black achievement in desegregated schools.

Regardless of the reasons it advanced, in deciding the *Brown* case the Supreme Court was well aware that school desegregation would be a massive undertaking that would likely provoke widespread opposition to any institutions and policies involved. Based on the contention that a cooling-off period was required after the initial decision, the Court issued a second ruling one year later (*Brown II*) that left the scope of remedy to the de jure segregation, already declared unconstitutional, open ended. In that decision the Court merely stated that school districts must eliminate desegregation with "all deliberate speed."

Due to the tenacity of racial discrimination in the South, fully thirteen years later the Supreme Court charged that there had been too much deliberation and not enough speed. As two leading experts of school desegregation recount:

Under fierce local political pressure, most Southern federal courts reacted to the vague mandates by delaying desegregation cases for long periods and then, in the end, ordering limited changes. Often these plans amounted to allowing a few black schoolchildren to attend a few grades in white schools, while maintaining a school district's essentially segregated character. Sometimes this meant that no whites were ever transferred to the previously all-black schools, faculties remained segregated, and black-and-white schools offered educational programs that differed in content and quality. (Orfield and Eaton, 1996:7)

As the federal courts began to shift toward implementing the desegregation decisions, the remedies they imposed on school committees across the nation institutionalized long-term controversy. The courts might never have been able to enforce the *Brown* rulings if not for Congress's power of the purse.

Congress provided a key compliance incentive in passing the Civil Rights Act in 1964 that later worked in accord with the judiciary's desegregation rulings. One of the provisions of the act, Title VI, made federal funding of education contingent upon elimination of educational discrimination:

Title VI prohibited racial discrimination in all schools receiving federal funds and empowered the Department of Health, Education and Welfare (HEW) to require segregated school systems to draw up plans for accomplishing substantial integration. Title VI became all the more important when, in the following year, Congress passed the Aid to Elementary and Secondary Education Act, which established for the first time a system of substantial federal aid to local school systems. . . . What the Supreme Court could not accomplish very well directly, it accomplished indirectly by bringing Congress into the picture with the carrot and stick of federal funds. (Johnson and Canon, 1984:258–59)

If the courts were finding school systems in violation of *Brown*, HEW could rather easily claim that these systems did not deserve federal aid. The combination of pressure from the lower federal district courts, HEW oversight, and the availability of federal aid for school districts working to comply with the *Brown* decision ended massive resistance and led to the widespread adoption of school desegregation plans.

TOWARD COMPULSORY RACIAL BALANCING: THE *GREEN* AND *SWANN* DECISIONS

The question of how the lower district courts would go about enforcing the *Brown* decisions to achieve desegregation remained unanswered until the late 1960s. The two pivotal Supreme Court cases that led to widespread controversy in the desegregation effort were *Green v. County School Board of New Kent County* (1968) and *Swann v. Charlotte-Mecklenburg Board of Education* (1971). As Rossell and Armor have noted:

[P]rior to the 1968 Supreme Court decision, *Green v. Board of Education*, substantial majorities of both Black and White students were enrolled in predominantly one-race schools (i.e., over 90% Black or White) in the South and, to a lesser extent, in the North. However, this began to change after *Green*, and the changes accelerated with *Swann v. Charlotte-Mecklenburg* in 1971. These Supreme Court decisions led to court-ordered racial balance remedies throughout the South and in the larger cities of the North during the 1970s. (Rossell and Armor, 1996:271–72)

The *Green* case was specifically directed at "freedom-of-choice" plans, which generally resulted in school districts going to great lengths to prevent black students from attending white schools even though they were supposed to be able to go (Rossell, 1990:3–6). In the *Green* decision Justice William Brennan stipulated that, pursuant to *Brown II*, school districts had an "affirmative duty to take whatever steps might be necessary to convert to a unitary system in which racial discrimination would be eliminated root and branch." Brennan stressed that the "burden on a school board today is to come forward with a plan that promises realistically to work, and promises realistically to work *now*" (391 U.S. 430, 439; emphasis in the original).

The *Green* decision did not elaborate on the types of remedies for previously segregated school districts. Generally, "school districts simply did what was necessary to achieve court approval of their plans, and that usually meant adopting the plaintiff's plan" (Rossell, 1990:8). What the federal courts would require to meet the criterion of "realistic" plans did not become clear until the *Swann* decision in 1971. At that time "the Supreme Court specifically addressed the issue of permissible remedies. *Swann* represented an innovation in the determination of both violation and remedy" (Rossell, 1990:8).

The *Swann* decision proposed forced integration through busing as one of several appropriate remedies to the persistent problem of school segregation. In spite of the *Brown I* and *II* decisions to desegregate schools with "all deliberate speed," Southern school districts succeeded in "keeping over three-fourths of the South's black students in schools that were ninety percent or more black" (Garrow, 1988:879). Thus in *Swann* the exasperated Supreme Court proclaimed:

All things being equal with no history of discrimination, it might well be desirable to assign pupils to schools nearest their homes. But all things are not equal in a system that has been deliberately constructed and maintained to enforce racial segregation. The remedy for such segregation may be administratively awkward, inconvenient, and even bizarre in some situations and may impose burdens on some; but all awkwardness and inconvenience cannot be avoided in the interim period when remedial adjustments are being made to eliminate the dual school systems. (402 U.S. 1, 28 [1971])

The Court also noted that the district court's use of a racial balance requirement, as "a useful starting point in the process of shaping a remedy" was "within [its] equitable remedial discretion" (402 U.S. 1, 25).

As Lino Graglia has pointed out, the Supreme Court continually avoided explicitly requiring racial balancing, which is itself another way of classifying by race, and merely reasserted that the elimination of dual school systems must be accomplished by the school districts, with the district courts supervising the process. Nevertheless, in *Swann* the district court approved, and the circuit court and the Supreme Court upheld, a comprehensive school desegregation plan that would be utilized as a blueprint for desegregation across the nation.

First, the district court relied on evidence that "as a group Negro students score quite low on school achievement tests . . . and the results are not improving under present conditions." Lower academic achievement, the judge continued, " 'cannot be explained solely in terms of cultural, racial or family background without honestly facing the impact of segregation.' . . . The solution was clear and simple: a 'dramatic improvement' in black performance could be 'produced' 'without material detriment to the whites' by 'transferring underprivileged black children from black schools into schools with 70% or more white students' " (Graglia, 1976:106–7). The most significant implication of the ruling was that the distinction between de jure and de facto segregation became a moot point in the face of the problem of black academic achievement, which integration through busing and other means would apparently alleviate. Academic achievement, along with racial balancing of schools, would now be litmus tests to be used by the federal courts in determining the extent of compliance with *Brown*.

In *Brown* the Court had declared that segregation was unconstitutional and that the schools would have to be desegregated. In practice, following *Swann*, the lower federal courts began to require busing as a means to raise black academic achievement. This was linked to the much broader goal of producing lasting racial integration, which ultimately involved a more complex array of social, economic, and political institutions and conditions. Thus the *Brown* decisions, which held de jure segregation unconstitutional, were transformed into a national integration strategy that involved mandatory busing for public schools.

Charles Johnson and Bradley Canon note that "following *Swann v. Charlotte-Mecklenburg County Board of Education* (1971), federal district courts began issuing detailed orders regarding cross-town busing, racial ratios among teachers and pupils, curriculum offerings, and other features of the school system thought necessary to achieve desegregation" (Johnson and Canon, 1984:218). Small school districts often redrew boundaries to achieve required racial balance. Larger districts required busing to achieve the levels of integration the courts wanted. "These plans frequently led to significant white flight and, in some cases, to resegregation" (Armor, 1995:47). To provide some idea of the magnitude of the change resulting from the *Green* and *Swann* precedents, from the years 1954 to 1975, 53 of a total of 208 (25 percent) judgments for desegregation plans were entered by the federal courts in 1968 and 1969. One hundred and seven of the total 208 judgments (51 percent) were entered in 1970–71 (U.S. Commission on Civil Rights, 1976:135). Thus the courts handed down more than three-fourths of all busing decrees from that period in the *Green* (1968) and *Swann* (1971) years.

Jennifer Hochschild, an authority on busing policy, noted in 1984 that school desegregation seemed to be moving in the right direction in the 1970s:

By the early 1970s, OCR [Office of Civil Rights] had investigated, negotiated with and arm-twisted over 3000 districts in the South. Courts had handed down desegregation orders in over 150 districts. As a consequence, racial isolation in the South dropped considerably.... Legislators, litigators, and regulators turned their attention to the North; the Supreme Court ruled in *Keyes v. School District No. 1 of Denver, Colorado* (1973) that Northern districts, even without a history of legislated dual school systems, could be found to have intentionally segregated their students and thus could be subject to the same mandates as the South. The problem of racial isolation seemed on the way to being solved. (Hochschild, 1984:28)

Nevertheless, Hochschild's identification of racial isolation as the source of the segregation problem suggests that the courts were really contending with a much more intractable set of underlying social and economic conditions in attempting to integrate the nation's schools. Indeed, the "problem of racial isolation" involves a complex and interrelated set of circumstances, including education, jobs, and housing—the entire social fabric.

Could the least democratic and least powerful branch of American government realistically expect to do much more than what it had already done in *Brown*, that is, to declare de jure segregation to be violative of the equal protection clause of the Constitution? In retrospect it seemed, even to the courts themselves, that addressing problems like minority academic underachievement and racial isolation through busing decrees actually had created more problems for everyone. Thus, as Hochschild implies, just as they began to pervasively influence the racial balance of public schools across the nation, the courts found a way to minimize their involvement, by limiting remedies to intradistrict integration, and backed off.

JUDICIAL RETRENCHMENT IN SCHOOL DESEGREGATION

Just as sweeping desegregation seemed to become a national priority, the Supreme Court decided *Milliken v. Bradley* (1974). In *Milliken* the Court ruled that "courts could not order busing across school district boundaries unless all the affected districts were found guilty of *de jure* segregation" (Hochschild, 1984:29). Here the Court acknowledged that integration efforts had practical limits and that white flight could not be remedied by endless busing decrees. David Armor notes that since this ruling "lower court decisions have tended to reinforce the principles of *Milliken I*, particularly regarding the requirement that remedies must be tailored to specific constitutional violations" (Armor, 1995:47).

In rejecting "cross-district transportation of pupils" in *Milliken*, Chief Justice Warren Burger stated that such a remedy "can be supported only by drastic expansion of the constitutional right itself, an expansion without any support in . . . principle or precedent" (418 U.S. 717, 748). The Court was not going to require further and further expansion of busing programs as a means of remedying white flight. Judicially mandated intradistrict remedies remained in force for many years after *Milliken*, but as long as white flight continued, either geographically or through white migration to private and parochial schools, desegregation goals were unattainable. In many Northern cities the problem of racial isolation worsened as white students left the inner-city schools.

In the early 1990s, in cities that had experienced some of the greatest difficulties achieving desegregated schools, the courts began to relax their imposition of busing and other remedies. In *Board of Education of Oklahoma v. Dowell* (1991) the U.S. Supreme Court ruled that formerly segregated school districts could be released from desegregation orders. Justice Rehnquist stated that school desegregation "decrees . . . are not intended to operate in perpetuity. Local control over the education of children allows citizens to participate in decisionmaking, and allows innovation so that school programs can fit local needs" (498 U.S. 237, 248). At the time of this ruling more than eight hundred school districts remained under decrees, and this case signaled a shift toward releasing local school boards from desegregation orders in the 1990s (Taylor, 1992:207).

A 1994 article in the *Economist* also noted that the courts had given up trying to force integration in De Kalb County around Atlanta in 1992: "[T]he city could not help it, said the court in effect, if its efforts had not worked" ("Back Where It All Began: School Desegregation," 1994:29). In the Atlanta case, *Freeman v. Pitts* (1992), the Court authorized an incremental dismantling of desegregation plans. The majority ruled that "good-faith" compliance with a consent decree could determine whether a school district in partial compliance with a desegregation order could be incrementally released from judicial oversight. The Court also held that demographic factors beyond the control of the school board should not be considered as sufficient to maintain jurisdiction. "Where resegregation is a product not of state action, but of private choices, it does not have constitutional implications. It is beyond the authority and beyond the practical ability of the federal courts to try to counteract these kinds of continuous and massive demographic shifts" (503 U.S. 467, 495 [1992]).

Following this trend, in *Missouri v. Jenkins* (1995) the Supreme Court struck down a district-court decision mandating that Missouri pay more than $1.4 billion for magnet schools. Proponents of the plan argued that these revenues were essential to help raise minority academic achievement in Kansas City public schools. Ruling against the plan, the Court held that if achievement differences are "not the result of segregation, they do not figure in the remedial calculus." The district court should therefore have limited its review to determining "whether the reduction in achievement by minority students attributable to prior de jure segregation

[had] been remedied to the extent practicable" (U.S. Supreme Court, 1995, 93-1823:30–31). In a concurring opinion, Justice Thomas criticized those who assumed that predominantly black schools necessarily provided an inferior education. "It never ceases to amaze me that courts are so willing to assume that anything that is predominantly black must be inferior. . . . The mere fact that a school is black does not mean that it is the product of a constitutional violation" (Justice Thomas concurring, U.S. Supreme Court, 1995, 93-1823:1–2).

Gary Orfield and John Yun, in their widely cited report on the status of desegregation, have presented data indicating that since the 1980s resegregation has occurred. Among their findings, the researchers observe that resegregation is occurring in the South and that urban blacks, Latinos, and suburban whites are becoming the most racially isolated groups of students. The authors partly attribute these trends to court cases limiting the force of desegregation plans. "Among school districts recently ending or phasing out their desegregation plans are Buffalo, NY; Broward County (Fort Lauderdale), FL; Clark County (Las Vegas), NV; Nashville–Davidson County, TN; Duval County (Jacksonville), FL; Mobile, AL; Minneapolis, MN; Cleveland, OH; San Jose, CA; Seattle, WA; and Wilmington, DE. A number of other major districts are now in litigation over the issue, with some of them struggling to be permitted to continue their desegregation plans" (Orfield and Yun, 1999:11).

The *Milliken* decision and its progeny limited and eventually terminated many prolonged efforts at achieving school desegregation through busing and other means. The federal courts have recognized that demographic change, with or without the acceleration associated with white flight, would make necessary "a permanent system of student assignment by racial quotas . . . with continuous redistricting or reapportionment to correct these imbalances" (Wolf, 1981:294–95). Judicially mandated busing profoundly influenced American education. In its wake a body of evidence began to accumulate that suggested that its central objectives had failed, that resegregation had occurred, and that the policy itself was increasingly opposed by both blacks and whites, particularly in Northern urban centers.

CONSEQUENCES OF SCHOOL DESEGREGATION

Implementation of a Judicially Mandated Racial-Balancing Policy

The first major study to examine trends in desegregation across the United States reported significant progress by 1980. Gary Orfield reported the following general impacts:

Nationwide, segregation of black students in public schools declined significantly between 1968 and 1980. . . . The most substantial decreases in segregation of black students came in the South and the border states. . . . The Northeast was the only region in which segregation of black students increased and, in 1980, had the highest level of any region. Nearly half (48.7 percent) of black students in the region attended almost all-minority schools in 1980, compared with less than a quarter (23 percent) of black students in the South. All other regions showed decreases in segregation, although the Midwest in 1980 was significantly more segregated than the nation as a whole. (Orfield, 1983:3)

Indeed, it was evident that by the end of the 1970s substantial progress had been made toward integrating schools. From 1968 until 1980 the percentage of black students in schools composed of more than 50 percent "non-Anglo students" declined from 77 percent to 63 percent. Schools comprised of virtually no Anglo students also "declined from two-thirds in 1968 to one-third in 1980" (Hochschild, 1984:30).

In the aggregate, these statistics suggest the extent to which desegregation altered the composition of the nation's public schools in the 1970s. While integration efforts in the South, where de jure segregation had long been practiced, were succeeding at mixing black and white students in public schools, the desegregation policy was failing in the North (Hochschild, 1984:30). In 1984 Hochschild reported that "we have the largest, most urban, and most heavily non-Anglo schools left to desegregate" (Hochschild, 1984:33). Why, in spite of widespread resistance, had desegregation worked in the South? What had happened in the North to prevent busing from achieving racially integrated public schools?

Social Protest and Interracial Conflict

Sociologists Susan Olzak, Suzanne Shanahan, and Elizabeth West have studied the incidence of antibusing events in Standard Metropolitan Statistical Areas (SMSAs) across the country from 1968 to 1990. The authors found that while "most SMSAs had no events, one-third of our SMSAs had at least one protest, and Chicago and Boston had over 40 anti-busing events during 1968–1990." Moreover, the researchers found that "anti-busing activity rises and peaks during the mid-1970s, but then its incidence declines sharply toward the end of that decade" (Olzak, Shanahan, and West, 1994:217). Perhaps the most important conclusion that the authors drew was that the degree of school desegregation itself, not the fact that it was imposed by federal mandate, directly affected the extent of social protest over busing. "The conventional view that federal-court-ordered busing sparked the grievances that led to anti-busing protest does not hold up under scrutiny. Instead, it appears that an urban area's history of racial events, interracial exposure in neighborhoods, residential isolation of whites, and the amount of change in interracial contact in schools intensified the rate of white mobilization against busing" (Olzak, Shanahan, and West, 1994:232). If this is true, it is likely that any form of integration policy would have generated some resistance among whites and blacks.

Selected Case Studies of Desegregation Efforts

In the case of Boston's South End these observations are borne out. Numerous incidents occurred in Boston after Judge W. Arthur Garrity handed down his busing decree in 1974. Rocks were thrown at buses; black students were attacked verbally and sometimes physically by white students and angry protestors outside the schools. In 1976 Judge Garrity placed South Boston High in receivership because the conditions he observed there were so bad. At the same time, conflicts were minimal in the rest of the city. "South Boston and Charlestown, the two communities that had been most racially isolated before busing, had the most racially motivated problems after busing. The resistance to busing was strongest in these areas, and the resulting inability of blacks to even enter the communities was largely confined to these two parts of the city" (Willie and Greenblatt, 1981:63).

The cases against desegregation decided by the Supreme Court in the early 1990s reflected frustration with the inability to overcome "housing patterns [that] were relentlessly segregated" ("Brown 40 Years On," 1994:15). Jared Taylor provides a telling account of how some Florida communities circumvented busing in their efforts to desegregate schools:

Palm Beach County schools were to be exempted from mandatory busing if enough blacks could be induced to move into white areas by 1995 and send their children to local schools. People dislike busing so much that towns were willing to rewrite housing codes to allow cheap apartments in million-dollar neighborhoods. Real-estate developers advertised heavily in black newspapers and offered rent subsidies and reduced-rate mortgages for blacks. (Taylor, 1992:195)

Richard Pride and J. David Woodard's study of school busing in Nashville, Tennessee, underscores the intensity of social resistance to desegregation efforts. Consequences of busing in Nashville school districts included substantial initial and protracted white flight, persistent, though unsubstantiated, fear of white declines in achievement in desegregated schools, general opposition from both whites and blacks in the community (though blacks were less likely to oppose busing), and the eventual rejection of busing in Nashville by the federal courts (Pride and Woodard, 1985:282).

Another study of desegregation efforts in Erie, Pennsylvania, concluded that the policy had failed. "In most desegregated classrooms, observers report that there is still an atmosphere of 'us' and 'them,' with children from another neighborhood being identified as outsiders" (Willie and Greenblatt, 1981:80). A study of Corpus Christi, Texas, schools also found that desegregation plans there had not brought about the desired results. "Most west side schools still remain virtually minority, a condition that will not necessarily change as the Mexican-American population continues increasing and the Anglo-American population continues decreasing. In addition, economic and housing patterns in minority communities remain virtually unchanged" (Willie and Greenblatt, 1981:152).

In Richmond, Virginia, the Supreme Court decisions had an immediate impact on the school system. After the *Swann* decision Richmond implemented District Judge Robert Merhige's busing plan for more than 21,000 students, but as Robert Pratt remarks, "[D]emographics made it highly unlikely that court-ordered busing would succeed. Just beyond the city limits lay Henrico and Chesterfield counties, both of which had overwhelmingly white school systems" (Pratt, 1992:58). Whites who could afford it either chose private or parochial schools for their chil-

dren or moved to the suburbs. Pratt notes that some black and white realtors capi-
talized on the strain of busing by practicing block-busting. He provides the
following description:

A white realtor finds a white couple who is willing to sell to a Negro. The couple is put into
contact with the Negro broker who sells the home to a Negro couple, at a higher price than a
white would pay, and sends one half commission to the white realtor. Surrounding home
owners are put in touch with the Negro broker, and so goes the block. Out to the country and
a new suburban home and school goes the white. (quoted in Pratt, 1992:62)

After the *Milliken* decision the interdistrict busing plan that Judge Merhige had ordered for Richmond and the surrounding white suburbs was struck down. As a result of this halt to desegregation efforts, "Richmond developed a new type of dual
education—a private school system for the affluent and white, and a public school
system for the poor and black" (Pratt, 1992:99).

Discussing the impact of busing in Boston, Jared Taylor emphasizes that all the
money spent in Boston's urban schools had little impact. By the late 1980s, long after a 1975 court order initiating busing, Boston schools were "spending more than
$7,000 a year per pupil (the national average is $3,752), [but] 40 percent of all
ninth-graders were dropping out before graduation." White flight had shifted the socioeconomic base of the schools to students from predominantly poor families.
"Middle-class students had steadily left the schools, and white attendance had
dropped from 60 percent in 1972 to only 22 percent in 1990. . . . So many children
came from poor families that 80 percent of Boston grade-school students got free or
cut-rate lunches." These changes, brought about by busing, led to even more bizarre
consequences. "With so few students left, students had to be bused for crazy distances to achieve racial balance. The president of the Boston Schools Committee,
who had been a supporter of busing, called it a process of 'shuffling black children
across the city to a mediocre school with other black children' " (Taylor, 1992:204).

As most of these case studies underscore, in the face of considerable resistance,
mandatory desegregation plans were effective in the South but not in the North.
David Armor summarizes the results of Southern desegregation: "For southern
districts with mandatory plans, racial imbalance dropped rapidly between 1968
and 1972, with little or no change after that time. Southern districts with voluntary
plans also show declines in racial imbalance, but not nearly to the degree shown by
mandatory plans" (Armor, 1995:186). Desegregation in Northern metropolitan areas was a different story. In the North considerable evidence accumulated that
linked desegregation itself to changing demographics that eroded policy gains and
worsened the racial-isolation problem.

THE WHITE-FLIGHT RESPONSE TO FORCED
INTEGRATION

James Coleman and colleagues created considerable controversy in the late
1960s in a study in which they concluded that school desegregation was associated

with a sharp drop in the number of white students enrolled in the school district (Coleman et al., 1966). Several researchers subsequently criticized Coleman's inference. However, more elaborate studies supported Coleman's findings. The study by Reynolds Farley helped to further clarify the white-flight phenomenon. Desegregation was more likely to contribute to white flight in the largest, central-city school districts with the highest concentrations of black students (Farley and Wurdock, 1977). Another study by Rossell corroborated these findings and also found that white-flight effects were strongest where white students were "reassigned to formerly black schools" (Armor, 1995:176). This occurs where desegregation is accomplished through two-way busing (whites bused to black schools and blacks bused to white schools). Rossell found that white flight was less pronounced where black students were reassigned to predominantly white schools. This is referred to as one-way busing (blacks bused to white schools).

Forced integration, especially by busing, apparently contributes significantly to white flight, but this does not necessarily lead to an out-migration of whites from desegregating districts. For example, Richard Hula found that in Dallas, Texas, desegregation did not influence residential housing patterns. Although Hula's work was based only on a single case study, it suggests that white flight does not necessarily involve geographic relocation but may frequently lead, for both more affluent blacks and whites, to increased student flight to private and parochial schools (Hula, 1984).

Reanalyzing data previously collected by Farley from 104 central cities until 1976, W.A.V. Clark found that white flight persisted over time following desegregation efforts. Clark found that white flight continued for up to four years after busing went into effect, "for 4 years in the matched city example and the 42 cities with court-ordered desegregation plans and for 3 years in the full sample of 104 cities" (Clark, 1987:222). Clark provided a specific example from Norfolk, Virginia, which experienced substantial white out-migration following a federal court decision implementing a desegregation plan. Comparing actual population changes with a model projecting white migration based on demographic trends in the absence of any desegregation, Clark found that "the losses were substantially in excess of the losses which might have occurred, especially during the year of implementation and the following year" (Clark, 1987:224–25).

David Armor's study of desegregation confirms the argument that the courts had a substantial impact on white attrition. Nevertheless, desegregation seems to have peaked in 1980 and declined thereafter. Armor concludes that "the opportunities for meaningful desegregation in larger public school districts are increasingly affected and limited by changing demographics and the declining proportion of white students" (Armor, 1995:170). Armor links some of the changing demographics of cities to forced integration itself. He notes that in "central city school districts with higher percentages of black enrollment . . . mandatory busing . . . raise[d] white loss rates by three to five times that due to underlying demographic processes" (Armor, 1995:176).

In *The End of Equality* Mickey Kaus remarks that busing in the 1970s helped to further impoverish the nation's urban centers:

Throughout this period, busing . . . had the clear effect of accelerating the flight of mid-dle-class whites from urban public schools. It made urban school districts, with their large underclass populations, unacceptable to ambitious parents, since even living in a "good" neighborhood no longer offered assurance of avoiding an underclass presence at your child's school. Simultaneously, because the Supreme Court refused to extend busing be-yond municipal boundaries, the suburbs were established as a safe haven. In Boston, busing left a public school system only 21 percent white out of a metropolitan-area school popula-tion 87 percent white. Almost 40 percent of the children in the Boston public schools now come from welfare families. In Seattle, public schools have lost a third of their students since busing began in 1978, cutting enrollment to half of what it was in the early seventies. In a city 79 percent white, whites are now only 46 percent of the public school population. In Los Angeles, the number of whites in the public schools dropped by 25 percent between the initial talk of mandatory busing in 1976 and its implementation two years later. (Kaus, 1992:54)

Although some of the findings may reflect higher black birth rates, these statistics suggest a strong correlation between busing policy and white flight to suburban areas. Once court-ordered busing appeared imminent to white parents, who believed that busing would jeopardize their children's education, they began to leave urban areas for the white suburbs. But why did whites believe that the presence of black students would detract from their children's education?

DESEGREGATION, BLACK NEIGHBORHOODS, AND THE BLACK UNDERCLASS

When critics of the post-*Milliken* era (characterized by substantial resegregation of public schools in large metropolitan areas) point to the worsening conditions in inner-city schools and the "virtually all-white rings around blacks-only ghettos," they tend to discount the evidence that forced integration itself caused the mass ex-odus of whites from public to private or parochial schools and the cities to the sub-urbs (Dimond, 1985:vi). As Kaus acknowledges, these whites were not running from black students per se, and public opinion surveys corroborate widespread support among whites for desegregation in principle (this will be discussed further in the conclusion to this chapter). It is more likely that middle-class whites and blacks were attempting to avoid the impact of problems of the underclass on their children's education.

Sociologist W.J. Wilson places the "underclass" phenomenon in the context of black migration to the Northern cities. Until the 1970s poor rural blacks moved into the industrial cities in numbers too great to be assimilated. During the 1970s, a second migration began; a substantial number of middle- and working-class blacks left the cities. The poorest of the poor, usually female-headed families, were left behind. The young age of this new inner-city population is an important char-acteristic: "[T]he number of central-city blacks aged fourteen to twenty-four rose by 78 percent from 1960 to 1970, compared with an increase of only 23 percent for whites of the same age. From 1970 to 1977 the increase in the number of young blacks slackened off somewhat, but it was still substantial" (Wilson, 1987:36). It is this age cohort that is responsible for, among other things, a disproportionate share of violent crime, drug abuse and alcoholism, single-parent families, out-of-wed-lock births, school dropouts, and welfare dependence.

Critical to understanding the societal response to judicially shaped and man-dated integration efforts, the out-migration of working- and middle-class blacks supports the notion that white flight is not simply racially motivated. It is largely a manifestation of the pervasive avoidance of the lowest class of inner-city resi-dents, who are mostly black, by the middle and working classes. Because this is so, argued Eleanor Wolf in *Trial and Error* (an insightful study of desegregation in Detroit), "[b]using may intensify the processes involved in middle-class attrition, both black and white" (Wolf, 1981:293).

In spite of this, there is the additional paradox of the reluctance of even middle- and upper-income blacks to move out of black neighborhoods when opportunities to move into white areas increase. Considerable evidence suggests that many blacks do not wish to live in predominantly white neighborhoods (Downs, 1970; Gans, 1969; Watts et al., 1964). Wolf mentions a study by Davis (1965:212) that found that reasons given by interviewed blacks for remaining in black neighbor-hoods were not related to perceived discrimination but " 'satisfaction with the area, attachment to friends and family, desire to stay close to work or other facili-ties and lesser costs.' Only 7 percent reported experiencing overt or covert actions in their search for alternate housing which were, or could be, suspected to be dis-criminatory" (Wolf, 1981:44).

Christopher Jencks and Paul Peterson's 1991 study of the urban underclass of-fers additional evidence supportive of the notion that class was more significant than race in explaining white and black flight from the inner cities. Between 1970 and 1980, the period of desegregation, black ghetto poverty increased by roughly 30 percent nationwide. Moreover, increased ghettoization occurred in large metro-politan Northern cities like New York, Chicago, Philadelphia, and Detroit. Ghetto poverty was actually on the decline for the same period in cities across the South. These trends suggest that working- and middle-class families were leaving North-ern cities at an accelerated rate at the same time that the ghetto poor, the very popu-lation that working- and middle-class parents believed would be impacting the quality of schools under desegregation orders, were increasing in number. More-over, the numbers of Hispanic ghetto poor were actually growing faster than black ghetto poor during the 1970s (Jargowsky and Bane, 1991:244–57).

DESEGREGATION AND ACADEMIC ACHIEVEMENT OF BLACK AND WHITE STUDENTS

If white flight eroded the chances of desegregation's success at achieving a more favorable racial balance within metropolitan schools, desegregation also seems to have been largely unsuccessful in improving the academic performance of black students. There is little evidence that desegregation has provided the kind of improvement in black educational achievement that its proponents had hoped for. Most research shows substantial improvements in achievement since the early

1970s, but not much progress can be attributed to desegregation itself. For example, a review of black academic performance edited by Christopher Jencks and Meredith Phillips finds that blacks in Southern integrated elementary schools read better than those from predominantly black schools, but racial mix seems to have little impact beyond sixth grade, and large achievement disparities remain even in integrated schools (Grissmer, Flanagan, and Williamson, 1998:206–11). Disparities persist despite the fact that average expenditures and resources for black and white students are roughly equal.[1] An interesting and important difference noted by researchers is that the academic achievement scores of black and white teachers in predominantly black schools were significantly lower than in other schools (Sanders and Rivers, 1996; Ferguson, 1998:273–317; Haycock, 2001). The research suggests that lower educational achievement among teachers tends to hinder student progress in inner-city schools.

Evidence from National Assessment of Educational Progress student testing is mixed. Black scores on these tests have improved over the past thirty years (Jencks and Phillips, 1998). When the tests were first administered in the early 1970s, the gaps between black and white educational test scores were of staggering proportions. Black seventeen-year-olds were six years behind whites in reading, four years behind whites in math, and five to seven years behind whites in science. This means that at graduation age blacks had developed fewer skills in these basic areas than whites entering high school as freshmen. In reading and science, blacks who should have been leaving high school had an education level comparable to whites finishing grade school. Today, on average, black students score at approximately the same levels as whites entering high school (Haycock, 2001; Johnston and Viadero, 2000).

The Thernstroms' summary of achievement data suggests substantial progress in black student performance during the 1980s, followed by setbacks in the early 1990s:

African Americans who were in high school made little educational progress, but scores rose perceptibly for students in the younger age groups—nine-year-olds and thirteen-year-olds. . . . A solid foundation for progress at the high school level was thus being laid in grade school and junior high during the 1970s. The scores of white students in the younger age brackets were level or declining a bit, while those of black students were rising. As these better-prepared black students reached high school in the 1980s, the racial gap began to narrow there as well.

Thus, the racial gap in reading competency shrank dramatically between 1980 and 1988, falling from 6 years to just 2.5 years, a truly remarkable, but, alas, short-lived, change. In 1980 only 7 percent of black youths could read at the proficient level; by 1988 the figure had jumped to 25 percent (as compared with 45 percent for whites). In mathematics a gap of 4.1 years in 1982 narrowed to 2.5 years in 1990. In science the gap fell from an appalling 7.1 years in 1982 to 4.4 years in 1986. The first assessment of student ability to write the English language was not attempted until 1984, but between 1984 and 1988 the gap narrowed from 3.1 years to 2.1 years. (Thernstrom and Thernstrom, 1997:356)

These gains are truly impressive, especially for the speed at which they were realized. Yet by 1994 the gap in reading had widened from 2.5 to 3.9 years. In math, from 1990 to 1994 black students had fallen from 2.5 to 3.4 years behind white students. In science blacks fell back to 5.4 years from 4.4 years in 1986. Finally, in writing, blacks regressed from only 2.1 years to 3.3 years behind whites (Thernstrom and Thernstrom, 1997:355, table 1). Black test scores have remained roughly the same since these setbacks were reported in the mid-1990s (Campbell, Hombo, and Mazzeo, 2000).

RESEGREGATION IN DESEGREGATED SCHOOLS

One of the more persistent problems in desegregated schools is the various processes by which black students end up segregated within the desegregated school itself. To provide an example from one Northern desegregated school without a tracking system, "over 80% of the students in the eighth grade scholars' program are white [and] nearly 90% of the children in educable mentally retarded (EMR) classes are black" (Rist, 1979:159–60). The same researcher concludes that "the unequal performance levels that students bring with them . . . appear to have the strong potential for reinforcing stereotypes about racial differences in intelligence and creating resentment and hostility between black and white children" (Rist, 1979:170). This research casts doubt on the notion that desegregated schools raise black students' self-esteem in any uncomplicated, unequivocal manner. Many researchers who have identified the problem of resegregation within desegregated schools tend to attribute it to insufficient emphasis on diversity and self-esteem building. This seems to be more an article of faith among them than an empirically validated conclusion. Indeed, after surveying the literature, Henry Louis Gates (1992) pointed out that there is no evidence that self-esteem contributes in significant ways to academic achievement.

If minority achievement was improving in desegregated and segregated schools throughout the 1980s, then progress was made with traditional programs largely in place. Minority students evidently benefited from the types of educational programs they received, whether they tended to have resegregated or not. Reviewing studies of black achievement, Crain and Mahard suggested that "special efforts" to enhance learning in reading comprehension were particularly beneficial to black students (Crain and Mahard, 1982). Yet others engaged in the same research have advocated doing away with many of these programs because they bring about resegregation within the schools:

Academic grouping practices that are commonly used to manage diversity include ability grouping and tracking, compensatory education, special education, and bilingual education. . . . Resegregation results from the pupil assignment practices and organization of these programs. . . . Traditional student assignment practices invariably result in the disproportionate channeling of minority students into low-ability groups and other programs addressing academic deficiencies (Eyler, Cook, and Ward, 1983:160).

A study conducted by the New York State Office of Education Performance Review in 1974 tends to confirm the assertion that black academic achievement does not depend upon desegregation of schools, white peer groups, or mainstreaming. The study compared two predominantly black, inner-city schools, one high-achieving and one low-achieving. "The study showed that the differences in student performance in the two schools could be attributed to factors under the schools' control." Specifically, among other things, "the more effective school had developed a plan for dealing with the reading problem and had implemented the plan throughout the school" (Bell, 1980:112).

Another study of a number of Michigan schools found that academically improving schools, unlike declining schools, placed substantially more emphasis on accomplishment of "basic reading and mathematical objectives," and faculty in the declining schools "spend less time in direct reading instruction than do teachers in the improving schools" (Bell, 1980:115). Other success stories from urban schools have emphasized a return to academic excellence among teachers and students and mastery of the basic curriculum (Northwest Region Educational Laboratory, 1999). Magnet schools, in particular, have shown considerable promise in raising black academic achievement above the national averages (Dentler, 1990; Mitchell, Russell, and Benson, 1989). These studies tend to corroborate what many observers of contemporary education have claimed, that a key factor influencing any student's achievement, minority or not, may be the extent to which educators themselves have mastered and effectively teach basic learning skills—reading, writing, math, and science.

MAGNET SCHOOLS AND SCHOOL-CHOICE PLANS

Before the *Missouri v. Jenkins* (1995) decision Kansas City had spent disproportionate amounts of money on magnet schools designed to attract white students from neighboring suburbs. Missouri journalist Blake Hurst explained that "Judge Clark's desegregation plan has affected every part of the budget of the state of Missouri. . . . Missouri spends 44.6 percent of its elementary and secondary education funds in Kansas City and St. Louis though the two districts contain only 9.1 percent of the state's students. Per pupil costs in Kansas City are two-and-a-half times the state average" (Hurst, 1995:55). Hurst went on to point out that the huge expenditures had not favorably impacted academic achievement in the Kansas City schools. "The costs borne . . . would be more bearable if the result was a better education for the kids. But as the school district freely admits . . . student performance has been disappointing" (Hurst, 1995:55). This conforms to the general findings about school performance and educational expenditures. "In a review of over 187 studies on educational funding and performance, University of Rochester professor Eric A. Hanushek concluded that there is "no systematic relationship between school expenditures and school performance. . . . [E]xpenditures per pupil in the United States have more than doubled in the last 20 years. During the same period, test scores have fallen" (Hurst, 1995:55).

Some magnet-school programs have showed more promise than others. Christine Rossell studied the effectiveness of controlled-choice plans in twenty school districts above 30 percent minority. Rossell found that these plans "produce significantly less white enrollment decline than mandatory plans but more than voluntary plans—about one-third more white enrollment decline than normal when implemented in districts that did not formerly have a mandatory reassignment plan" (Rossell, 1995:67).

Moreover, Rossell concluded that controlled choice was less beneficial from the parents' standpoint than voluntary plans with magnet-school incentives, due to a "lack of predictability regarding a child's school assignment and a lack of control over whether a child can attend the neighborhood school" (Rossell, 1995:69). Rossell clearly favors neighborhood schools with magnet incentives over controlled choice, remarking that "as far as parents are concerned, controlled-choice plans have too much control and not enough choice" (Rossell, 1995:69).

CONCLUSION: TO ABANDON OR RESTORE THE PROMISE OF *BROWN*?

Large majorities of blacks and whites remain committed to the goal of desegregation. Just as clearly, substantial majorities are opposed to busing as the remedy. Americans appear to have virtually reified the *Brown* decision. Public opinion surveys suggest that the goal of desegregation still enjoyed widespread support in the 1990s among blacks and whites:

A national Gallup Poll in 1994 found that 87 percent of Americans believed the Supreme Court's decision in *Brown* was right, a 24 percent increase since the peak of the civil rights movement. Change in the South was even more dramatic. In 1954, 81 percent of Southerners thought the Supreme Court was wrong in mandating desegregation. Although the South experienced far more coercion and is more desegregated than other regions, only 15 percent of Southerners in 1994 said they thought the *Brown* decision was wrong.

A growing majority, 65 percent of the public and 70 percent of blacks, said integration "improved the quality of education for blacks"—a large increase since the beginning of busing in 1971. Forty-two percent of Americans also believed that "integration has improved the quality of education for whites." Fifty-six percent in 1994 believed that efforts for desegregation should be intensified. Eighty-four percent of blacks supported more efforts. (Orfield and Eaton, 1996:108)

Nevertheless, in virtually every survey conducted, large majorities of whites opposed busing to achieve school desegregation, both before and after its implementation (Raffel, 1985; Sears, Hensler, and Speer, 1979). As Glenn Loury has poignantly observed, "Busing is dead as social policy" (Loury, 1997:146).

Many of the same questions that were being asked in the 1960s and 1970s are still being asked with respect to desegregation today. The courts began to implement some sweeping changes and encountered strong resistance, prompting a substantial retreat from the process. The courts were powerful enough to launch a massive social experiment but seemed unwilling or unable to fully execute it.

Meanwhile, reformers continue to search for a means of securing a more meaning-ful and lasting integration of schools and society.

For example, Orfield and Eaton have concluded that one of the most important steps toward integration is to concentrate policy "on the housing issues in combi-nation with school desegregation" to create "more powerful remedies." Further, they assert that the "goal of better integrated schools in integrated neighborhoods with less busing fits much better with the values that huge majorities of Americans express than turning back to segregation." They point out that "most Americans strongly support integrated schools but want educational reform, choice, and more direct parent and community involvement in schools. African-American parents want integrated schools in the communities where they live" (Orfield and Eaton, 1996:356). One of the most persistent claims made to support desegregation ef-forts is that "both blacks and whites who attended desegregated schools were more likely to function in desegregated environments in later life. More of them lived in desegregated neighborhoods, had children who attended desegregated schools, and had close friends of the other race than did adults of either race who had at-tended segregated schools" (Braddock, 1985:11).

These are very important reasons to value and to strive for more comprehensive racial integration. The slow and painful process of integration should reinforce the essential validity and importance of the principle of equal educational opportunity enshrined by the *Brown* decision, but the deeply flawed desegregation efforts that followed are still cause for concern. As Pride and Woodard conclude in their anal-ysis of Nashville busing, "[T]he problem with busing, and perhaps with other forms of affirmative action, is that it reinforces racial thinking. Racial ratios and school enrollment percentages dominated the courtroom debates on desegrega-tion. People became so caught up in racial concerns that other common interests were submerged" (Pride and Woodard, 1985:284).

The remaining question is what can now be done to improve the education of in-ner-city students given that (1) white and minority fear of the underclass has tended to further isolate the poorest urban blacks, Hispanics, and whites from edu-cational and economic opportunities; and (2) these students and their parents are now the most likely victims of urban underclass crime and social pathology. Given the realities of inner-city public schools, it is understandable that more affluent white and black families, frustrated by the burdens of forced integration, fre-quently placed their children in private or parochial schools or left for the suburbs.

In important respects, as Jennifer Hochschild has pointed out, desegregation had the ironic effect of reinforcing racial stereotypes. In Northern metropolitan ar-eas desegregation only succeeded in "removing ghetto blacks from their local schools, transporting them long distances, and depositing them in overwhelmingly white schools." Once the courts accomplished this, the experiment merely rein-forced racial stereotypes of blacks as "poor, uneducated, and unmotivated" com-pared with middle-class whites, because "ghetto blacks almost inevitably [fell] short" in academic performance (Hochschild, 1984:164). Clearly, there remains residual opposition to forced integration, in large part because the widespread adoption of busing remedies, resulting from court pressure to desegregate "now,"

produced a heavy-handed, artificial, and in many respects counterproductive social integration.

Not all the costs of desegregation efforts are easily quantifiable. For example, in
some of his concluding thoughts about the troubled legacy of desegregration, Lino
Graglia emphasizes the price of losing neighborhood-school advantages for both
blacks and whites:

> Students lose the comfort and security of familiar surroundings, of closeness to home, and
> of the presence of siblings and neighborhood friends. The need to conform to bus schedules
> seriously interferes with participation in school-centered activities before and after the
> usual school hours. Of utmost importance to many parents is the "strongly felt" need . . . for
> "direct control over decisions vitally affecting the education of one's children." The aban-
> donment of neighborhood schools tends to limit parental participation in, and supervision
> of, the operation of the school system and lessens the importance of the school as a center of
> community concern and cohesion. (Graglia, 1976:265)

In placing too much faith in school desegregation alone to accomplish more lasting
racial integration, policy makers may have overlooked many alternative approaches for improving black academic performance, particularly in inner-city
schools.

Although Justice Clarence Thomas has been roundly criticized for pointing out
that inner-city black schools are not necessarily inferior just because they are racially unbalanced by desegregation standards, his point bears repeating. If there
are steps that can be taken to enhance the education of black students in predominantly black schools now, they should certainly be implemented. As Derrick Bell
has also argued, "[E]ven for those who adhere to the belief that racial balance is the
only appropriate outcome of *Brown*, it is likely that the establishment and maintenance of effective all-black schools is the best means of moving toward that goal"
(Bell, 1980:127). Nevertheless, these are education policies, not matters of constitutional law.

As for the courts and their role in the integration experiment, Lino Graglia's
warning of the danger of *Brown*, stated more than twenty years ago, should be regarded with a renewed sense of concern:

> The appeal and general acceptance of a simple prohibition of all official racial discrimina-
> tion are so great, indeed, that it is hardly possible to quarrel with the *Brown* decision—as
> distinct from the opinion—except on the ground that so important a social change should
> not have been made by unselected, lifetime appointees. The *Brown* case was less a tradi-
> tional lawsuit than a call for a social revolution, and in a healthy democracy social revolu-
> tions are made by elected representatives authorized to effectuate their political views and
> accountable for the results. The fact that this revolution was made, or greatly advanced, by
> judges soon led to many other revolutions, much less justifiable, being made in the same
> way. (Graglia, 1976:32)

If anything, evidence amassed from studies, while mixed and complex, suggests
that court-ordered busing was an extremely narrow, simplistic response to the

problem of racial segregation that may have preempted more successful and less divisive policies.

Cases subsequent to *Brown*, both in the Supreme Court and the lower federal courts, established busing as the predominant remedy to segregated school systems. During the Warren and Burger era the federal courts were more frequently intervening in the political process, finding constitutional violations in areas as diverse as employment laws, voting districts, prison administration, law enforcement, and the operation of state mental hospitals. As in the *Brown* case and the busing experiment, the principles advanced by the courts were less problematic than the remedies that they often imposed in their wake. These led to unintended consequences that did not necessarily serve even the interests of the intended beneficiaries of these changes in law and policy. Today the legacy of pervasive judicial involvement in social policy making leads us to reassess the nature and limits of judicial review in our political system.

NOTE

1. Though the myth is still widely believed and is propagated by writers like Jonathan Kozol (1991), it is simply not true that funds spent per student on African American students are lower than those spent on white students. This conclusion is often based on comparing very rich suburban (largely white) schools that spend a great deal of money on students with the inner city. However, most white students do not attend such schools, In fact, as early as 1966 a massive study by James Coleman and colleagues demonstrated that per capita expenditures were about the same for white and black students. A 1989–90 study by the National Center for Educational Statistics (1995) found that on average, the larger the proportion of black students in a district, the larger the per capita expenditure per student, with special-need expenditures held constant. The 10 percent of students who attend very well-to-do suburban schools are the one exception. Incidentally, expenditures for education, including expenditures for predominantly black schools, have risen very sharply in the past twenty years. The United States now spends more per student in elementary and secondary schools than just about any country in the world (Nappi, 1999). In 1994–95 Newark, New Jersey, spent more per pupil than any other school district in the country, and Washington, D.C., ranked third. Students in both districts are predominantly black, and both systems were, in 1995, total disasters. Indeed, the Newark system was taken over by the state because of its massive failure (Peterson, 1994:24). Of course, a good argument can be made that given the problems of central cities, predominantly black schools need more money than do predominantly white schools.

Chapter 3

Affirmative Action and the Consequences of Racial Preference

RACE NEUTRALITY OR RACIAL PREFERENCE IN HIRING?

At a public policy forum of the American Enterprise Institute, former NAACP director Benjamin Hooks provided a vivid account of the legacy of discrimination in Alabama and the impact of affirmative action in the state highway patrol:

Judge Frank Johnson, having been exasperated by their failure to hire a single black [from the 1930s to 1972], directed that henceforth they hire one black applicant for every white applicant.

Now around the time the *Allen* suit was filed, a suit was also filed against all the departments of the Alabama state government for failure to hire black applicants. But in that case, *U.S. v. Frazer*, the judge did not require any goals to be met. And a strange thing happened. After the passage of a few months—a few years, in fact—more black people were hired by the Alabama highway patrol than by all the seventy-five departments of the state government put together (Goldwin, Schambra, and Kaufman, 1987:111).

Hooks's remarks underscore the dilemma associated with efforts to remedy employment discrimination, particularly in the South. While in many cases there has been a clear historical pattern of discrimination, which the government has undertaken to alleviate, to impose quotas or goals as a remedy creates an obvious hiring preference based on racial identity alone.

Affirmative-action policies were principally initiated through presidential leadership and aggressive executive-agency enforcement. Subsequent judicial reinterpretation of civil rights laws in the early 1970s was also instrumental in altering the course of affirmative action to favor result-oriented hiring practices. By the 1980s the courts had generally swung back in the direction of race neutrality. Judicial intervention has thus contributed to the persistent controversy surrounding affirmative-action policies for more than thirty years. Shifting political and legal trends reflect deep divisions in American society about the meaning and appropriate scope of equal protection remedies to discrimination.

Critics of affirmative action argue that the practice of imposing racial hiring preferences through affirmative-action policy runs counter to the spirit of the civil rights movement and the Civil Rights Act. Civil rights laws were intended to prohibit any discrimination based on race. While the gradual acceptance of racial hiring preferences defies the logic of various provisions of actual antidiscrimination laws, affirmative action is regarded by its supporters as a pragmatic strategy to fulfill the ultimate goal of civil rights reforms, genuine equality of opportunity for all races (Greene, 1989; Edwards, 1995; Drake and Holsworth, 1996; Edley, 1996).

Prior to the civil rights era of the 1960s blacks were denied opportunities to advance through systematic educational, housing, and employment discrimination. "African Americans, even if they were college-educated, worked as bell-boys, porters and domestics, unless they could manage to get a scarce teaching position in the all-black school. . . . In higher education most African Americans attended predominantly black colleges, many established by states as segregated institutions" ("2. Affirmative Action," 1). Because progress for minorities was slow, even after passage of the Civil Rights and Voting Rights acts, "both the courts and Republican and Democratic administrations turned to race- and gender-conscious remedies as a way to end entrenched discrimination" ("2. Affirmative Action," 2). Direct government coercion of state and local agencies and private institutions led to significant increases in minority hiring. These successes eventually led to the widespread adoption of hiring goals, quotas, and timetables—a system of mathematically determined hiring preferences designed to remedy past racial discrimination.

Another historical factor spurring the adoption of affirmative-action policies was the wave of riots that swept America's urban centers in the 1960s. Andrew Kull points out that the riots and the Kerner Commission report on their causes led to a "conviction that the whole [remedial] process would cost too much and take too long. . . . The obvious alternative was to address the results directly, rather than the preconditions; though the 'equality of results' that could be achieved in this manner would necessarily be something different. Expenditure was minimized, because the really expensive part of the traditional prescription—substantial government intervention to alter the lives of the truly disadvantaged—was being abandoned" (Kull, 1992:188).

If equal opportunity was considered to be attainable through result-oriented hiring policies, then presumably affirmative action would have a finite life span. At some point hiring preferences would no longer be required to counteract past discrimination. In the 1978 *Bakke* decision Justice Harry Blackmun hoped that "the time will come when an 'affirmative action' program is unnecessary and is, in truth, only a relic of the past." Blackmun felt that the goal could be reached "within a decade at the most" (438 U.S. 265, 403). Opponents of affirmative action dispute this goal-oriented approach to progress for blacks. For example, Jared Taylor argues that "in some cases, blacks may have quickly caught up with the mainstream, but all too often they did not. What might have been intended as a temporary relaxation of standards hardened into permanent racial preferences. The gap in black/white achievement refused to go away, and what came to look more and more like reverse discrimination had to be justified by claiming that the persistent racial gap in achievement could be due only to persistent white racism" (Taylor, 1992:124). Of course, many critics still oppose affirmative action as a matter of principle; but, much of the recent controversy does not concern the legitimacy of past minority hiring preferences but whether employment discrimination has diminished to a point where affirmative action should come to an end (Eastland, 1996; Bolick, 1996; Skrentny, 1996).

Philosopher and outspoken opponent of affirmative action Carl Cohen has characterized affirmative action as both wrong and bad:

[P]reference is wrong because it is a violation of fundamental moral principles, a violation of the U.S. Constitution, and a violation of the civil rights laws of the United States. It is bad because it does serious injury to all concerned. It corrupts the colleges and the companies that employ it, and it fosters the resentments and hostilities that now tear our society apart. Perhaps worst of all, racial preference does direct and serious harm to the very minorities it was designed to assist. However honorable the character of those who support it, preference by race is morally indefensible and socially counterproductive. (Cohen, 1995:5)

Affirmative action remains a central and complicated issue in American public life not only because it arose as a well-intended remedy to the shameful legacy of chattel slavery, white supremacy, and invidious racial discrimination, but also because it essentially views with suspicion what were once seemingly inviolable majoritarian ideals—liberty, equality of opportunity, individualism, and democratic participation.

Defending affirmative-action policy, Herbert Hill has summarized the controversy from a highly critical perspective. He comments, "The current conflict over affirmative action is not simply an argument about abstract rights or ethnic bigotry. In the final analysis it is an argument between those who insist upon the substance of a long-postponed break with the traditions of American racism and those groups that insist upon maintaining the valuable privileges and benefits they now enjoy as a consequence of that dismal history." Proponents such as Hill argue that affirmative action "without numbers, whether in the form of quotas, goals, or timetables, is meaningless" (Hill, 1989:248–49).

The thirty-year legacy of quotas, goals, and timetables notwithstanding, it is important to recognize that affirmative action had quite modest origins. If not for its quite radical reinterpretation, implementation, and enforcement by executive agencies, Congress, and the federal courts from the late 1960s to the present, it would scarcely have become the lightning-rod national political issue that it is today. In the words of Frederick Lynch, affirmative action "has been an administrative revolution imposed by judges and bureaucrats." Lynch points out that the implementation of affirmative action contradicted the stated intentions of those who enacted civil rights laws and notes that the "vague legal framework" resulted in "an amazing degree of discretion" to bureaucrats and judges (Lynch, 1989:172–73). We must next turn to the origins of affirmative action to determine how racial preference, rather than race neutrality, became the legacy of this government policy.

ORIGINS OF THE TWO COMPETING AFFIRMATIVE-ACTION IDEAS

Seymour Martin Lipset identifies the two conflicting origins of affirmative action that continued to influence the historical development of affirmative-action policies and views of its legitimacy as a civil rights policy. The first conception involved the notion that blacks had been systematically excluded from the privileges of education, training, housing, job opportunities, and career advancement as a result of discrimination. Therefore, affirmative action would consist of race-neutral "policies to remove these chains so that [blacks] could compete equally" (Lipset, 1995:2). William Bennett and Terry Eastland noted that in fashioning remedies based on this vision of affirmative action, race-neutral affirmative action meant "taking such measures as would ensure that tests to discern employment qualifications were free of racial or cultural bias; or that a recruitment net was flung far and wide so that anyone conceivably interested might find his way into the applicant 'pool' " (Sutherland, CEO, 1998:7). The second notion is the more problematic one involving racial preference. Lipset points to the views of black scholar Harold Cruse as representative of the more aggressive conception of affirmative action. Cruse "argued that equality of opportunity and formal integration were not enough for blacks. Given the history of oppression and continued discrimination against blacks, African Americans required recognition as a unique national minority and group rights above and beyond those sought by other minorities and the non-black poor" (Lipset, 1995:2).

Under the former, race-neutral conception, elimination of de jure hiring discrimination and policies ensuring that blacks had equal access to educational and economic opportunities would be enough to create a just socioeconomic order. Under the latter conception, blacks continued to be disadvantaged as a direct result of past discrimination, regardless of formal, legal equality of opportunity. Therefore, remedial policies were necessary to help them attain genuine equality of opportunity.

Beginning with the presidency of Franklin Roosevelt and up to the Johnson administration, affirmative-action initiatives, however modest, conformed to the race-neutral or what some refer to as the "color-blind" vision. Antecedents of affirmative action can be found as far back as the Freedmen's Bureau, which provided various social, health, and economic relief services to former slaves, but it did not actually emerge as a significant national policy until the 1960s (Franklin and Moss, 1994:228–29). In the 1940s and 1950s several presidents made inroads by unilaterally advancing civil rights policies within the federal government. For example, in 1941 Roosevelt issued Executive Order 8802 "to prohibit racial discrimination in defense industries" during World War II. "Roosevelt's order barred discrimination against blacks by defense contractors, and established the first Fair Employment Practices Committee. However, federal compliance programs were routinely understaffed, underfunded and lacked enforcement authority" ("2. Affirmative Action," 3). Both Harry Truman and Dwight Eisenhower extended antidiscrimination provisions to all government contractors (Lynch, 1989:11).

As the civil rights movement progressed in the late 1950s and early 1960s, "President John F. Kennedy created a Committee on Equal Employment Opportunity in 1961 and issued Executive Order 10925, which used the term 'affirmative action' to refer to measures designed to achieve non-discrimination" ("2. Affirmative Action," 4). These measures were all modest steps intended to ensure race neutrality in government contracting and hiring, but they did little to change the overall opportunity structure for blacks. Without legal prohibitions against discrimination they were little more than symbolic gestures. Robert Detlefsen argues that presidents have employed executive orders partly to avoid major legislative battles and the rigidity of statutory law. Affirmative-action orders had a flexible, experimental quality that minimized political conflict and accountability (Detlefsen, 1995:60; Morgan, 1970:84).

Stephen Wasby breaks down the history of civil rights policy over the past fifty years into four distinct periods:

(1) a lack of presidential enthusiasm for civil rights initiatives and congressional resistance to civil rights legislation, coupled with the Court's increasing support for civil rights, through (2) a brief period of tripartite support for major elements of the civil rights community's agenda, into (3) a period of presidential and legislative withdrawal coupled with moderated judicial support, and then to (4) presidential opposition to civil rights claims and efforts to roll them back through the courts, with Congress ultimately giving shelter to civil rights organizations by legislatively reversing the Court over the president's objections. (Wasby, 1995:83–84)

Affirmative-action policy, a major initiative of the civil rights movement after 1970, conforms reasonably well to Wasby's chronology. The role of the courts is particularly important in the first, third, and fourth periods. The courts were an initial catalyst of preferential affirmative action following the *Griggs v. Duke Power Co.* (1971) ruling (where the courts shifted the burden of proof in employment discrimination cases to the employer under a disparate-impact rather than a discriminatory-intent standard). In the late 1970s the courts began a slow retreat from earlier positions as reverse-discrimination cases increased in number and political opposition mounted. Nevertheless, the judiciary managed to preserve affirmative action well into the 1990s in the form of minority business set-asides (e.g., the 1990 *Metro Broadcasting* case) and under the banner of diversity in higher education and corporate culture (Katyal, 1995; MacDonald, 1993). Finally, President Clinton was able to salvage much affirmative action policy by administrative action that countered the more conservative directives of the Supreme Court.

One of the most powerful expressions of the convictions of the civil rights movement was the enactment of the Civil Rights Act of 1964. The language of what has become the most controversial component of this legislation seems to clearly prohibit any race-based hiring preferences. Title VII, Section 703(j), of the Civil Rights Act of 1964 states unequivocally: "Nothing contained in this title shall be interpreted to require any employer . . . to grant preferential treatment to any individual or to any group because of race, color, religion, sex or national origin of such individual or group on account of an imbalance." As clear as this provision seemed at the time, by 1970 preferential hiring practices were becoming more and more commonplace. By 1980 they were instituted for federal and state employees, most government contracts, and college and university faculty hiring and student recruitment and within most corporations.

In 1965 Lyndon Johnson also used the term "affirmative action" in Executive Order 11246. Johnson's initiative directed government contractors to take "affirmative action" to promote the hiring of blacks and other minorities (Lynch, 1989:11–12). "Order 11246 . . . established color-blind hiring rules for federal contractors. It says, 'The contractor will take affirmative action to ensure that applicants are employed, and that employees are treated during employment, without regard to their race, color, religion, sex, or national origin.' Here too the emphasis was on equal treatment, not on special preferences" (Taylor, 1992:126). In spite of the race-neutral language, by 1969 racial preferences were being instituted at the federal level. To understand how this came about, one must first review the bold actions taken by two agencies created by the Civil Rights Act, the Equal Employment Opportunity Commission (EEOC) and the Office of Federal Contract Compliance (OFCC).

IMPLEMENTATION AND JUDICIAL ENFORCEMENT OF AFFIRMATIVE ACTION

New Civil Rights Agencies and Proportional Representation

The first difficulty that the new federal agencies charged with implementing the Civil Rights Act confronted was the legislation itself. The statute authorized no more than a piecemeal attack upon intentional discrimination that had to be proved on a case-by-case basis. The EEOC was simply not authorized to take broad measures to discover and eradicate discriminatory practices over a broad spectrum of economic enterprises, at least not until it redefined its mission.

The primary objective was to find private firms that were not hiring minorities, and in order to do this, the EEOC needed to develop an effective means of counting by race. By 1965, through bureaucratic wrangling and creative interpretation of state equal employment opportunity reporting, required by the Civil Rights Act, the EEOC established a national race reporting system for government contractors and employees. Some 60,000 firms were now required to file annual reports including data on racial composition of their workforces (Graham, 1990:191–96). Despite its almost immediate reversal of an important civil rights objective, to eliminate race counting that had perpetuated discrimination against minorities, EEOC's national reporting system became a crucial tool for developing a full-blown proportional representation scheme for federal and state employment and contracting. In 1966 the Civil Service Commission followed suit, resolving that it would "henceforth require each federal agency to maintain records of their employees' race" (Graham, 1990:199).

For its part, the OFCC used its substantial leverage in the preaward stage of the government-contract bidding process to increase minority hiring. OFCC encouraged contractors "to provide a 'manning table' [that] . . . would list the specific number of minority workers to be hired in each trade." Once one contractor was persuaded to agree to this, obviously greatly improving the chances of a contract award, "his competitors could scarcely afford to remain far behind. Once the low-bid protocol was breached, contractors would scramble to meet the new criteria" (Graham, 1990:286–87). By changing the bidding process to favor contractors who promised to hire greater numbers of minorities, the OFCC was able to make the bidding pool for federal contracts fall like a house of cards in favor of affirmative-action initiatives.

In May 1968 the OFCC promulgated administrative regulations requiring an affirmative-action compliance program for every major contractor and subcontractor with more than fifty employees and contracts greater than $50,000. To enforce these regulations, the EEOC and the OFCC began arguing that disparities between minorities in the workforce and in "surrounding labor pools" were prima facie evidence of discrimination by an employer. These two offices pushed for goals and timetables and good-faith efforts at compliance (Lynch, 1989:12).

In the 1970s litigation became the most important mechanism for enforcing regulations, and the lower federal courts became a major instrument in implementing affirmative action in government and private-sector employment. Pursuant to the 1972 Civil Rights Amendments, the EEOC was authorized to "bring suit on behalf of plaintiffs" for violations of Title VII (Welch, 1989:153). Finis Welch has compiled summary statistics of the volume of affirmative-action litigation from 1966 to 1982. Welch reports that in 1970 only 340 cases were filed in federal courts under Title VII. By 1975 this figure had jumped to 3,930 and rose to 7,689 by 1982 (Welch, 1989:156, table 7.1). "[E]mployers could be found guilty by the numbers unless they could prove otherwise, such as by having pre-existing, vigorous affirmative action programs. Therefore, starting and maintaining affirmative action quotas became the best defense against EEOC, OFCC, civil rights groups, and employee discrimination lawsuits" (Lynch, 1989:12). Under the circumstances it seems a gross distortion of the facts to consider the vast majority of affirmative-action policies instituted by employers as "voluntary."

In 1969, with President Nixon's approval, the Department of Labor implemented the so-called Philadelphia Plan requiring "government contractors in that city [to] come up with minority hiring goals in order to be considered for government contracts" (Taylor, 1992:126–27). Apparently the Philadelphia Plan was born of mixed motives. By at least one historical account Nixon and Secretary of Labor George Shultz wished to split the labor movement along racial lines "in order to free the construction industry from the guildlike grip of craft unions" (Graham, 1992:59). Nixon also appeared to genuinely believe that this plan could bring about real progress for blacks. In his memoirs he later wrote,

A good job is as basic and important a civil right as a good education. . . . I felt that the plan Shultz devised, which would require such [affirmative] action by law, was both necessary and right. We would not impose quotas, but would require federal contractors to show affirmative action to meet the goals of increasing minority employment. (Nixon, quoted in "2. Affirmative Action,":4).

The Philadelphia Plan soon influenced most major firms contracting with the federal government. Early in 1970 the Labor Department "issued a new set of rules that would extend the Philadelphia Plan's model of proportional representation by race and selected ethnicity in employment to basically all of the activities and facilities of all federal contractors—which . . . covered from one-third to one-half of all U.S. workers" (Graham, 1990:341). In 1971 the Court of Appeals for the Third Circuit held that the Philadelphia Plan model instituting minority hiring preferences "did not violate the Civil Rights Act," and the Supreme Court denied certiorari (review on the merits of the case), allowing the ruling to stand (Graham, 1992:59).

While the EEOC and OFCC did not systematically coerce private sector firms into hiring on a proportional representation basis, they seized enough leverage to achieve that end by seemingly less drastic means. The regulatory climate that the two agencies established, with the help of the judiciary, rigged the market to make it almost impossible for firms to win federal contracts without employing a representative number of minorities. Similarly, if labor unions wanted to continue securing jobs for their members, they would have to offer up enough positions to minorities to provide the correct racial mix in the labor force. Through these practices the two very small civil rights offices were able to exert a considerable influence over the American economy.

The Judiciary and the Tortured Logic of Affirmative Action

Part of the explanation for the tremendous energy within the new civil rights agencies lies in the fact that a substantial number of activists who had fought hard for the breakthrough legislation of 1964 were now staffing them. "By 1967 the OFCC, like the EEOC but on a smaller scale, was accumulating a staff of activist blacks and white liberal reformers whose zeal for enforcement mirrored that of their young, attractive, and aggressive leaders" (Graham, 1990:285). Yet it is tempting to attribute too much power and independent success to the various new civil rights agencies created under the Civil Rights Act of 1964. The pervasive impact these agencies have had on America's workforce would have been impossible if it had not been for the intervention of the federal courts.

In fact, the EEOC and OFCC were fledgling agencies that wielded little clout compared to the much larger mission agencies that had been around for many years. Moreover, traditional power relations were problematic for advancing affirmative-action policy.

Congress had proliferated subcommittees to foster programs for veterans, farmers, small business entrepreneurs, the elderly, non-English speakers, the physically handicapped, the hungry—and such groups found many friends and few enemies in Congress. But minority groups seeking to displace non-minorities from jobs according to a controversial model of proportional representation, and doing so through a network of bureaucratic intrusion backed by federal coercion, could count on stiff opposition from congressional conservatives, whose ranks included many senior committee chairmen. (Graham, 1990:365)

What made the difference for the EEOC and OFCC was the sympathetic ear of the federal courts.

As a *Forbes* article noted in 1993, "The number of discrimination suits in federal courts is rising astronomically—by 2,166 percent between 1970 and 1989, when some 7,500 were filed, versus an increase of only about 125 percent in the general federal caseload. . . . Preliminary reports are that since the 1991 Civil Rights Act and the 1990 Americans with Disabilities Act . . . filings have jumped some 30 percent. Both acts for the first time allow punitive damages, an explicit incentive to contingency fee trial lawyers" (Brimelow and Spencer, 1993:96). Key Supreme Court decisions provided the legal foundation to legitimate the objectives and tactics of a growing civil rights bureaucracy. In 1971, the same year the Supreme Court allowed the Philadelphia Plan to stand, the high court handed down a decision that would transform the regulatory climate governing civil rights. In *Griggs v. Duke Power Co.* (1971) the Supreme Court ruled that employment entrance exams would have to be discarded unless they were required by business necessity. Given the legacy of the poll tax and literacy tests as a barrier to black voting, some of the justices could reasonably argue that entrance exams were merely more subtle barriers to blacks in the job market. This was especially true in the actual case at hand, but as Hugh Graham notes, "[W]hile discriminatory motives on the part of Duke Power Company were not only historically demonstrable and subsequently probable, they were also irrelevant. What mattered was not discriminatory motive but the racial effect of employment provisions—whether their impact fell disparately upon blacks and whites, whether their results were racially proportionate" (Graham, 1990:386).

The court ruled in *Griggs* that the reasonableness of entrance exams, to ensure a certain level of performance to employers, was an insufficient justification for such rigid barriers to entry. Once the threshold was crossed here, that is, from discriminatory intent to discriminatory effect, any exams would have to prove that they were justified by "business necessity." In practice, this became an almost insurmountable barrier to employer utilization of entrance exams. Thus all at once the *Griggs* decision sanctioned the idea that where entrance exams were concerned, discrimination would be defined in terms of effect, not intent. This amounted to judicial sanctioning of proportional representation writ large. Subsequent to the *Griggs* decision Congress amended the Civil Rights Act in 1972, in part to facilitate class-action lawsuits in affirmative-action cases.

The act retained the individual's right to file suit (and thus the idea that discrimination is also intentional), but it also enhanced the EEOC's enforcement power, enabling it to initiate litigation. This also reflected the assumption that discrimination is systemic and that eradicating it is, as a congressional report states, a "major public interest" beyond the interest of any individual person. The major rationale advanced for the bill was results-oriented: it stressed the need to improve the economic status of blacks. (Taylor, 1992:23)

Perhaps the best-known case regarding preferential admissions policies in education is *Regents of the University of California v. Bakke* (1978), in which the Court ruled in a fragmented decision that race could be one criterion, but not the only factor, for selection of students at universities and professional schools. *Bakke* was a landmark case in which the Court seemed to split between supporters of clear-cut quotas and others who wished to hold the line on the extent to which affirmative action strayed from the intentions of civil rights legislation. The decision was a compromise rather than a victory for either point of view. The split on the Court can perhaps be characterized best by distinguishing between a "class" and a "classification" approach in applying equal protection to affirmative action (Farber, Eskridge, and Frickey, 1993:142–43).

Brennan and others on the Court who had viewed the racial-preference version of affirmative action favorably regarded past discrimination as a sufficient cause for remedial policies for minorities. They took a class approach to enforcing the equal protection clause. Because blacks and other minorities were a "suspect class," these jurists looked more favorably on remedial laws and policies favoring minorities and were more likely to intervene where minorities might be adversely affected. Remedial policies designed to remedy past discrimination were not viewed with strict scrutiny. Thus in *Bakke* Brennan wrote, "Davis' articulated purpose of remedying the effects of past societal discrimination is, under our cases, sufficiently important to justify the use of race-conscious admissions programs where there is a sound basis for concluding that minority underrepresentation is substantial and chronic, and that the handicap of past discrimination is impeding access of minorities to the Medical School" (438 U.S. 265, 363).

By contrast, those who favored a classification approach, such as Lewis Powell, adhered to the original statutory intent of Title VII (or the Title VI provision at issue in *Bakke*)—any racial classifications were suspect. If a classification was used, the burden of proof was upon the party using the classification to show a compelling governmental interest for its existence, and the means must be narrowly tailored to accomplish that end. This was Powell's reasoning in rejecting the University of California Medical School's reliance on race as an overriding admission criterion. Powell wrote, "[All] legal restrictions which curtail the civil rights of a single racial group are immediately suspect. That is not to say that all such restrictions are unconstitutional. It is to say that courts must subject them to the most rigid scrutiny" (438 U.S. 265, 290).

Remarkably, while Powell applied strict scrutiny to race as a factor in admissions, his opinion was pivotal in establishing a constitutional basis for preferential admissions policies. He argued that racial preference was a method that colleges, professional schools, and universities could employ to further the First Amendment goal of academic freedom. Powell stated that "the attainment of a diverse student body . . . is a constitutionally permissible goal for an institution of higher education. Academic freedom, though not a specifically enumerated constitutional right, long has been viewed as a special concern of the First Amendment" (438 U.S. 265, 311–12). Thus race and ethnicity could be justified as one aspect of admissions criteria because a diverse student body furthered First Amendment objectives in the "robust exchange of ideas" (438 U.S. 265, 313).

Justices John Paul Stevens, Potter Stewart, and William Rehnquist did not regard the case as reaching the level of a constitutional question. They argued that the statute clearly prohibited any discrimination based on race and rejected the admissions policy accordingly. "[T]he meaning of the Title VI ban on exclusion is crystal clear: race cannot be the basis of excluding anyone from participation in a federally funded program" (438 U.S. 265, 419).

Similar divisions are also recognizable in the later "reverse-discrimination" employment cases. In *United Steelworkers v. Weber* (1979) Justice Brennan upheld a voluntary affirmative-action plan negotiated between an employer and a labor union. Brennan interpreted the Civil Rights Act as follows: "[N]othing contained in Title VII 'shall be interpreted to require any employer [to] grant preferential treatment [to] any group because of the race [of such] group on account of a de facto racial imbalance in the employer's work force.' " But since Title VII "does not state that 'nothing in Title VII shall be interpreted to permit' voluntary affirmative efforts to correct racial imbalances,' " preferential minority hiring plans are not barred by the statute (443 U.S. 193, 205–6). Brennan reasoned that they simply could not be compelled by law. Justices Rehnquist and Burger vehemently disagreed:

We have never wavered in our understanding that Title VII "prohibits all racial discrimination in employment, without exception for any particular employees. . . . " Today, however, the Court behaves much like the Orwellian speaker earlier described, as if it had been handed a note indicating that Title VII would lead to a result unacceptable to the Court if interpreted here as it was in our prior decisions. Accordingly, without even a break in syntax, the Court rejects "a literal construction of 703(a)" in favor of newly discovered "legislative history," which leads it to a conclusion directly contrary to that compelled by the "uncontradicted legislative history" unearthed in *McDonald* and our other prior decisions. Now we are told that the legislative history of Title VII shows that employers are free to discriminate on the basis of race: an employer may, in the Court's words, "trammel the interests of the white employees" in favor of black employees in order to eliminate "racial imbalance. . . . "

Thus, by a tour de force reminiscent not of jurists such as Hale, Holmes, and Hughes, but of escape artists such as Houdini, the Court eludes clear statutory language, "uncontradicted" legislative history, and uniform precedent in concluding that employers are, after all, permitted to consider race in making employment decisions. (443 U.S. 193, 220–21)

Neither Justice Rehnquist nor Chief Justice Burger could see any justification for a departure from the intent of the legislation as previously determined by the Court. Title VII meant what it said. No preferential treatment was permissible for any group, whether it was voluntarily instituted by an employer or not.

Rehnquist's objections notwithstanding, the following year Supreme Court decisions continued to favor quotalike programs. In *Fullilove v. Klutznick* (1980) the Court upheld a federal provision requiring 10 percent funding set-asides for minority business enterprises. The Court conceded that any racial classification is subject to strict scrutiny and requires a compelling governmental interest and a sufficiently narrow (not under- or overinclusive) means-to-end relationship. Yet the Court again strayed from the "race-neutral" approach to civil rights. In a concurring opinion Justice Powell pushed beyond principle to more pragmatic concerns. "The time cannot come too soon when no governmental decision will be based upon immutable characteristics of pigmentation or origin. But in our quest to achieve a society free from racial classification, we cannot ignore the claims of those who still suffer from the effects of identifiable discrimination" (448 U.S. 448, 516). Again, the Court relied on substantive rather than procedural notions of equal protection and in doing so continued its venture into result-oriented equal protection jurisprudence.

Objecting to the decision on pragmatic grounds, Justice Stevens decried the hopelessly politicized outcome of the case. Stevens understood just how toothless strict scrutiny was becoming for congressional remedies reviewed by the Court:

We can never either erase or ignore the history that Mr. Justice Marshall has recounted. But if that history can justify such a random distribution of benefits on racial lines as that embodied in this statutory scheme, it will serve not merely as a basis for remedial legislation, but rather as a permanent source of justification for grants of special privileges. For if there is no duty to attempt either to measure the recovery by the wrong or to distribute that recovery within the injured class in an evenhanded way, our history will adequately support a legislative preference for almost any ethnic, religious or racial group with the political strength to negotiate "a piece of the action" for its members. . . . Preferences based on characteristics acquired at birth foster intolerance and antagonism against the entire membership of the favored classes. For this reason, I am firmly convinced that this "temporary measure" will disserve the goal of equal opportunity. (448 U.S. 448, 539)

While Stevens perceived many of the dangers of the Court's acceptance of minority set-asides, his opinion does not acknowledge that the very conception of equal opportunity had shifted decisively toward proportional representation as the only reliable measure of racial justice.

REAGAN, BUSH, CLINTON, AND THE SUPREME COURT

Just as the victory for affirmative action appeared to be won by Congress and the federal courts, conservative presidents Ronald Reagan and George Bush began to challenge the ascendancy of racial preference as the foundation of affirmative-action policies. As a Clinton administration White House report on affirmative action recounted, "OFCCP [Office of Federal Contract Compliance Program] enforcement was greatly scaled back during the 1980s. For example, the real budget and staffing for affirmative action programs was reduced after 1980. Over the same period, fewer administrative complaints were filed and back-pay awards were phased out. Perhaps not surprisingly, available evidence suggests that OFCCP did not have a noticeable impact on the hiring of minority workers by contractor firms in the early and mid-1980s" ("3. Empirical Research":3).

Other measures were taken by the Reagan administration, but as Herman Belz sees it, they had mixed results due to the differing orientations of agencies involved in policy implementation:

The Department of Labor and OFCCP reformed the administration of the executive order goals and timetables policy in response to business criticism of the Carter Administration's overly aggressive affirmative action program. The Department of Justice, the government's chief law enforcement agency, vigorously pursued an anti-quota policy. The Equal Employment Opportunity Commission, the stronghold of militant affirmative action in the 1970s, was slower to change: in the second Reagan Administration, though, it opposed quotas and adopted a policy of full relief for individual victims of discrimination. (Belz, 1991:183)

As we shall see, this retrenchment was not absolute, nor did it seem to slow educational or economic progress for blacks. This suggests that educational gains, the impact of civil rights laws on the macroeconomic opportunity structure, and temporary affirmative-action benefits substantially improved economic opportunities for working-class, middle-class, and wealthy blacks. By the early 1990s problems of the black underclass appeared to be worsening and threatened to erode progress by adversely impacting inner-city communities and schools.

In the 1980s and 1990s the more conservative Supreme Court also began to more frequently oppose affirmative-action programs. In the late 1980s the Court began to tighten the circle around affirmative-action policies, applying strict scrutiny to any racial classifications. In *Richmond v. J.A. Croson Co.* (1989) the majority of the Court struck down a 30 percent minority set-aside program imposed by Richmond, Virginia, on the ground that it failed to show a past history of racial discrimination. In striking down the law, the Court invoked strict scrutiny in the "classification" as opposed to "class" paradigm:

[T]he purpose of strict scrutiny is to "smoke out" illegitimate uses of race by assuring that the legislative body is pursuing a goal important enough to warrant use of a highly suspect tool. The test also ensures that the means chosen "fit" this compelling goal so closely that there is little or no possibility that the motive for the classification was illegitimate racial prejudice or stereotype.

Classifications based on race carry a danger of stigmatic harm. Unless they are strictly reserved for remedial settings, they may in fact promote notions of racial inferiority and lead to a politics of racial hostility. (488 U.S. 469, 493)

The case was limited to "State" action and left federal set-aside programs intact, but the impact was substantial. "The inefficiencies of set-asides became immediately obvious after the Court ruling. In Philadelphia, before the ruling black-owned companies were getting 25 percent of the city's contracts. When normal competitive bidding was restored, blacks got 3.5 percent" (Taylor, 1992:139–40).

At the same time, *Richmond* in no way signaled an end to affirmative action. The following year the Court decided *Metro Broadcasting v. F.C.C.* (1990) in favor of congressionally sanctioned minority set-asides in the broadcasting industry. Justice Brennan, writing for the majority, asserted that the FCC's set-aside policies for broadcasting were examples of "benign racial classifications" that did not impose "undue burdens" on the white majority.

[J]ust as we have determined that "as part of this Nation's dedication to eradicating racial discrimination, innocent persons may be called upon to bear some of the burden of the remedy," *Wygant* (opinion of Powell, J.), we similarly find that a congressionally mandated benign race-conscious program that is substantially related to the achievement of an important governmental interest is consistent with equal protection principles so long as it does not impose undue burdens on nonminorities. (497 U.S. 547, 596–97)

Justices O'Connor, Rehnquist, Scalia, and Kennedy dissented, arguing that the FCC's racial preferences did impose indefensible burdens and that they represented a means of implementing a proportional representation scheme on the basis of race that violated the equal protection clause. "Like the vague assertion of societal discrimination, a claim of insufficiently diverse broadcasting viewpoints might be used to justify racial preferences, linked to nothing other than proportional representation of various races" (497 U.S. 547, 614). The four dissenters argued that since there was no "identified racial discrimination" in this case, the law failed to appropriately tailor means to ends.

Abruptly changing course again in 1995, the Supreme Court in *Adarand Constructors Inc. v. Pena* (1995) went as far as it has ever gone in reforming affirmative-action programs both within the federal government and among federal contractors. In *Adarand* the Court overruled *Metro*, stating that any federal program that classified people by race must be subject to strict scrutiny and would have to be "narrowly tailored" and serve a "compelling national interest." The Court thus extended the strict-scrutiny standard from *Richmond v. J.A. Croson Co.* to the federal government. Nevertheless, the Court went on to make some exceptions to the ruling, pointing out that "programs that seek to diversify institutions like law enforcement agencies or colleges, which may have the added goals of improving interaction with a diverse public or providing a richer cultural experience, may be acceptable." Subsequent to the ruling the Justice Department issued a memorandum stating that affirmative-action initiatives within the federal government must "now be justified by evidence of particularized discrimination in a specific sector rather than a general assumption of widespread racism or sexism" (Holmes, 1995:A1, A16). Although affirmative-action programs have been in effect for two or three decades, the Court's decision suggests recognition that programs to benefit minorities are considered temporary, remedial measures and that at least some of them may no longer survive under the broad justifications they once did.

At Senator Bob Dole's request, in 1995 the Congressional Research Service (CRS) compiled a list of all government programs with specific mention of minority preference provisions (Dale, 1995). CRS discovered 171 programs with hiring provisions. "All of the 171 programs it lists categorize people by the color of their skin, or categorize a company according to the race of 51 percent of its owners. . . . Almost 95 percent of the 171 programs ensure favorable results based on those categories" (Sutherland, 1998:7). These programs demonstrate the persistence of racially preferential policies in affirmative-action programs.

The Clinton administration's response to *Adarand* suggests the limits of court-ordered race neutrality in the face of an entrenched affirmative-action bureaucracy. Daniel Sutherland of the Center for Equal Opportunity has argued that the Clinton administration's legal strategy has been to "twist the holding in *Adarand*, counting on the skills of its lawyers and on the fact that it will take years for cases challenging the Clinton legal interpretation to reach the Supreme Court" (Sutherland, 1998:8). The memorandum on *Adarand*, issued by Assistant Attorney General Walter Dellinger in 1995, appears to provide the dozens of federal agency programs employing affirmative-action measures with a blueprint for defending against strict judicial scrutiny. Generally, it directs that "*Adarand* makes it necessary to evaluate federal programs that use race or ethnicity as a basis for decision making to determine if they comport with the strict scrutiny standard. No affirmative action program should be suspended prior to such an evaluation" (U.S. Department of Justice, 1995:20). It goes on to recommend various forms of evidence to be "marshaled to support the conclusion that remedial action was warranted when the program was first adopted." Among the evidence would be "statistical and documentary evidence . . . testimonial or anecdotal evidence of discrimination" (U.S. Department of Justice, 1995:22). The memo recognizes the special burden *Adarand* places not only on preferential policies based on generalized allegations of discrimination but also on nonremedial programs. "At a minimum, to the extent that an agency administers a non-remedial program intended to promote diversity, the factual predicate must show that greater diversity would foster some larger societal goal beyond diversity for diversity's sake. The level and precision of empirical evidence supporting that nexus may vary, depending on the nature and purpose of a non-remedial program." The same type of evidence would have to be mustered to defend these programs (U.S. Department of Justice, 1995:22).

CONSEQUENCES OF AFFIRMATIVE-ACTION POLICIES

Given the controversial legacy of affirmative action and the judiciary's expansive interpretation of legitimate remedies under Title VII, it is somewhat surprising that more attention has not been directed at the actual consequences of the preferential policies. Ostensibly, affirmative action bestowed clear benefits on blacks and other minorities—more and better jobs and improved access to education. But affirmative action imposed certain costs: white employees lost jobs as goals and timetables were met; minorities faced opposition in the workplace that often translated into hostility after they were hired; minorities themselves expressed mixed views about preferential policies; affirmative action helped some minorities more than others; and perhaps worst of all, poorer, less skilled minorities seemed to be passed by completely.

White Males

Frederick Lynch explores the consequences of affirmative action utilizing Robert Merton's analytical approach of considering not only the "manifest" function of affirmative-action policy but also the "latent" function. The manifest, or intended, impact of affirmative action is to place more minorities and women in various positions through the use of quotas, or goals and timetables. The latent function is to displace primarily white male competitors in the labor pool. Lynch is more interested in the impact of affirmative action on white males. Relying on extensive studies of white males affected by affirmative-action policies, Lynch concludes that they have been "invisible victims" of discrimination:

[W]hite males have not been accorded the status of victims of unjust social policies. Instead, their accounts of reverse discrimination, if voiced, have been met with awkwardness, disbelief, skepticism, or a discouraging "there's nothing you can do" response. Only half the subjects have been offered social support by friends and co-workers. The mass media have preferred to ignore the issue or belittle the complaints of white males. Corporate employers have responded with blaming the victim affirmative action seminars designed to demonstrate that white males have been wrong to resent discrimination. (Lynch, 1989:72)

Under the veil of proportional representation, advocates of affirmative-action programs argue that there are no white "victims" of discrimination, everyone ultimately benefits from diversity, and whatever slight burden is shouldered by whites is necessary and justified without legal recourse.

One of the more insidious by-products of affirmative action has been a majority suspicion of minority incompetence in the workplace.

Majority members typically view . . . minorities selected through [affirmative action] to be less competent than those selected without affirmative action, and this effect may generalize to evaluations of the target group as a whole. Such findings occur when affirmative action is operationalized as strong preferential treatment and when affirmative action is not defined procedurally, that is, when affirmative action is simply mentioned. (Kravitz et al., 1997:2)

These findings confirmed prior studies comparing majority responses to black job or student candidates when they were told that the position was or was not an affirmative-action opening (Nacoste, 1994; Northcraft and Martin, 1982; Garcia et al., 1981).

Corporations

Since the late 1970s the Court has struck down many affirmative-action laws as more and more white plaintiffs have brought reverse-discrimination suits before the courts. Yet corporations themselves have been reluctant to scale back affirmative-action programs. In the private sector the nearly thirty-year legacy of affirmative action has so bureaucratized race-based hiring that many commentators believe that curtailing it would create tremendous difficulties for large corporations. In 1985, as the Reagan Justice Department attempted to dismantle affirmative-action directives, the National Association of Manufacturers actually lobbied in favor of continuing affirmative action (Taylor, 1992:157).

Behind this structural inertia lie the industry of diversity consulting and training and also the threat of litigation. A 1995 article in the *Economist* reported that 75 percent of the fifty top U.S. firms employed "directors of diversity" or "diversity managers," but also noted that while employers remained enthusiastic about diverse workforces in the international market, problems of mismatching employees with jobs for which they were unqualified remained a potential problem ("A Strong Prejudice: Affirmative Action," 1995:69–70). The demands of civil rights agencies, legitimated by the federal courts, essentially forced the private sector to conform to proportionate racial representation in the workforce. "If an employer were so foolish as to ignore race and hire only the best-qualified workers, it could be seen as a betrayal of stockholders' interests. This was because the gains of having competent workers could be wiped out if the company had to fight a discrimination suit—brought by the EEOC at taxpayers' expense. . . . Supreme Court cases of the late 1960s and early 1970s had essentially forced employers to institute racial hiring quotas" (Taylor, 1992:143). Today it is a commitment to diversity, rather than affirmative action, that is more deeply embedded in American corporate culture. In 1985 *Fortune* magazine reported that more than 95 percent of *Fortune* 500 business executives would continue to use "numerical objectives to track the progress of women and minorities . . . regardless of government requirements" (Fisher, 1985:28). On top of the fact that affirmative-action policies take on a bureaucratic life of their own in the private sector, as they have done in the public sector, corporate executives see practical advantages to affirmative action. "Once a company has an affirmative action policy, it cannot stop or even retreat noticeably without stirring grievances and impairing morale among women and minorities on the payroll. On the positive side, affirmative action can enlarge the pool of talent for companies to draw on. . . . Affirmative action can also have practical business value in customer relations. . . . Why would someone want to be a customer of an all-white male company?" (Fisher, 1994:271).

One important means for corporations to achieve a safe level of compliance is to lower standards for minority applicants. This practice of "race norming" is widespread. "By 1986 about forty U.S. state governments and myriad private companies were race norming their test results" (Taylor, 1992:158). The 1991 Civil Rights Act formally condemned race norming, but the practice allegedly continues (Taylor, 1992:158–59).

Higher Education

While achieving affirmative action objectives in higher education has proved especially promising for enforcement agencies and less problematic to the courts, considerable evidence suggests that many black students are more likely to underachieve in higher education because of the strong diversity emphasis fostered by racial-preference policies. Under contemporary diversity programs in higher education, black students are often selected at double the percentage rate of white students (Zelnick, 1996:128–31, tables 3 and 4). The problem is that these policies do not take into account some persistent racial gaps in academic achievement. For example, in selected elite colleges Scholastic Aptitude Test (SAT) gaps range from 80 to 270 points (Zelnick, 1996:132, table 5). Thernstrom and Thernstrom report that the mean gap in SAT scores narrowed from 119 points in 1976 to 90 in 1991 and remained in that vicinity until 1995. In mathematics the gap was 139 in 1976 and 104 in 1991, widening to 110 in 1995 (Thernstrom and Thernstrom, 1997:398, table 3). The *Journal of Black Higher Education* projects that absent racial preferences, the 3,000 of 45,000 places reserved for black college freshmen in the "highest-ranked universities" would decline to about 900 (reported in Zelnick, 1996:126).

The inflated rates of admission for academically disadvantaged black students help to explain a substantially lower graduation rate among them. At thirty large state universities black student graduation rates averaged 21 percentage points lower than for whites six years from entry (Zelnick, 1996:133, table 6). In 1994 at more than three hundred major colleges and universities the black dropout rate was 66 percent compared to 43 percent for whites (Thernstrom and Thernstrom, 1997:392). Black graduation rates also correlate quite strongly with the strength of their SAT scores, suggesting that adequate preparation for college provides much greater assurance of the success of black students than simply increasing the number of entering freshmen. Arguably the latter will simply raise the expectations of black students beyond what can be realistically expected of them. Only 38 percent of students with SAT scores of 700 or less graduated from colleges with median student SAT levels of 900. Only 26 percent graduated from colleges with median student SAT levels of 1,000. Percentages of black students graduating were significantly greater when their SAT scores ranged from 701 to 850: 56 percent for 900-median schools and 39 percent for 1,000-median schools. Students in the 851 to 1,000 range fared even better, graduating at rates of 77 percent and 51 percent in 900- and 1,000-median SAT colleges, respectively. The figures were the same for those with scores over 1,000 (Thernstrom and Thernstrom, 1997:410, table 10).

William Bowen and Derek Bok's study *The Shape of the River* attempts to demonstrate that preferential admissions policies for blacks in elite schools are highly beneficial (Bowen and Bok, 1998). However, critics of the study point out that blacks at elite schools are more successful than blacks at other schools only because they come from more affluent and better-educated families. Moreover, the dropout rate among blacks at these institutions is still nearly 21 percent, compared to about 6 percent for whites (Thernstrom and Thernstrom, 1999:47).

While percentages of graduates of these schools do go on to obtain professional and doctoral degrees, in these schools preferential policies are often weighted even more heavily to increase black admissions. This has had some adverse consequences for black students. For example, Linda Wightman found that one-quarter of black law students who received law degrees were unable to pass a bar examination within three years. The failure rate is nearly seven times the rate for white law-school graduates (Wightman, 1998).

In spite of Bowen and Bok's optimistic conclusions, then, their study actually seems to reinforce our observation that in upholding preferential admissions policies the federal courts have contributed to exaggerated dropout and failure rates among black college, graduate, and professional students. This can hardly be considered a benefit to blacks who succeed on their own merits, or to those who do not succeed because they are mismatched to these institutions, or to the white and other minority students who have been displaced by preferential policies. Finally, at least one study has shown that failing out of a better school was considerably less likely to be as financially rewarding as graduating from a less selective school. "In 1986, fourteen years after leaving high school, black college dropouts were earning one-quarter less than their counterparts who went to less selective schools in the first place but managed to graduate" (Thernstrom and Thernstrom, 1997:411). Thus the intended beneficiaries of preferential admissions, and these are as many as two out of three black students admitted, are likely to end up worse off financially as a direct result of racial-preference policies.

A similar pattern also holds among medical students. As reported by the *Journal of Blacks in Higher Education*, in 1994 average grade point average (GPA) "for blacks accepted to medical school was 3.05 compared to 3.50 for whites" (Zelnick, 1996:150). On the National Board exams in 1988 " 'pass rates were 88 for whites, 84 for Asians, 66 for Hispanics, and 49 for blacks.' The mean score for black females was 369; for black males, 392; for white females, 467; and for white males, 499." As might be expected, the study found a high correlation between the performance on the boards and early scores and grades on the Medical College Admission Test (MCAT) and various science courses (Zelnick, 1996:150–51). Another study by Gail Heriot confirms these findings for medical students: "[O]nce in medical school, the special admissions students received much lower grades on average, were three times less likely to be selected for medical honors societies and were three times less likely to graduate. . . . Special admittees were eight times more likely to flunk National Board of Medical Examiners' tests" (National Center for Policy Analysis, Idea House, 1997c:2).

A parallel can be found among faculty. Faculty hiring is inflated by affirmative action, and yet tenured black faculty are only a small fraction of faculty at top schools. Of twenty-nine institutions such as Brown, Harvard, Cornell, and Vanderbilt, tenured black faculty represented only 0.4 to 2.7 percent of the faculty (Zelnick, 1996:135). The demand for black instructors far exceeds the supply of Ph.D.s "In 1986 only 820 blacks earned Ph.D.s in the whole country, and half of those were in education." The dearth of black doctoral degree earners is particularly acute in the hard sciences: "In 1987, of the 290 doctorates granted in electrical engineering, not one went to a black student. Blacks earned 3 of the 281 doctorates in chemical engineering, 2 of the 241 doctorates in mechanical engineering, and 5 of the 698 doctorates in astronomy and physics. . . . The first real increase in black Ph.D. degrees since 1977 did not come until 1991, when 933 were awarded" (Taylor, 1992:166). The percentage of black professors hovered at 4.3 percent throughout the 1980s (Shull, 1993:199).

One of the more unfortunate consequences of affirmative action for black college students is that they are frequently mismatched to institutions because of educational achievement that is statistically lower than for whites. In 1990 more black students were graduating from high school than a decade earlier, 77 percent compared to only 60 percent in 1980. White high-school completion rates rose from 81 to 83 percent in the same period (Shull, 1993:199, table 8.5). Certainly this is good news and indicates that in secondary education blacks are beginning to narrow the achievement gap significantly. Unfortunately, at the postsecondary level affirmative-action goals seem to generate a demand for black students that outstrips the supply at any given achievement level.

Black students are continually recruited to schools where they will have greater difficulty succeeding. For example, Myron Magnet notes that a "quarter of the blacks at MIT don't graduate; those who do often have below-average grades. Nearly 60 percent of the black students at Berkeley never graduate. . . . Of the total number of black students nationwide, only 26 percent succeeded in graduating six years after matriculating. So preferential policies have not helped blacks rise up the social and economic ladder as much as alternative approaches might" (Magnet, 1993:191). More evidence for this problem can be seen from the repeal of racial preferences in California institutions of higher education:

When unqualified students were admitted on the basis of race, the results proved disastrous. Only 58 percent of African American students from the freshman classes entering Berkeley between 1987 and 1990 managed to complete their degree requirements within six years. . . . Experts say that under the new admissions system the number of blacks eventually graduating statewide should increase by a solid 19 percent. . . . Thus the total number of blacks graduating would still be about the same as under preferences—even though fewer were admitted. (National Center for Policy Analysis, Idea House, 1998b:1–2)

Another consequence of affirmative action in higher education is the uneven distribution of minorities, particularly at elite institutions. Ron Unz reports that at Harvard blacks and Hispanics are somewhat underrepresented in relation to their numbers in the population with 8 percent and 7 percent enrollment, compared to 12 percent and 10 percent in the population, respectively. Asians, representing only 2 to 3 percent of the population, account for nearly 20 percent of the Harvard student body. Jews account for 25 to 33 percent, compared with a 2 to 3 percent population representation. One of the results of this commitment to affirmative action is that "non-Jewish white Americans represent no more than a quarter of Harvard undergraduates, although they constitute nearly 75 percent of the general population—and thus they are far more underrepresented than blacks, Hispanics or any other minority group" (National Center for Policy Analysis, Idea House, 1998a:1–2).

Education has a direct bearing on minority experiences in the job market. In education several factors other than race may account for persistent underachievement for blacks, leading to persistent wage gaps. Citing Thernstrom and Thernstrom, one report noted that "black men earned 19 percent less than comparably educated white men, but measured on performance on basic tests of word knowledge, paragraph comprehension, arithmetical reasoning and mathematical knowledge, black men earned 9 percent more than white men with the same skills" (National Center for Policy Analysis, Idea House, 1997b:2). This suggests that educational achievement measures may be more important than discrimination in explaining wage differentials.

A particularly telling example of the educational skills factor is apparent in the armed forces, where blacks have been more successful at career advancement than in almost any other area. Charles Moskos has reported that the "number of blacks who are promoted from captain to major, a virtual prerequisite for an officer seeking an army career, is usually below the goal. . . . The most plausible explanation is that a disproportionate number of black officers lack the writing and communication skills for promotion to staff jobs. In all other ranks, including colonel through general officers, promotions show little racial difference" (Moskos, 1995:22). This suggests that educational factors often explain apparent racial disparities in economic opportunities.

Economic Progress

James Smith and Finis Welch, authors of a RAND Corporation study, *Closing the Gap: Forty Years of Economic Progress for Blacks* (1986), concluded in the mid-1980s that black wage gains over the previous forty years had very little to do with affirmative action and were attributable to steady improvement in the quality of black education. The authors offer the following assessment:

Affirmative action cannot be the whole story, however, nor for that matter, a very large part of it. The principal reason is that the increase in the economic benefits of black schooling began long before the affirmative action pressures of the last two decades. More than half of the narrowing of the gap in income benefits from schooling between the races took place before 1960. As a result, the narrowing of racial differences in the benefits from education was as large during the twenty years from 1940 to 1960 as it was in the twenty years after 1960. (Smith and Welch, 1991:504)

Smith and Welch conclude that long-term improvements in black education were the primary determinants of black economic progress. The greatest progress made by blacks resulted from dramatic improvements in the quality of primary and secondary education, where affirmative action had little or no impact. In higher education the diversity emphasis, a deeply entrenched extension of the affirmative-action policies embraced by minority interest groups, congressional sponsors, federal agencies, and the courts, appears to be providing few tangible benefits compared to the frequently substantial academic and economic costs it is imposing on black students.

An overview of the aggregate data available showing trends for blacks in the labor market suggests that affirmative-action policies, particularly as reviewed and revised by the courts, have been, at best, a mixed blessing. Since the civil rights initiatives of the 1960s blacks have divided into three roughly equal parts: a middle class, a working class, and a large underclass. The black middle class appears to have benefited most from affirmative-action policies from the late 1960s until at least the early 1980s (Donohue and Heckman, 1991:1603). In fact, supporters would argue that affirmative action was important in creating and sustaining a black middle class since the 1970s, but it appears that the Civil Rights Act itself was more important than affirmative-action policies (Freeman, 1973; Leonard, 1991).

Enforcement of Title VII cases by the federal courts initially seemed to be contributing to the economic advancement of blacks: "Once Title VII went into effect, black workers who were members of industrial unions filed many charges with the EEOC and initiated lawsuits in the federal courts against the unions to which they belonged because they had learned that what exclusion was to the craft unions, separate lines of job promotion and seniority were to the industrial unions" (Hill, 1989:242–43). Numerous rulings against the Steelworkers Union resulted in an industry-wide consent decree in 1974. Other unions faced similar legal battles throughout the 1970s. "Such litigation involved labor organizations in papermaking and communications, in the tobacco industry, in aircraft and automotive manufacturing, . . . in longshore, in public utilities, and in the transportation industry, among others" (Hill, 1989:243).

Nevertheless, the impact of affirmative action appears to have been marginal and temporary. Smith and Welch point out:

During the initial phases of affirmative action, there was a remarkable surge in incomes of young black males. . . . The large shift in black employment was concentrated during the years 1966–70 and was largely completed by 1974. During these early years, EEOC-covered firms rapidly increased their demand for black workers, bidding up their wages. However, once the stock of black workers had reached its new equilibrium, this short-run demand increase was completed and wages returned to their long-run levels. (Smith and Welch, 1994:174)

Since the major legislative victories in civil rights, long-range macroeconomic trends seem to have impacted black economic progress more significantly than affirmative action. For example, during the 1980s, at a time when affirmative-action initiatives were being less strongly enforced by the Reagan administration and were treated more ambivalently by the courts, real median black family income rose by 17 percent. In fact, as one economist noted in 1995, "[b]etween 1983 and 1989, real wealth among white families rose 24%—but it increased 35% for blacks and 54% for Hispanics" (National Center for Policy Analysis, Idea House, 1995a:1).

Another study reported that "[a]fter controlling for age, IQ and gender, the average black fulltime worker actually earns 1% more than his white counterpart" (National Center for Policy Analysis, Idea House, 1995b:1). Another study reported that personal annual income was 50 percent higher among blacks as of 1997 than in 1980 and that in 1996 "the 28.4 percent of blacks living below the poverty line represented the lowest proportion since the Census Bureau started keeping such data in 1955" (National Center for Policy Analysis, Idea House, 1997a:1). Census Bureau data also indicate that from 1987 to 1992 "the number of black-owned firms in the U.S. surged 46 percent. . . . This was during a time that the overall number of businesses increased just 26 percent. The number of wealthier black households—with annual incomes of $75,000 or more—increased from 1.7 percent in 1970 to 5.2 percent in 1993" (National Center for Policy Analysis, Idea House, 1996:1).

One of the consequences of enforcement strategies targeting government and government contractors was that government jobs tended to offer more favorable earning ratios for blacks and other minorities than jobs in the private sector. Black professionals and managers therefore gravitated heavily toward government jobs throughout the late 1960s and 1970s, making impressive gains. According to census data blacks comprised only 1.9 percent of all officials and managers in 1970. By 1980 blacks had reached 4 percent and by 1988, 5.6 percent. Blacks comprised 2.6 percent of all professionals in 1970, 4.3 percent in 1980, and 6.7 percent in 1988 (Shull, 1993:196). Two-thirds of all black managers and professionals worked in the public sector, compared to only 17 percent among the general population.

While it seems obvious that affirmative action created opportunities for many qualified blacks in government, it left them particularly vulnerable to the fiscal constraints imposed at local, state, and federal levels in the 1980s. Moreover, as Thomas Sowell points out, "the employment of blacks by private employers without government contracts declined between 1970 and 1980, while increases in black employment in various government and government-related sectors were being hailed as indicators of the general progress of blacks under affirmative action" (Sowell, 1990:142; see also Dometrius and Sigelman, 1984). In the 1980s some of the laid-off black government employees found jobs in the private sector and became members of a small black elite, with growing opportunities. Many others did not find comparable work, and this partly explains a black unemployment vulnerability twice that of white middle-class workers (Dawson, 1994:31).

Thus affirmative-action gains for black professionals in the 1970s may have drawn the best-educated and qualified blacks away from the private sector, simply resulting in a subsequent reshuffling. This reshuffling may explain the temporary decline in black income levels relative to those of whites in the early 1980s. One case study of affirmative-action programs in Atlanta, Georgia, reported in the *Economist*, found that during a two-decade period minority contract awards rose from less than 1 percent to 35 percent, but that the city's business enterprises remained segregated and that minority firms thriving from minority business contracts had turned into a system of nepotism ("But Some Are More Equal than Others: Affirmative Action," 1995:21–23).

By contrast, the black working class seemed to benefit significantly in the early years of aggressive affirmative-action enforcement by the EEOC and OFCC. The pervasive reach of these organizations into the labor unions and trade organizations contracting with the federal government provided many opportunities for blacks who had been previously overlooked or overtly discriminated against in the job market. James Heckman provides a cautiously optimistic assessment for the impact of affirmative action in the South from 1960 to 1970: "Very little reliable information is available about the negative or positive effects of affirmative action and equal rights programs on the status of blacks in the aggregate. Evidence from the South Carolina labor market indicates that these programs at the very least facilitated the breakthrough in black employment that occurred in the traditional manufacturing sector of the state" (Heckman, 1989:77). One critic of this study suggests that because the improvements came largely before the goals and timetables period, and because it focused on the South, it was more likely that "the Civil Rights Act itself . . . produced the large increase in relative earnings" (O'Neill and O'Neill, 1992:97).

Also focusing on employment discrimination in the South, Alfred Blumrosen studied the decisions of Southern appellate justices who rejected the narrow construction of Title VII by Southern district courts:

The southeastern states had "open and notorious" job segregation, dual lines of seniority and officially segregated school systems which tended to assure inferior education and employment for minorities. The district judges sitting in those states, with some notable exceptions, were unsympathetic to Title VII. With almost monotonous regularity, they adopted a narrow construction of the statute and made findings of fact in favor of defendants. Thereupon the Fourth and Fifth Circuit Courts of Appeal wrote a remarkable chapter in the history of statutory interpretation. They created a jurisprudence of Title VII which was calculated to simplify the attack on segregated employment systems. (Blumrosen, 1994:241)

Blumrosen found that in 1978 and 1980, after the first phase of aggressive Title VII interpretation by the courts had already ended (by 1975–76), the occupational distribution of blacks remained substantially more favorable than if pre-affirmative-action trends were projected from 1966 until that time. He concluded that in spite of the judiciary's repudiation of more aggressive affirmative-action measures after 1976, "the pattern of continued inclusion of blacks which began under the regime of southern jurisprudence persisted at least to the end of the decade" (Blumrosen, 1994:244). Thus, according to Blumrosen, affirmative-action gains in the South were not reversed by a relaxation of judicial and executive enforcement of affirmative-action policy in the late 1970s.

Blumrosen also compiled data on various occupational categories of minority workers. The data suggest that black workers made the greatest advances in semiskilled and skilled trade occupations from 1965 to 1975. Blumrosen presented ratios of minority versus white inclusion in a number of occupational categories from 1950 to 1980. Blacks in semiskilled occupations improved relative to whites from a ratio of 117 in 1965 to 136.9 in 1975 (100 would mean parity with whites). Blacks in skilled blue-collar occupations moved from a ratio of 49.6 in 1965 to 65.7 in 1975. Growth slowed from 1975 to 1980 but did continue (Blumrosen, 1994:239).

For the most part, enhanced employment opportunities persisted throughout the 1970s, with a "lower proportion of terminations relative to hirings among blacks as compared to other workers" (Belz, 1991:251). Nevertheless, some groups of blacks benefited more than others. For example, while blacks enjoyed absolute gains in employment opportunities, black females appear to have benefited more than black males. Jonathan Leonard's widely publicized 1983 study of affirmative action, drawing on a sample of 16 million employees at 69,000 firms, is the most authoritative to date. Leonard found that black employment opportunity was greater in firms that contracted with the government (and hence were subject to affirmative-action compliance review) than in those that did not. He also found substantial differences among various cohorts of minority and nonminority employees. "Over a six-year period [1974–80] the employment of members of protected groups grew significantly faster in contractor than in noncontractor establishments. The growth rate is 3.8 percent faster for black males, 7.9 percent for other minority males, 2.8 percent for white females, and 12.3 percent for black females. A summary measure, white male employment, grew 1.2 percent slower in the contractor sector" (Leonard, 1991:495).

Leonard's study strongly suggests that affirmative action disproportionately benefited black women and other minority males while providing very marginal benefits to black males and white women. Given that white women lagged behind black men, these data at least raise the possibility that factors other than racial discrimination explain the disparate relative gains of the subgroups. For example, macroeconomic conditions may have favored black women and other minority members more. This is the conclusion drawn by O'Neill and O'Neill in their assessment of the impact of affirmative action on the labor market. The researchers attribute "the lack of convergence in the black-white earnings gap among men and the strong rise in the earnings of women relative to men" to wage differences between skilled and unskilled workers since the mid-1970s. Because blacks tend to be less skilled than whites, they "suffer disproportionately from a shift in demand against low-skilled labor." Women fared better in the 1980s largely because "cohorts of working women are relatively more educated and have acquired more continuous years of work experience than was true of women in the past" (O'Neill and O'Neill, 1992:97, 101).

The fact that black men appear to have gained least from affirmative-action programs and black women gained most may have had undesirable consequences for black families in the 1980s. Greater income disparities between black men and women could have further eroded the black "male marriageable pool" and perhaps have contributed to a rise in black female-headed households at higher economic echelons. This argument is at least plausible, although we are unaware of any studies that evaluate this possibility.

The declining male marriageable pool has been well documented by sociologist William J. Wilson in his study of the black urban underclass, though he certainly does not link the trend to affirmative action (Wilson, 1987). Nevertheless, Wilson recognizes that the out-migration of middle- and working-class blacks from the inner city eliminates "the mainstream role models that help keep alive the perception that education is meaningful, that steady employment is a viable alternative to welfare, and that family stability is the norm, not the exception" (Wilson, 1987:56).

Wilson attributes the rise of female-headed households, which have grown from 17.6 percent in 1950 to 41.9 percent in 1983, to a "sharp rise in separation and divorce rates and the substantial increase in the percentage of never-married women" (Wilson, 1987:67).

Like many other analysts of black economic trends, Wilson links the decline of the male marriageable pool to an economy that has shifted to require higher levels of education and has decreased the number of low-level entry positions available to blacks. Wilson continues to emphasize the structural conditions as explanations of the growth of the underclass, and the reforms he prescribes are in employment and labor-market policies: job-training programs to move underclass individuals into secure positions, a dispersion of low-income housing to limit the effects of underclass concentration, and a child-support program to bring about full employment and balanced economic growth.

As Wilson and others would probably concede, affirmative-action programs seem to have provided very minimal changes in the structure of economic opportunity for the black underclass. Black poverty rates declined most before affirmative-action policies really took hold. They declined substantially from 1960 to 1974, from about 55 percent to 30 percent; however, they rose slightly to 36 percent by 1982 and then dropped back to 30 percent by 1987. As of 1996 rates dropped again to 28.5 percent, suggesting that macroeconomic conditions are more important than affirmative action in advancing black economic opportunity. Poverty rates for whites declined from 23 percent in 1960 to 9 percent by 1974 and remained between 10 and 12 percent until 1987 (Dawson, 1994:28–29). While reverse-discrimination cases were beginning to partially undermine preferential policies for minorities after 1976, black poverty rates were affected very little. In fact, they seem not to have been affected by either affirmative-action setbacks under the Reagan and Bush administrations or by the courts. From 1982 until 1987 conditions for low-income blacks actually improved. Again, the significantly brighter macroeconomic picture following the 1982 recession probably had a more direct impact on black poverty rates than affirmative action. This again seems to have been the case in the 1990s economy.

As Herman Belz argues in *Equality Transformed* (1991), the black underclass was left largely untouched by affirmative action. "Criminal activity, drug dependency, illegitimate teenage pregnancies, and high unemployment among young black males are some of the problems that constitute the social pathology of ghetto existence, for which affirmative action does not appear relevant" (Belz, 1991:253–54).

For black youth, the larger socioeconomic picture also seems to tell most of the story. As America shifted more from a manufacturing to a service-based economy, many blacks were disadvantaged in a market with high demand for "well-educated, technologically-oriented workers, technicians, managers, and professionals and a declining demand for unskilled and semiskilled labor." Black youth unemployment in the early 1980s had "soared to over 50 percent . . . [and] in 1985, in the midst of a strong recovery, the official black teenage unemployment rate was 39 percent, almost triple the 15 percent rate of white teenagers" (Dawson,

1994:25). The unfortunate fact is that affirmative action is unlikely to reach the vast majority of black youth. The jobs they are qualified to fill have left the inner city. As Lipset has noted, "Preference policies or quotas are not much help to an illegitimate black ghetto youth who grows up in poverty and receives an inferior education" (Lipset, 1995:7).

Public Opinion and Preferential Treatment

Not only do the economic data suggest affirmative action's unimpressive performance, but the American public has largely opposed racial-preference policies. Perhaps most surprising, until the late 1970s large majorities of women and minorities objected to affirmative action, believing that merit alone should govern education and employment decisions. In 1977 a Gallup Survey asked the following question: "Some people say that to make up for past discrimination, women and members of minority groups should be given preferential treatment in getting jobs and places in college. Others say that ability, as determined by test scores, should be the main consideration. Which point comes closest to how you feel on this matter?" Overall, 83 percent of respondents felt that ability should be the main consideration. Only 10 percent felt that women and minorities should be given preference (7 percent had no opinion). Among "nonwhites," 64 percent favored ability versus 27 percent favoring preferential treatment. Among women, 82 percent favored ability as against 11 percent favoring preference for women and minorities.

In a 1996 assessment of trends in public opinion of affirmative action Charlotte Steeh and Maria Krysan conclude that since 1965 it remains "clear that white adults do not favor preferences, quotas, or economic aid for blacks when these questions are generally phrased. However, this support is considerably greater than it was in 1963" (Steeh and Krysan, 1996:140). Seymour Martin Lipset concludes that public opinion remains largely opposed to affirmative action:

White men and women are fairly consistently and overwhelmingly in opposition; they favor meritocracy and individual competition. Blacks, however, vary in their reaction when queried in national polls. They are invariably more supportive of group rights, quotas, or special preferences than whites, but they differ in their response pattern depending on how the question is posed. More often than not, however, a majority or plurality supports meritocratic principles, usually by a much smaller percentage than among whites. African-Americans are pulled to favor group rights, but they still respond favorably to the individualistic ethos. (Lipset, 1995:3)

Public opinion polls have continuously underscored the fact that affirmative action, in the form of racially preferential hiring and admissions policies, is an elite-driven government entitlement program lacking majoritarian support. Blacks, the intended beneficiaries of most of these policies, are not as opposed to affirmative action as whites, but significant numbers still express ambivalence or opposition to affirmative action. So too do they embrace a variety of meritocratic principles of economic organization. Undoubtedly, large numbers of blacks and whites support race-neutral policies because they are consistent with the pervasive

American belief in individual merit and competition over group identity as determinants of economic advancement.

CONCLUSION: THE UNCERTAIN FUTURE OF
AFFIRMATIVE ACTION

During the years that the courts and federal agencies have defended preferential policies in employment and admissions they have helped to create a constituency of beneficiaries and also a moral expectation among many blacks that these policies are necessary and justifiable in fighting societal discrimination. We cannot know what public policies would have arisen had the bureaucracy and the courts not redirected the civil rights movement away from race neutrality and toward racial hiring and admissions preferences, but clearly the public's perception is that something is very wrong with this type of remedial policy. Even though many blacks recognize that the policies may be beneficial to some, substantial numbers of them (and large majorities of whites) still believe that preferential policies are unfair.

Moreover, the supposed benefits of affirmative action appear to be unimpressive. Empirical research on the consequences of affirmative action suggests that preferential policies aimed at improving the overall educational and economic opportunity of black Americans tend to favor some cohorts over others, provide only temporary advantages, and build certain vulnerabilities into black economic progress. Further, affirmative action tends to mask the more problematic aspects of black poverty and educational underachievement and has done almost nothing to improve opportunities for poor, urban blacks. In spite of their problematic legacy, preferential policies have become entrenched in the federal bureaucracy, in part due to the support of the federal courts. This is so in spite of the supposed temporary character of affirmative-action policies.

In the 1970s the racial-preference conception became the predominantly employed version of affirmative action, largely as a result of administrative actions of the federal government and judicial reinterpretation of civil rights law. As "reverse discrimination" became a more widespread criticism of affirmative action's racial hiring preferences, controversy over race neutrality and racial preference returned. Liberals and conservatives, blacks and whites, and Congress and the federal courts became more divided over which conception should predominate. This fundamental disagreement continues to characterize affirmative-action controversies to the present. This debate has proceeded largely among the elite levels of government in the context of strong popular opposition to preferential policies, even among a plurality of African Americans.

It would be a mistake for anyone attempting to understand the policy career of affirmative action to discount the decisive role of the federal courts and especially the Supreme Court in determining how far in the direction of quotas the federal government would go. The Supreme Court's initial embrace of executive-branch proportional representation programs and the disparate impact approach to remedy the evils of a past history of discrimination against minorities endorsed an aggressive enforcement policy by federal civil rights agencies.

The implementation of affirmative-action policy has been a social and economic experiment of immense proportions, ultimately affecting hundreds of thousands of employers and more than half the total American workforce (Brimelow and Spencer, 1993:82). Yet far from demonstrating that affirmative action has been an unqualified success, aggregate economic data suggest that the programs have yielded limited benefits and created some unfavorable social and economic consequences for minorities themselves. For more fortunate blacks who have benefited from racial preferences, the data seem to corroborate Thomas Sowell's observation that affirmative action tends to cream off blacks with the best skills, education, and credentials. Ironically, this has in some unintended ways jeopardized their well-being, for example, when they are mismatched to educational institutions where they will not perform optimally, or when they are disproportionately laid off by shrinking local, state, or federal government agencies.

Working-class blacks have perhaps gained the most from affirmative-action policies, particularly in the South; however, much of what blacks gained in the 1960s and 1970s would not be forfeited if affirmative action came to an end. The private sector relies on blacks in the labor force and would be unlikely to reverse this trend. As for racial preferences within the corporate economy, Richard Epstein argued that "affirmative action would not disappear if Title VII were repealed tomorrow; the political support for the current status quo would still exert extensive power within private firms" (Epstein, 1992:420).

The black underclass has not been, and will not be, helped by affirmative-action programs. Drugs, crime, violence, illegitimacy, and related problems are social pathologies that have become more widespread in the inner cities, and employment programs alone cannot do much to alleviate them. Black inner-city youth are also unlikely beneficiaries of preferential hiring. The jobs that youth need to enter the workforce are far from home and frequently require skills that they do not yet possess. Certainly court-ordered progress has been uneven, and the data for women and Asian Americans indicate that racial discrimination alone does not provide a compelling explanation for the slow progress of blacks in the labor force.

With a substantial number of more conservative judges staffing the federal judiciary since the 1980s, the support for affirmative action has declined. The retrenchment evident in decisions since the late 1980s reflects not only ideological polarization on the Court but conflicting visions of the American constitutional order in the society:

The Living Constitution has left us with two mutually exclusive versions of democracy. Either democracy is the affirmative action vision writ large—a society is democratic because all groups are proportionally represented in all its parts, from university faculties to death row—or it is democratic because all are equal in the eyes of the state, free to excel and succeed regardless of what group they were born into. Both cannot be true. And standing bewildered between them, we feel, quite accurately, that we have lost our bearings. (Magnet, 1993:194)

Given the extent to which affirmative action has already been instituted, the support it enjoys among civil rights advocacy groups such as the NAACP, and the litigation industry it continues to fuel, it seems unlikely that racial-preference policies will quickly lose their political support. The Clinton administration elected not to comply with the *Adarand* precedent.

Still, the very fact that some aspects of affirmative action have been challenged on constitutional grounds probably forecasts a period of greater resistance and more open debate over the means and ends of remedial policies for racial minorities. More than thirty years after passage of the Civil Rights Act the principle of a society that allocates opportunity on the basis of individual merit remains an elusive ideal whose elusiveness has been ironically delayed by affirmative-action policies themselves. Affirmative action seems to have made race a more conspicuous and troublesome issue than either opponents or advocates had anticipated. It is also an issue that can polarize various racial and ethnic groups, heightening the possibilities of conflict and weakening the social fabric which binds the society together (Sniderman and Piazza, 1993).

A review of the consequences of affirmative-action programs as a remedy to racial discrimination suggests that the intended beneficiaries may have suffered certain adverse impacts from the policies themselves. Preferential policies have not produced a more genuine equality of opportunity. Instead, they appear to have damaged race relations, benefited minorities marginally and unevenly (largely bypassing poor, urban blacks), exposed many blacks to risks of under- or unemployment in the labor market and underachievement in higher education, and challenged widely held public attitudes toward individual merit and equal opportunity without regard to race. Given these social, political, and economic costs, the actions of the civil rights agencies and the federal courts appear more difficult to defend on both pragmatic and theoretical grounds.

Chapter 4

Prisoners' Rights and the Consequences of Correctional Reform

ORIGINS OF JUDICIAL ACTIVISM IN PRISON REFORM

Prison populations have expanded enormously in the past forty years. In 1960 the total number of prisoners incarcerated in state and federal prisons was estimated at 213,000. By 1980 the prison population had increased to 330,000. Since 1980 the number of inmates in the United States has more than quadrupled, with nearly 1.3 million inmates residing in state and federal prisons in 1996 (U.S. Department of Justice [DOJ], Bureau of Justice Statistics, 1997; U.S. DOJ, Bureau of Justice Statistics, 2001). In 1980 approximately 2 million Americans were either in custody, on parole, or on probation. In 1993 that figure had climbed to nearly 5 million, with one-third of these individuals behind bars. The prison population explosion has been fueled in part by a large increase in convicted drug offenders. The numbers of those incarcerated for drug-related offenses increased from 19,000 to 172,300 from 1980 to 1993 (Bureau of Justice Statistics, 1994:1).

These rising populations help explain the tremendous increase in prisoner litigation in the federal courts. Critics of inmate litigation point out that many of these new cases are frivolous lawsuits brought by jailhouse lawyers. "In 1995, Senator Robert Dole introduced the PLRA, citing prisoner lawsuits involving such grievances as 'insufficient storage locker space, a defective haircut by a prison barber, . . . and yes, being served chunky peanut butter instead of the creamy variety,' all filed 'free of charge. No court costs. No filing fees' " (Third Branch, 1999:1). Many critics of the judiciary argue that the courts have been much too sympathetic to these lawsuits, and that they have interfered too often and for too long in the administration of the nation's prisons.

Judicial intervention in prison administration and the dramatic increase in civil rights litigation have angered Congress and prompted passage of the Prison Litigation Reform Act (PLRA) in 1996. As one commentator described it, the law "substantially changes almost every aspect of federal court procedures currently used in non-habeas prisoner litigation, including procedures for filing and reviewing *in forma pauperis* (IFP) petitions [for poor plaintiffs], court-ordered remedial relief for prison conditions, and appointment and payment of federal special masters" (Third Branch, 1996:1). At the time of its passage Senator Bob Dole applauded the measure, stating that the new law "will work to restrain liberal Federal judges who see violations of constitutional rights in every prisoner complaint and who have used these complaints to micromanage state and local prison systems" (Prison Litigation Reform Act, 1996:4). Senator Edward Kennedy took a less sanguine view of the new law, stating that "the PLRA is a far-reaching effort to strip Federal courts of the authority to remedy unconstitutional prison conditions. The PLRA is itself patently unconstitutional, and a dangerous legislative incursion into the work of the judicial branch" (Prison Litigation Reform Act, 1996:3). In spite of opponents' fears, the law has hardly shut down prisoner litigation, though it evidently has brought about a significant reduction of cases. Since the PLRA's enactment there has been a 25 percent decline in the previously more than 40,000 prisoner lawsuits per year. In order to place the prison-reform movement and trends in prison litigation in perspective, we must first explain the changing jurisprudence of the federal courts with regard to cases involving prisoners and correctional institutions.

From Hands-off Prisons to Judicial Intervention

Less than thirty-five years ago it could be said without exaggeration that the last contact a typical inmate had with the legal system was the day he was sentenced. Today most correctional facilities in each of more than forty states operate under some degree of judicial supervision. This dramatic change in prison politics has had far-reaching effects on correctional administration. Undoubtedly, the worst conditions and practices existing in prisons have been eliminated, staff are better trained and equipped, and safety and living conditions have improved for inmates. Nevertheless, judicial intervention has altered correctional administration in ways that have imposed certain costs, not only on the institutions themselves, but also upon the larger social, economic, and political system.

Summarizing the involvement of federal courts in the highly controversial area of prison reform, John DiIulio, Jr., emphasizes the enormity and complexity of the tasks undertaken by the judiciary. "[By] now virtually every facet of institutional life has been constitutionalized in ways that directly affect prisons and jails in all fifty states" (quoted in Feeley and Hanson, 1990:13). Consent decrees and injunctions govern prison administration in more than forty states. "In these cases courts have ordered improvements in institutional services, required the expenditure of vast sums of money, ordered the early release of thousands of inmates, and appointed special masters to design and implement detailed administrative plans to affect these and other aspects of institutional life" (Feeley and Hanson, 1990:12–13).

Edgarto Rotman emphasizes that initial perceptions of correctional-system failure were partially attributable to the widely publicized wave of prison riots of the 1950s. In that decade riots took place in prisons in New Jersey, Michigan, Ohio, Illinois, California, Oregon, New Mexico, Massachusetts, Washington, and Minnesota. "The usual complaints that triggered the riots were the deficiency of prison facilities, lack of hygiene or medical care, poor food quality, lack of treatment, and guard brutality. All the demands of the rebels generally coincided with what in the next decade would become rights recognized by the courts" (Rotman, 1995:188). Beginning in the late 1960s and 1970s, while the increasingly vocal and active inmate populations agitated for better living conditions and privileges, many members of the legal profession shifted from a deferential to an interventionist orientation with regard to prisoners' claims.

Despite attempts by various advocacy groups to establish legal precedent to the contrary, before the 1960s most courts refused to give favorable consideration to the claims of prisoners (Rotman, 1995:191). As a *University of Chicago Law Review* article noted in 1972:

The traditional role of the judiciary in correctional matters was merely to interpret statutes and to review a narrow range of administrative actions. Even in these cases, the judiciary granted only limited relief to specifically named inmate-plaintiffs. Whenever judicial intervention threatened to step beyond these narrow bounds, it aroused a plethora of objections, which led eventually to a policy of "hands-off." (Atkins and Glick, 1972:146)

Prisoners were viewed as "slaves of the state," a characterization drawn from the 1871 case *Ruffin v. Virginia,* and were considered to have experienced a kind of civic death. The opinion in this case states that "as a consequence of his crime, [a prisoner] not only forfeited his liberty, but all his personal rights except those which the law in its humanity accords to him. He is for the time being the slave of the state" (quoted in Wallace, 1992:333).

As Christopher Smith points out in his study of judicial policy making, *Courts and Public Policy,* the courts did not begin to intervene to a significant extent in the area of prison administration until the mid-1960s. Prior to that "judges responded by declaring either that prisoners were 'slaves' of the state and therefore possessed no rights or that judges must defer to the decisions of prison officials who are society's experts on correctional administration" (Smith, 1993b:93–94). While conditions in prisons prior to the 1960s were considered quite shocking by many outside observers and led to widespread rioting within, the federal courts continued to uphold a "hands-off" jurisprudence. The political branches would have to resolve difficulties in prison administration. As a *Yale Law Journal* article critical of the judiciary's "hands-off" jurisprudence noted, problems of prison administration were simply perceived by jurists as "beyond the ken of the courts" (*Yale Law Journal*, 1963:506).

Changing American Legal Culture and Prison Reform

Smith and others point out that a changing American legal and political culture explains the shift to increased judicial activism in prison administration. The 1960s were "an era in which American courts became more receptive to claims from political minorities seeking judicial protection of constitutional rights" (Smith, 1993b:94; see also Jacobs, 1983:35). The prisoners' rights movement drew substantial momentum from the larger civil rights movement, which "gave support and inspiration to the pioneers of prisoners' rights litigation" (Rotman, 1995:193). The civil rights movement itself was part of a larger sociopolitical transition that made civil rights and, later, prison reform possible.

C. Ronald Huff provides an insightful sociological perspective in explaining the rise of a prisoners' rights movement. Huff incorporates James Jacobs's (1977) analysis of changing prison conditions, which relied on Edward Shils's (1962) theory of the emerging dynamics of mass society, to explain greater sympathy for prisoners and prison conditions. Huff links the trend not only to the civil rights movement but also more generally to the extension of "predominant social and institutional norms and values . . . to include previously marginal groups" (Huff, 1980:50–51). The rights universe expanded, and advocates of change succeeded in extending further protections to marginal and institutionalized groups such as prisoners.

In applying this theory to judicial activism on behalf of "heretofore powerless segments of American society" in the 1950s and 1960s, Huff points out that it was the "activities of the Warren court which had such a profound impact on criminal law more generally" (Huff, 1980:51). Problems in prisons continued to be viewed as intractable and redressable only through systemic reform. Largely as a result of the perceived successes of the Warren Court, legal advocates began to see a need and an opportunity to more effectively reform correctional institutions through public law litigation. As previously noted, law-review articles critical of judicial deference in prisoners' rights cases were already being written in the early 1960s. Reformers viewed prisoners as a class of individuals who were particularly vulnerable to rights violations because of the highly insular nature of prison administration. It was highly unlikely that legislative majorities or public opinion would ever favor prison reform. This was another type of minority population suffering prejudice from the larger society that progressive members of the bench and bar believed required protection.

LANDMARK CORRECTIONAL RULINGS OF THE 1960s

A number of key court decisions of the 1960s provided breakthroughs in prisoners' rights jurisprudence and rather quickly swept away the "hands-off" approach of the 1950s. They led the way to widespread federal court intervention in the administration of prisons. As Samuel Pillsbury remarked, "Informed by the ideology of rights, the Supreme Court abandoned the deference to social science expertise which it had displayed earlier and undertook a careful review of penal decision-making. The Court began to legalize decision-making throughout the penal system" (Pillsbury, 1989:754).

First, in 1962 the Supreme Court ruled in *Robinson v. California* that the Eighth Amendment's prohibition of cruel and unusual punishment was applicable to the states under the Fourteenth Amendment's due process clause. Following this incorporation of the Eighth Amendment under the Fourteenth, prisoners' advocates were prompted to file suits alleging cruel and unusual punishment violations for a myriad of prison conditions. Throughout the 1960s and 1970s cases were filed in many states. Some of the most important precedents were established in lower federal court rulings in Alabama (*Pugh v. Locke*), Arkansas (*Holt v. Sarver*), and Mississippi (*Gates v. Collier*), where plaintiffs charged Eighth Amendment violations in state prisons (Yackle, 1989:43, 52). Court decisions finding violations of the Eighth Amendment's prohibition against cruel and unusual punishment rested on a number of different legal rationales in these cases. Some decisions relied upon a finding that the "totality of the circumstances" in the prisons constituted Eighth Amendment violations. Others found that conditions "shocked the conscience" and were therefore violative. Still others relied upon the Supreme Court's "evolving standards of decency" rationale articulated in *Trop v. Dulles* (1958).

A second major advance for prison reform came in *Cooper v. Pate* (1964). According to Christopher Smith, "Prisoners achieved a major legal breakthrough when the Supreme Court decided in 1964 that prisoners could utilize a federal statute as the basis for lawsuits to challenge the conditions of their confinement . . . , a statute that permits suits against state officials to be filed in federal courts, in order to assert claims of constitutional rights violations" (Smith, 1993b:94). The applicable section of the 1871 civil rights law reads as follows:

Every person who, under color of any statute, ordinance, regulation, custom, or usage, of any State or Territory or the District of Columbia, subjects, or causes to be subjected, any citizen of the United States or other person within the jurisdiction thereof to the deprivation of any rights, privileges, or immunities secured by the Constitution and laws, shall be liable to the party injured in an action at law, suit in equity, or other proper proceeding for redress. (quoted in Thomas, 1991:11)

Charles Thomas depicts this section of the statute as defining "the parameters of correctional law for more than a quarter of a century. Deprivations in such diverse areas as exercises of religious freedom, food services, medical services, disciplinary proceedings, transfers from correctional to mental health care facilities, physical abuse by staff, and facility overcrowding can be attacked by prisoner plaintiffs in Section 1983 suits" (Thomas, 1991:8).

A widely cited Bureau of Justice Statistics report on Section 1983 litigation underscores the pivotal nature of the *Cooper* decision for the past three decades of prison litigation. The volume of prisoner lawsuits rose dramatically after *Cooper*. "The Administrative Office of the U.S. Courts (AO) counted only 218 cases in 1966, the first year that state prisoners' rights cases were recorded as a specific category of litigation. The number climbed to 26,824 by 1992." As of 1995 this figure represented an astonishing 10 percent "of all civil cases filed in the nation's U.S.

District (trial) Courts" (Hanson and Daley, 1995:1–2). While *Cooper* granted prisoners access to the courts, it remained for the judiciary to adopt a jurisdictional mechanism allowing plaintiffs to prevail on constitutional grounds.

PRISONERS' RIGHTS AND THE LIVING CONSTITUTION

Historically it has been predominantly the responsibility of the judiciary to articulate the parameters and even the substance of constitutionally protected rights, including the scope of a prisoner's rights under the First, Fourth, Eighth, and Fourteenth Amendments. At this level of analysis it is arguably impossible to make judgments about the propriety of judicial involvement in prison policy without interjecting one's preferences for or against an organic, evolving constitution, but we can at least attempt to explain how this has occurred. For example, in the application of the Eighth Amendment's prohibition against cruel and unusual punishment, courts have independently determined whether specific practices or conditions violate this standard, essentially redefining the standard itself.

As a 1970 *University of Chicago Law Review* article noted, the meaning of cruel and unusual punishment has "evolved" during the twentieth century. "The immediate incentive to the passage of the eighth amendment was a desire to prevent the recurrence of such torturous punishments as pillorying, disemboweling, decapitation, and drawing and quartering. Indeed a number of early cases implied that only punishment physically barbarous in nature was subject to the proscription of the amendment" (*University of Chicago Law Review*, 1971:656).

By the early twentieth century the Supreme Court had begun to accept the more progressive legal community's sense of the fluidity of meaning in constitutional law in *Weems v. United States* (1910). "In that case, the Court held that the eighth amendment ' . . . is not fastened to the obsolete but may acquire meaning as public opinion becomes enlightened by human justice.' The court stated in dictum that the drafters of the amendment must have realized 'that there could be exercises of cruelty by laws other than those which inflict bodily pain or mutilation' " (quoted in Atkins and Glick, 1972:147).

This fluidity in Eighth Amendment interpretation continues to predominate in contemporary constitutional law cases. Phillip Cooper remarks that "[s]ince the benchmark for evaluating cruel and unusual punishments is society's 'evolving standards of decency' and other similarly open textured language, the problem for the judge has generally been just how to determine whether a particular prison is unconstitutionally overcrowded" (Cooper, 1988:217). Cooper's remark suggests how quickly a judge's determination of right is drawn into the realm of policy. As with many other aspects of penology, administrators may have very different notions than judges about the point at which overcrowding becomes a constitutional violation, particularly where prison conditions have otherwise gradually improved. For more than three decades, although they may have no better information and little or no experience in corrections, judges have determined when to intervene and when to defer to the expertise of corrections administrators.

COURTS AND THE COMPLEXITY OF INSTITUTIONAL INTERACTION

On the more pragmatic, policy-making level, when judges have elected to intervene on constitutional grounds, prison administrators have found themselves in a disadvantaged position relative to the courts because the judiciary has developed the means to enforce the constitutional standards it expounds. Part of the reason for this has to do with the way in which cases are argued before the courts and how they are resolved. Bradley Chilton notes that as in many other civil rights cases, in prison-reform cases those "who seek redress for an infraction of their civil rights by government authorities now more commonly seek structural changes in the governmental institutions themselves, not merely damages." The courts are thus invited by the nature of the litigation to render more "precise remedial decrees . . . specifying the protection of rights and structural changes in the institutions themselves." In the process of doing this, the courts become "an ally with the plaintiffs for administrative reforms" (Chilton, 1991:5). The courts have thus become part-time administrators of many correctional institutions.

Prison bureaucracies are subsequently confronted with numerous difficulties in complying with court orders. They may develop some means of resisting this new layer of administration. State legislatures sometimes compound the problem by refusing to appropriate funds needed to ensure full compliance. Nevertheless, the courts determine the nature of prisoners' rights, and ultimately administrators must see that these rights are protected. Through continuous litigation the courts engage in protracted oversight, frequently for many years, to ensure compliance.

To the extent that legislators and the public may believe that the courts have gone too far in the day-to-day administration of prisons, they may wrest some or all of that responsibility from the courts. The fact remains, however, that the legislature and the public have relegated to the courts the authority to determine what is generally permissible and impermissible in the treatment of inmates. Short of massive legislative and executive defiance of judicial authority, the courts will eventually prevail in conflicts with prison bureaucracy. They determine the meaning of constitutional provisions and the extent to which they can be applied to prison administration. Because they have extended constitutional rights to prisoners, courts now define the nature of legitimate treatment of inmates. Administrators are no longer judges in their own cause, as they were under the "hands-off" doctrine prior to the 1960s. This is perhaps a welcome change. Nevertheless, we cannot necessarily assume, as many legal-reform advocates do, that courts can do a better job and that they are any more capable of balancing rights claims against the public's interest in institutional efficacy.

Discussing the role of judges as managers of prison reform in Alabama, Tinsley Yarbrough observes that judicial impact in cases subjecting institutions to widespread reform becomes highly complex and difficult to determine:

Budgetary constraints and other limits to judicial power, the scope and complexities of the policy changes sought in omnibus cases, and related factors mean that the changes mandated and implemented are typically much more the products of compromise and negotiation than a pure reflection of unfettered judicial will. Moreover, the judge in such cases may well be more interested in pushing defendants in what he considers the "right" direction than in securing jot for jot compliance with his decrees. (Yarbrough, 1985:664)

Thus the contemporary role of "judges as catalysts for change" is readily apparent, but at the same time that power is circumscribed due to larger political forces influencing legislative decision making, public interest strategies, budgeting, implementation by administrative organizations, and public opinion.

John DiIulio, Jr., observes that "court-induced changes in how prisons operate have helped to increase the complexity of the corrections officers' work by vesting them with ever greater discretionary authority, personalizing their relationships with inmates, and obliterating the guards' once simple, paramilitary routine of numbering, counting, checking, locking, monitoring inmate movement, frisking convicts, searching cells, and so on" (DiIulio, 1987b:73). The courts are critical and controversial additional participants in the administration of correctional facilities. Those who have observed changes in prison administration would argue that courts have complicated the business of managing prisons, sometimes with detrimental consequences.

FORMS OF JUDICIAL INTERVENTION

The case of prison reform is another of the more noteworthy examples of large-scale judicial intervention in public institutions. From the standpoint of many advocates, prisoners, and critics of the penal system, prisons were ripe for reform. Overcrowding, corruption, violence, rioting, inadequate medical care, filthy cells, and generally poor living conditions had all become serious issues for prison administrations to contend with. In the 1960s few observers would have predicted that within twenty years nearly every prison facility in the country would be impacted by one or more judicial rulings mandating prison reform (Smith, 1993b:95).

Discovery of Prisoners' Rights and Legalization of Prison Administration

Perhaps the most immediate impact that judicial intervention has had on prison administration is to change the climate from one of an insular network of corrections administrators working with very little judicial or public scrutiny to one in which judicial oversight is a ubiquitous characteristic of administration. Just a few key cases decided in the 1960s unleashed a flood of litigation brought by inmates and public law advocates, completely transforming the bureaucratic environment of prison administration. Since the 1964 Supreme Court decision *Cooper v. Pate*, which recognized prisoners' rights to "file suits against state corrections officials under the Civil Rights Act of 1871 . . . subsequent cases contain over 230 citations to the . . . *Cooper* decision . . . prisoners filed 23,697 civil rights cases in federal courts in the 12-month period ending in June 1987" (Smith, 1993a:141).

The ongoing process of judicial oversight has certainly been widespread in correctional facilities during the past twenty-five years. Partly in response to the flood of prisoner litigation, in 1968 Congress created the office of U.S. magistrate. These newly appointed magistrates were authorized to hear civil rights cases of prisoners and actually routinely hold hearings within many prisons to facilitate their resolution (Smith, 1988:13–18).

Responding to the proliferation of civil rights litigation, most prison administrators have instituted formal grievance procedures designed to curtail judicial intervention. In an examination of prisoners' rights litigation in a number of Southern states, Dean Champion drew the following conclusions:

[P]risons in the states examined have established administrative grievance procedures and internal policies designed to nip this type of litigation in the bud. Also the growth of guard unions during the 1970s and the increased susceptibility of prison and jail administrators to lawsuits has created an atmosphere of greater awareness of legal liabilities and responsibilities. Thus, the likelihood has increased that arbitration will be used as a tool for resolving problems and conflicts between guards, prisoners, and administrators rather than subjecting their disputes to court litigation. (Champion, 1988:46)

This lower tier of mediation and arbitration reflects the systemwide adoption of remedial law that extends even to the most minute details of prison operation.

Federal Judges as State Administrators

One of the bureaucratic side effects of judicial intervention in prison reform is that it has considerably blurred the lines of authority between executive and judicial departments, substantially eroding state control of corrections facilities. When federal district judge Frank Johnson declared that taking account of the totality of circumstances, the Alabama prison system was in violation of the Eighth Amendment, he went much further than merely interpreting the Constitution and directing Alabama to reform its correctional system. "Indeed, he set forth a list of things to be accorded to inmates and identified them as the 'Minimum Constitutional Standards for Inmates of [the] Alabama Penal System' " (Yackle, 1989:102). Johnson was clearly administering prison reform as a result of what he perceived to be, and may well have been, the institutional failure of the legislative and executive departments of the state of Alabama. He declared at the University of Alabama Law School that the court would be forced to step in where the "legislature [had] clearly expressed its intention to once again abdicate its authority" (quoted in Yackle, 1989:99).

To oversee enforcement of the court-ordered reforms, Johnson commissioned an independent Center for Correctional Psychology to classify inmates and a Human Rights Committee to monitor standards (Yackle, 1989:103–4). Judges have frequently appointed officers or committees to oversee, monitor and enforce prison compliance efforts. These agents constitute a direct line of authority from the judge to correctional system administrators.

Special Masters

Special masters are perhaps the most widely used intermediaries in court-ordered reform of prisons. Special masters are able to oversee the daily operation of prisons and administer the details of court orders after the case is decided. They enable the judge to wield a more pervasive control over correctional institutions. In California county jail cases Wayne Welsh found that special masters were involved in the most complex, conflict-ridden, and prolonged cases. These were more likely to "involve orders to reduce overcrowding . . . raise staffing levels . . . improve pretrial release procedures . . . and release sentenced inmates early." Welsh notes that the "intrusive nature of such remedies may demand labor-intensive observation which can best be provided by a skilled special master" (Welsh, 1992:617). Special masters are thus instrumental in achieving more pervasive institutional reforms, broadening the reach of judges in the administration of prisons. "[C]ases involving special masters were more likely to have named the board of supervisors as defendants . . . and were more likely to have occurred in federal courts. . . . There is little doubt that judges needed help to monitor these complex cases. Cases involving special masters lasted nearly twice as long as other cases" (Welsh, 1992:617). Special masters enable the courts to achieve a high level of compliance with a lesser commitment of energy and expertise.

Retaining Jurisdiction

Another means employed by the courts to stay in control of correctional reform is to retain jurisdiction. Courts will frequently retain jurisdiction over a case after the initial decree to achieve greater compliance. Retaining jurisdiction extends judicial authority over the administration of prisons by allowing for long-term oversight of prison conditions and practices. "Retaining jurisdiction is frequently accompanied by an increase in supervision in order to monitor compliance. . . . Contempt citations are the conventional mechanisms used to enforce remedial decrees" (Chilton, 1991:55). Leaving the case open and utilizing contempt proceedings to enforce judicial rulings affords the judge, rather than the prison administrator, the final discretion to decide whether a condition, practice, or procedure is legitimate.

In a case involving prison medical care in Massachusetts, federal district judge W. Arthur Garrity issued a consent decree to retain jurisdiction. Curtis Prout and Robert Ross note the prolonged intrusiveness of the decree and the way in which it differed from the more typical resolution of a case. "The document hammered out in these negotiations . . . allowed for alterations in its execution and allowed for supervision and enforcement to assure the rights of both parties. . . . This court would . . . function, in some ways, as an executor or administrative agency" (Prout and Ross, 1988:105).

The consent decree was not the only catalyst for change in this instance. Many factors had played a part in Massachusetts prison reform, including the evolving campaign of reform groups to improve living conditions for inmates:

Without a doubt, the suit and threat of further litigation jogged the Department of Correction into action, but times had changed, as well. The general feeling of wanting to do good for the prisoners that had so ambiguously motivated the Prison Health Project just a few years earlier was replaced by a more sober and realistic desire for responsible budgeting, strict managerial accounting, and executive responsibility. (Prout and Ross, 1988:113)

Outside forces of reform were crucial to the sustained interest in improving prison conditions in Massachusetts. Advocacy groups also played a key role in most other states.

Empowering Legal-Reform Advocacy Groups

As the impetus grew for an extension of civil rights to a wide variety of groups perceived to be disadvantaged in American society during the 1960s and 1970s, the courts themselves became more sympathetic to the idea of prison reform. The desegregation experiment had already set a precedent for extensive judicial oversight of administrative procedures. Judges sensed that they could achieve compliance with newly interpreted constitutional mandates as long as they remained active participants in bureaucracy. As in the case of busing and affirmative action, judicial activism itself encouraged advocacy groups to organize and pursue long-term litigation strategies. "The federal courts . . . demonstrated extraordinary capacity to manage elaborate lawsuits whose design was not merely to vindicate constitutional rights but, in a real sense, to reform the operations of complex public institutions." The courts were thus instrumental in encouraging advocacy groups and a constituency of inmates "to seek the federal courts out for new service" (Yackle, 1989:4–5).

The American Civil Liberties Union (ACLU), in particular, and, to a lesser extent, the NAACP Legal Defense Fund were instrumental in broadening the scope of the prison-reform movement and extending it state by state. Phil Hirschkop, a lawyer and advocate for prisoners' rights in Virginia, coauthored a law-review article in 1972 that denounced the prison system as inherently unconstitutional (Hirschkop, Crisman, and Milleman, 1972). He encouraged challenges to prison conditions as violating the First, Eighth, and Fourteenth Amendments. The ACLU's fledgling litigation teams operating in New York and Virginia in the 1960s "were merged to form the National Prison Project with offices in Washington, D.C." (Yackle, 1989:4–5). The ACLU's interest in prison reform generated a sudden and widespread demand for litigation among inmates in the 1970s. Employing class-action litigation utilized successfully by the NAACP in civil rights reform, the ACLU won key court cases aimed at pervasive institutional reform.

In his comprehensive history of the ACLU Samuel Walker describes the impact that early interest in prisoners' rights litigation had on the ACLU. "By 1972, prison litigation was exploding across the country, and the ACLU [created] the National Prison Project . . . , organized the first national conference of prisoners' rights lawyers, and the first law casebook appeared in 1973." Headed by Al Bronstein, the National Prison Project (NPP) initiated "suits in forty-five states . . . challenged the entire prison system in ten states and closed the state penitentiary in Vermont" (Walker, 1990:311). Because of the length and expense of these class-action lawsuits, the NPP proved essential in providing the financial resources to see the cases through. Throughout the 1970s the NPP was sustained financially "by grants from the Edna McConnell Clark Foundation, as general ACLU revenues could not sustain Bronstein's project" (Walker, 1990:312).

In a study of California county jail-reform litigation Wayne Welsh found that although the ACLU represented prisoners in only a small proportion of cases (eight of forty-three), "doing so may [have facilitated] a long-term litigation plan aimed at establishing legal precedents through several important test cases" (Welsh, 1992:605). This observation is borne out by Welsh's finding that the majority of ACLU cases were filed in federal, as opposed to state, court, that federal court cases tended to be characterized by "greater judicial persistence, resources, and independence from local political environments," and that ACLU cases lasted much longer than private-firm cases "as a result of greater experience, resources, and resolve than other counsel" (Welsh, 1992:607, 616).

The ACLU relied more extensively on federal courts because they were much more likely to render favorable decisions in prisoners' rights cases. In a comparative sample of state and federal decisions in prisoners' rights cases Kenneth Haas finds that from 1969 to 1979, on a wide array of civil rights issues, federal judges ruled for prisoners in two-thirds of the cases, compared to less than one-third of state decisions in favor of prisoners (Haas, 1982:738). Statistically, federal judges were far more likely to follow the more liberal precedents set by the Supreme Court and other federal appellate courts. "In every state in the union, therefore, the wisest and most advantageous strategy for prisoners and their attorneys was to bypass, if possible, the state judicial process and file complaints directly in federal court" (Haas, 1982:740). The courts seem to have been quite effective at prolonged intervention in the administration of prisons. Many procedural reforms might not have been instituted at all in the absence of judicial enforcement mechanisms. Nevertheless, some research indicates that judicial oversight imposed substantial costs as well as benefits.

JUDICIAL IMPACT ON THE PRISON ENVIRONMENT

Increased Violence

A number of studies have suggested that judicial intervention resulted in increased violence in prisons. There are several different explanations for this. Engel and Rothman have argued that increased violence resulted from the breakdown of the informal order among inmates and the diminished authority of correctional officers resulting from the prisoners' rights movement (Engel and Rothman, 1983:91–105). Larry Sullivan argues that "court decisions emboldened the prisoners to take further measures, but they also caused a smoldering resentment among prison officials. The latter were no longer obeyed or given any respect solely because of their positions" (Sullivan, 1990:92). On the other hand, Stastny and Tyrnauer's study of the Washington State Penitentiary suggests that judicial intervention may have quelled some of the violence in that prison by improving living conditions somewhat and reducing overcrowding. "By spring 1981 some apparent improvements had been made in WSP's living conditions. The population has been brought down below 900; almost all the inmates were occupied in jobs or education; the prison staff had been enlarged; mental cases had been moved to another facility; and violence had nearly dropped from the statistics" (Stastny and Tyrnauer, 1982:114).

One of the most widely cited instances of increased violence in prisons as a result of court intervention occurred in the Texas prison system, where in the early 1980s a federal judge ordered sweeping changes in Texas prison administration. According to a 1992 *National Review* article, a wave of violence ensued as a direct result. "As the old system was uprooted and new guards hired and trained, prison gangs formed and took over. Homicides among inmates, virtually unknown previously, soared to 52 in just two years. By late 1985, homicides were occurring at the rate of one a day" (Methvin, 1992:37).

Analyzing compliance with the Texas court-ordered reform, Ekland-Olson and Martin note that prison administrators challenged the legitimacy of the court ruling, arguing that "prison administrators had independently initiated a set of reforms that had brought the TDC from one of the worst to one of the best prison systems in the United States" (Ekland-Olson and Martin, 1988:372). Substantial noncompliance through various means characterized the Texas Department of Corrections' response to judicial intervention for several years. The case, *Ruiz v. Estelle*, was finally decided in 1980, and in 1981, Judge Justice established a special master, Vincent Nathan, to oversee implementation of the consent decree. Nathan's involvement was a turning point for the TDC's compliance record (Ekland-Olson and Martin, 1988:375). By May 1982 the legislature had appropriated $5 million "for construction and staffing increases." Following Director W.J. Estelle's resignation in 1983, due to his inability to secure sufficient funds from the legislature and unwillingness to "compromise further on court-ordered changes," "Large-scale turnover of high-level TDC officials took place" (Ekland-Olson and Martin, 1988:380–81). The climate of uncertainty and disruption of prison administration autonomy seems to have incited greater violence in the Texas prison system.

Some court decisions undoubtedly have made it more difficult for prison officials to contend with the most violent criminals. In *Kelly v. Brewer* "the Eighth Circuit Court expressly disregarded Warden Brewer's assertion that an inmate convicted of killing a member of the prison staff thereby became a 'fit subject for administrative segregation for a prolonged and indefinite period of time and perhaps for the duration of his term of imprisonment.' " (Kinnamon, 1985:76). The court required frequent review of the inmate's "attitude and behavior" and thus opened avenues for further litigation from inmates and instituted a loosening of controls and punishments of recalcitrant individuals within the Iowa prison system. This kind of litigation may deter correctional officers from abusing their authority in handling violent inmates, but greater intermingling of the most hardened and violent prisoners with the general prison population increases the likelihood of violence.

Officer Authority and Autonomy

Judicial supervision of correctional systems has apparently had significant impacts upon correctional officers, both attitudinally and behaviorally. In a study of Massachusetts prison officers Kelsey Kauffman remarks that increased judicial scrutiny of prisons adversely affected officer authority and morale:

Although only a fraction of suits succeeded . . . , officer-inmate relations were widely affected. The scope of officers' authority was diminished as constraints were placed on what they might lawfully do, and their status as authority figures was undermined as they faced censure, individually and collectively, in courts across the nation. At the same time, inmate "jailhouse lawyers" achieved status as alternate sources of authority within the cell block. "They can go right to a book and quote it to you, 'You can't do this and here's why you can't do it. I'm telling you you can't.' " Often seeing themselves personally empowered by the courts, jailhouse lawyers assumed a much applauded role of telling the officers what to do. (Kauffman, 1988:72)

At the Washington State Penitentiary compliance with a "totality-of-conditions" ruling in 1981 became highly problematic. High-level administrators in the prison system resisted the ruling. "Amos Reed [warden] dislikes any kind of supervision, judicial or otherwise. . . . He firmly believes that optimum administration flows from an autonomous secretary and department" (Stastny and Tyrnauer, 1982:197). To make matters worse, before an appeal from the state (the defendant) could be resolved by the Ninth Circuit Court of Appeals, the Supreme Court ruled in *Rhodes v. Chapman* that "celling arrangements" were best left to the deliberations of legislatures and the discretionary authority of administrators. A more conservative Supreme Court majority seemed to be curbing court intervention in prison administration, and the Ninth Circuit "harshly rejected [Judge] Tanner's 'totality of conditions' approach, terminated WSP's court mastership, and returned the case to the district court for separate determination of each alleged constitutional violation" (Stastny and Tyrnauer, 1982:198).

Qualified Immunity for Prison Officials and the Section 1983 Exception

Qualified immunity, the exemption of prison officials from personal liability for actions involving prison administration, provides a good example of the complexity of litigation, the subjective nature of judicial decisions, and the frequently difficult operational environment it creates for prison officials. In *Anderson v. Creighton* (1987) the Supreme Court decided that the question of whether a prison official is "protected by qualified immunity [from personal liability for damages] turns on the objective legal reasonableness of the action, in light of legal rules clearly established at the time the action was taken; contours of the right allegedly violated must be sufficiently clear such that a reasonable official would understand that what he or she was doing violated that right" (Chapman and Dorkin, 1998:sect. 9, 1). In *Harlow v. Fitzgerald* (1982) the Supreme Court also ruled that prison officials "performing discretionary functions, generally are shielded from liability for civil damages insofar as their conduct does not violate clearly established statutory or constitutional rights of which a reasonable person would have known" (Chapman and Dorkin, 1998:sect. 9, 1). In practice this has been a fairly deferential judicial standard, but the large number of Section 1983 cases brought by prisoners do not afford this protection. In *Owen v. City of Independence* (1980) the Supreme Court ruled that qualified immunity was not available to prison officials in these Section 1983 cases (Chapman and Dorkin, 1998:sect. 9, 1). These cases apparently trigger a more careful review on the merits by federal judges.

Some prisoners have prevailed in Eighth Circuit cases on this issue. Qualified immunity has been denied in some First Amendment cases where Muslim religious beliefs in the handling of pork were considered to be clearly established according to an "objective legal reasonableness" standard by prior judicial establishment of Muslims' rights not to handle pork (*Hayes v. Long*, 72 F.3d 70, 8th Cir. 1995). The Seventh Circuit ruled that an officer's excessive use of force with "intent to punish" rendered qualified immunity inapplicable. The officer had grabbed an inmate by the hair, slammed his head into cell bars, punched him in the face, and kicked him in the groin (*Hill v. Shelander*, 992 F.2d 714, 7th Cir. 1993). Other cases denying qualified immunity to officers involved prisoners kept in unheated cell blocks during subzero weather conditions and denial of textbooks and legal materials to inmates (Chapman and Dorkin, 1998:sect. 9, 2–3).

Examples of cases granting qualified immunity involved a "prison's disclosure of [an inmate's] HIV-positive status and the resulting differential treatment." The reasoning was that at the time there was very little case law on the issue (Chapman and Dorkin, 1998:sect. 9, 3). In another case prison officials who for five years forced a prisoner to take psychotropic drugs against his will were granted immunity for actions taken before constitutionally admissible procedures for such drug treatments were established in *Harper v. Collins* (1994). Officers were also immune in the use of a "black box" to restrain segregated prisoners, since the practice was "allowed by established case law" (Chapman and Dorkin, 1998:sect. 9, 3).

In *Steidl v. Gramley* (1998) the Seventh Circuit clarified the general liability rule for prison officials, making it more difficult for prisoners to allege constitutional violations on the basis of isolated prison policy violations resulting in harm to inmates. The appeals court held that "the warden (and other supervisory personnel) could be liable under the Eighth Amendment if he was aware of a systemic lapse in enforcement of a policy critical to ensuring inmate safety. The liability would stem from condoning a constitutional deprivation, and it would be direct, not vicarious. A warden is not liable for an isolated failure of his subordinates to carry out prison policies, however—unless the subordinates are acting (or failing to act) on the warden's instructions" (Chapman and Dorkin, 1998:sect. 12, 1). At the very least it seems reasonable to conclude that the inconsistency of rulings across circuits and over time has significantly confused standards and guidelines involving appropriate officer conduct, acceptable types of discipline for inmates, and procedures for suppressing inmate violence and misconduct.

BUDGET WOES, SETTLEMENTS, AND CONSENT DECREES

One of the more obvious problems resulting from judicial oversight of prisons is the courts' lack of authority to fund whatever reforms they impose. This is frequently a serious obstacle to compliance. State legislatures are notoriously unsympathetic to the budgetary dilemma that corrections administrators face in attempting to bring prisons up to judicially imposed minimum standards. "While the administrator may desire to bring about certain changes, the primary obstacle is often the acquisition of adequate funding from a legislature whose priorities rarely include upgrading the prison system" (Leeke, 1980:113).

While the evidence is mixed, the overall tendency seems to be for prolonged judicial intervention to raise prison expenditures somewhat. In a study of fourteen states under court orders throughout the 1970s Harriman and Straussman found that capital expenditures did increase after court decisions. Corrections as a percentage of the total state budget also increased. Where per capita spending was initially lower in states with court orders compared to those without, court orders brought spending in the former more into line with the latter (Harriman and Straussman, 1983). Other studies found less impressive budgetary gains for corrections resulting from court orders. For example, studying the impact of court decisions on correctional budgets, William Taggert found fairly minimal independent impact on state expenditures. Corrections "spending was found to be a historical function of previous spending patterns. Scholarly claims to the contrary, the judiciary's ability to overcome these tendencies should not be overestimated" (Taggart, 1989:268).

Negotiated settlements appear to be a primary vehicle for breaking the stalemate that frequently develops between courts and legislatures on bringing correctional facilities up to minimum constitutional standards. "Full litigation of an inmate's civil rights action may result in the desired changes, but full litigation can be an enormous financial burden on the state. Sometimes, the negotiated settlement is a more economical alternative for effecting changes in conditions and practices in correctional institutions" (Leeke, 1980:113). "Reaching a negotiated settlement in 1978, the South Carolina Department of Corrections received immediate funding from the legislature to comply with terms of the settlement" (Leeke, 1980:124). Judges, attorneys, agencies, and legislatures perceive negotiated settlements as a means for avoiding budgetary crises. They are less obtrusive than instances where courts unilaterally order reforms and take over administration of prisons. Nevertheless, some evidence suggests that they may have a ratcheting impact on prison expenditures overall.

Consent decrees have also become a common means of resolving the more complex and comprehensive institutional-reform cases. As one legal analyst describes it, a consent decree is a "hybrid of a contract and an injunction. Two litigating parties fashion a prospective remedy and then request the court to enter a judgment based on that agreement. As it would in the case of an injunction, the court then monitors the agreement to ensure that the parties comply with its terms" (Fieweger, 1993:1025). Consent decrees are a mechanism used by courts to make remedial actions less adversarial and promote institutional compliance. "The advantages of a consent decree are reasonably straightforward. First, it eliminates costly litigation. Second, it allows the state to retain administrative control of the corrections system. Third (and this is only conjecture), it may be less costly than court-mandated spending if it takes less—in a budgetary sense—to comply with the courts' concern for prisoners' rights" (Harriman and Straussman, 1983:350).

One of the problems with consent decrees is that historically the Supreme Court has been unwilling to allow for their modification. As a result, courts do not adequately account for, nor do prison administrators get credit for, long-term progress in improving prison conditions. In 1986 a *Harvard Law Review* article pointed out that the Court's "long-standing resistance to consent decree modifications fails to take account of the distinctive characteristics of institutional reform litigation. As a result the Court runs the risk of tethering plaintiff parties and defendant institutions to outmoded, ineffectual, or unfair decrees" (*Harvard Law Review*, 1986:1039). The Supreme Court addressed this problem in a 1992 case, *Rufo v. Inmates of Suffolk County Jail*, suggesting that courts should be more willing to modify consent decrees (Fieweger, 1993:1024–54; Lemov, 1993:23).

Consent decrees carry with them an inherent tendency for prolonging judicial administration of prisons that stems from the political realities of judicial oversight. "One reason is that governments typically fear opening the question of compliance, for which they bear the burden of proof. . . . Asking a court to terminate a decree opens governments to the risk of failure, entailing possible new obligations and public exposure of the compromises that are inevitably made in public institutions" (Sandler and Schoenbrod, 1996:65). The tendency of prison administrators to avoid judicial scrutiny usually lengthens the period of judicial oversight whether the prison is actually largely in compliance with court-ordered reforms or not. Thus, while settlements and consent decrees hold some promise for more cooperative management of correctional reform, they have practical limitations.

HANDS OFF AGAIN? PRISONERS' RIGHTS IN FLUX

Countertrends: Increased Deference to Prison Administrators

Most prisons are now administered according to systemwide procedures instituted to protect the inmate population's array of constitutional rights, yet since the early 1980s the courts have continuously shifted ground in reviewing the constitutionality of prison administrative policies and actions. One of the consequences of this equivocation is the indeterminacy and instability of prisoners' rights. This appears to have encouraged frivolous litigation, has created regional and ideological differences among courts in prisoners' rights cases, and has also created considerable confusion about the legitimate scope of rights retained by prisoners.

Commenting on the Supreme Court's increasing unease with lower federal court intervention in correctional policy, Carter, Glaser, and Wilkins observe that "the Court's opinion in [*Bell v. Wolfish*], and in *Rhodes v. Chapman* decided 2 years later, was obviously antagonistic to the activist approach taken by the lower courts. In both cases, [the district and circuit courts] had found overcrowded conditions unconstitutional . . . , yet the Supreme Court overturned these decisions" (Carter, Glaser, and Wilkins, 1985:102). The Supreme Court appears to be attempting to curb federal involvement in the administration of prisons. Nevertheless, it is not entirely clear that deference to prison administrators is as widespread as the more conservative Supreme Court rulings of the 1980s and 1990s suggested.

A 1992 article in *Federal Probation* remarked that *Wolfish* may have signaled a less activist approach to correctional litigation, but interventionist rulings lingered on:

Out of the 49 published cases since *Wolfish* in which the court ruled in favor of the inmate-plaintiffs, the court invited the input of the defendants (and often the plaintiffs) in nearly half (21). In actual practice, however, the apparent "deference" to prison administrators may be illusory in many of these cases. By the time the court has described in minute detail what the conditions are, whether they pass constitutional muster, and, if not, how they fail to measure up, the discretion which the defendant has in crafting the proposed remedy is quite circumscribed. (Cole and Call, 1992:34)

The lower federal courts have not abandoned their quest for prison reform, although in many cases litigation was heading in a more conservative direction in the 1990s.

In 1991 the Supreme Court further limited remedies to prisoners alleging Eighth Amendment violations. In *Wilson v. Seiter* the Court ruled that even when various aspects of living conditions fall below minimum standards that are the product of court orders, consent decrees, or legislative mandates, inmates must prove "deliberate indifference" of administrators in order to prevail ("Supreme Court Increases Inmates' Burden in Correctional Lawsuits," 1991:187). To some extent it appears that the Supreme Court's call for greater restraint in prisoners' rights cases has been mirrored by various circuit courts, which in turn attempt to rein in more interventionist district judges. A number of Fourth and Fifth Circuit cases in the 1980s and 1990s either reversed restrictive district-court rulings or evidenced a concern that district courts impose "the least intrusive remedy possible" when engaging in correctional reform (Cole and Call, 1992:35).

The Prison Litigation Reform Act of 1996

New legislation has also addressed the perceived excesses of past and present prison reform efforts. As previously noted, in 1996 Congress passed the Prison Litigation Reform Act to curtail the influence of federal courts over state correctional facilities. A major objective of the law is to place two-year time limits on consent decrees. The law also requires that courts more directly link remedies to constitutional violations in order to restore substantial discretionary authority to corrections administrators (Sandler and Schoenbrod, 1996:62–63).

CONTINUED JUDICIAL INTERVENTION IN PRISON ADMINISTRATION

As the following federal court cases illustrate, in spite of legislative backlash, the courts continue to exert a tremendous influence over many facets of prison administration. Of course, the courts do not always favor prisoners' claims, but they clearly have a strong impact on correctional standards. This trend was evident both before and after passage of the Prisoner Litigation Reform Act.

Overcrowding and the Eighth Amendment

A number of recent cases have addressed the issue of overcrowding. Since at least the 1980s, double-celling as an administrative response to overcrowding has not generally been considered cruel and unusual punishment. The controlling case is still *Rhodes v. Chapman* (1981), but there have been some recent modifications of this general allowance of double-bunking.

In one recent case, *Jensen v. Clarke* (1996), the Eighth Circuit did rule that double-celling violated the Eighth Amendment "when cell assignments were done randomly . . . in an institution with a rising incidence of violence" (AELE Law Library, 1998:1). Other cases involving overcrowding also favored prisoners' claims of constitutional violations. In *Harris v. Angelina County, Tex.* (1994), the Fifth Circuit affirmed a district-court injunction limiting the inmates in a county jail to the number of bunks it was designed for. The Tenth Circuit upheld an early-release law intended to remedy prison overcrowding as not violative of equal protection in *Keeton v. State of Oklahoma* (1994).

Prisoner's Exhaustion of Remedies

In *McCarthy v. Madigan* (1992) the Supreme Court ruled that a prisoner does not need to exhaust prison administrative grievance procedures before bringing claims for monetary damages before the courts. In *Pratt v. Hurley* (1996) the Court of Appeals for the Seventh Circuit held that prisoners also do not need to exhaust administrative remedies "when damages are sought for past harms because prison grievance procedures are not capable of compensating prisoners for those harms" (Chapman and Dorkin, 1998:sect. 6, 1).

Excessive Force by Corrections Officers

The Ninth Circuit ruled in 1995 that an officer who inadvertently wounded an inmate while shooting at another was liable and not entitled to qualified immunity "despite officer's lack of specific intent to injure him" (AELE Law Library, 1998:1). In 1994 the Eighth Circuit ruled that an officer who struck an inmate for no obvious "legitimate penological reason violated the prisoner's Eighth Amendment rights" and the prisoner was entitled to judgment for suffering pain (AELE Law Library, 1998:1). In 1993 a Fourth Circuit court found that an officer who "swung keys on brass ring at inmate's face only in response to his smoking, and subsequently hit inmate's hand" had employed excessive force. An Eighth Circuit court ruled in 1993 that an officer was not entitled to qualified immunity for "failing to intervene" when another officer attacked a prisoner. The court ruled that the standard to be applied to officer conduct was "deliberate indifference" rather than the more permissive "malicious and sadistic" standard (AELE Law Library, 1998:2–3). These cases demonstrate the continued tendency of the courts to uphold a high professional standard even in the treatment of recalcitrant prisoners and a continued commitment to protecting a wide array of prisoners' rights. They cut against the grain of more conservative rulings of the Supreme Court and some circuit courts and underscore the dissensus among federal courts with respect to the scope of prisoners' rights.

CONCLUSION

In the 1960s a constellation of landmark cases brought to the Supreme Court on various constitutional grounds began to change the landscape of American prisons and jails. From the mid-1960s until the present the federal courts have extended progressive civil rights guarantees to prison inmates. Liberal legal advocacy groups had come to regard inmates as perhaps the most disenfranchised minority group in modern American society. Becoming increasingly sympathetic to this vein of legal reform throughout the 1970s and 1980s, the federal courts rejected a jurisprudence that had previously been almost totally deferential to the discretionary authority of correctional administrators (under the so-called hands-off doctrine) and undertook a massive judicial effort to reform the American penal system.

The objective of this undertaking was to bring correctional facilities up-to-date with the Warren Court's "procedural revolution in American law" (Pillsbury, 1989:753–54). The Supreme Court opened the door to judicial intervention in prison cases by granting prisoners access to the courts through Section 1983 of the Civil Rights Act of 1871. Lower courts then began to apply more modern conceptions of what constituted cruel and unusual punishment and the procedural guarantees of the due process clause of the Fourteenth Amendment in cases brought by inmates objecting to prison conditions. Disposition of these cases was not limited to remedying particular grievances of individual parties.

The cases were brought before the courts as class-action lawsuits, frequently with the aid of public law litigators such as the ACLU. The prisoners' rights movement thus contributed to a growing body of institutional-reform cases adjudicated by the federal courts throughout the 1970s. Far from generating a smooth pattern of compliance, court rulings led to a diverse array of consequences affecting the judicial system itself, agencies, inmates, state budgets, and public perceptions of the penal system. Reviewing a number of case studies to illuminate some of the consequences of judicial intervention, we have found mixed outcomes.

Courts and Caseload

Clearly, the volume of litigation that resulted from the courts granting access to prisoners has been overwhelming and had crowded the federal docket. The courts requested and Congress specifically authorized magistrates to handle many of these claims. The courts have also developed some restrictions to filter more frivolous claims. Moreover, in the 1980s the Supreme Court began to substantially curtail judicial intervention in prisons by instructing lower courts that Eighth Amendment violations must involve deliberate indifference on the part of administrators, and by ruling that prison overcrowding does not necessarily constitute cruel and unusual punishment.

Inmates, Officers, and Administrators

For the most part, and not surprisingly, inmates have welcomed judicial oversight. Most observers believe that prison conditions have improved over the long term as a direct result of judicial intervention. Nevertheless, it is evident that at least for a period of time litigation generated more violence in prisons. Reforms broke down past systems of order maintenance among inmates, politicized and emboldened prisoners, raised inmate expectations beyond what could be realistically provided, upset the delicate balance of authority between inmates and staff, and altered lines of authority from upper-level administrators. Prisoners' rights advocates argue that prison conditions were bad enough to justify the negative consequences of rapid court-ordered reform.

Budgets

The few studies examining the impact of judicial intervention on prison finance yield contradictory findings. Some find that correctional budgets did in fact increase following court rulings. Others dispute these claims and assert that correctional budgets simply follow an incremental pattern. Case studies suggest that over time negotiated settlements and consent decrees, because they contain some voluntary agreements entered into by the state, tend to be associated with at least modest increases in state appropriations for improvements to correctional facilities.

Rights

The impact of judicial intervention in prison reform on the universe of civil rights appears to be one of expansion and then at least partial contraction and confusion. The fact that the Supreme Court has not consistently applied a "hands-off" or an activist approach to prisoners' rights has also meant that lower federal courts apply the Constitution unevenly from circuit to circuit and district to district. Those who contemplate the quixotic nature of judicial reasoning in the area of prisoners' rights may begin to question the capacity of judges to interpret the Constitution in a coherent manner. Many court rulings appear contradictory and confusing even to members of the bench and bar.

First, after remaining virtually silent on the question of prisoners' rights, the courts themselves became key reformers of correctional institutions. The courts were spurred on by public litigants such as the ACLU's National Prison Project. Then, largely as a result of ideological shifts in the wake of the Reagan-Bush judicial appointments, and what seems to be a tacit recognition of the myriad problems associated with implementation of judicial decrees, the courts backed away from a massive reform initiative they themselves had started. We can at least raise the question of whether the courts and the Constitution suffer some loss of prestige when judicial pronouncements appear so transparently political in nature.

Prisons under a Living Constitution

In the early 1980s Second Circuit judge Irving Kaufman warned against excessive intervention by courts in prison administration. While he recognized a role for the courts, he also emphasized that they must respect constitutional boundaries and the independent authority of other institutional actors:

The principal actors—courts, legislatures, and prison officials—ought to recognize a clear division of labor that allows each to exercise its special expertise. While legislatures and courts bear the responsibility for determining appropriate punishments and defining the limits of these punishments, they should make clear that they do not pretend to possess a more sophisticated knowledge of penology than the jailors. Courts, in particular, must avoid the temptation to transform their obligation to decide whether actions taken by the state against criminals meet the requirements of constitutionally guaranteed due process into an opportunity to dictate personally favored programs of reform. (Kaufman, 1981:1471)

Kaufman recognized that widespread judicial intervention in prison policy can prevent legitimate democratic control of institutional reform.

Employing the language of rights in making a convincing-enough case for the urgency of their intervention, courts have brought the due process revolution into the prisons. The courts have interpreted the meaning of the Constitution in a manner that a majority of the justices believe is in keeping with the spirit of American justice. Yet some of the problems associated with judicial intervention in prison administration raise questions as to the efficacy of the course taken by the courts.

Were the courts really forced to intervene to the extent that they did, or could other more representative institutions have brought about change? Prisons do seem to represent a special problem of accountability. Legislatures have alternately given little regard to prisons or exacerbated overcrowding conditions by getting tougher on criminals without providing funding for new prisons. For their part, administrators have been left to be judges in their own cause. This would appear to leave little opening for democratic reform.

Some commentators have suggested that bureaucratic forces within prisons themselves were gradually working in the right direction, and a less heavy-handed approach by courts might have achieved as much by working more cooperatively and less intrusively with administrators. Clair Cripe argues that the professionalization of corrections officers and the organizational imperatives of jail management under the pressure of overcrowding were already bringing about the kind of changes in prisons that the courts imposed by decree:

Rather than giving the courts so much credit for being the innovators of reform, I argue that most of the credit should go to the prison leaders themselves. . . . To take one example, in 1965 several central office Bureau of Prisons staff members, including me, were called into the office of the director, Myrl Alexander. Mr. Alexander had a group discussion of the process we were then using for the disciplining of federal inmates who broke the rules in our institutions. He gave us the specific assignment to come up with a new policy, one which would give procedural protections to inmates, depending on the level of action taken. As an aside, this policy was also to anticipate any court requirements of due process which we might think would be forthcoming from the courts. A new policy was adopted; it provided basics of procedural protection in disciplinary hearings, which were later referred to in court opinions, and which essentially met the due process requirements described by the Supreme Court nearly ten years later. (Cripe, 1990:280–81)

What Cripe describes is, broadly speaking, characteristic of sociologist Max Weber's notion of the rationalizing forces common to modern bureaucratic organizations. The courts have played a role in this iterative and incremental process, but in many cases they may have inhibited reforms by creating a backlash against institutional change.

In most organizations change is disruptive and inconvenient, however necessary it may be. In prisons sudden changes can be and have been catastrophic, bringing about prisonwide crises. To put it another way, where incrementalism might have been most needed, far-reaching constitutional rulings may have in some cases proved injurious to prisoners, prison officials, and institutional stability.

John DiIulio's general observations of judicial intervention in prison-reform cases is highly instructive, suggesting the limits that organizational structure impose on implementation of court-ordered reforms:

The costs of an intervention are increased where the judge's actions stir popular and bureaucratic resistance . . . it seems that one thing judges can do to reduce such resistance and the costs it entails is to proceed incrementally but decisively. This suggestion implies many things. It implies that "totality of conditions" interventions are to be avoided whenever possible in favor of specific remedies aimed at specific institutional problems. It also implies the need to frame the substance, tone, and timing of an intervention in light of whatever popular and bureaucratic pressures may arise, and to physically go "where the action is," meaning into the prisons and jails where the problems exist and where the people who will be most directly affected by the intervention live and work. (DiIulio, 1990:317)

Whether the courts tend to follow these kinds of prescriptions or not, it is evident that they will continue to be heavily involved in the daily operations and administration of the nation's prison systems for the foreseeable future. Courts have been decisive actors in determining the nature and scope of the remedies necessary to bring prisons into compliance with the variable civil rights claims of the prison population.

Chapter 5

Mental Health and the Consequences of Deinstitutionalization

DEINSTITUTIONALIZATION OF THE MENTALLY ILL

For the first half of the twentieth century the mental hospital was regarded as a progressive and humane institution, providing essential treatment and care for the mentally ill. In David J. Rothman's classic, *The Discovery of the Asylum*, the author points out that the mental institution was designed to "re-create fixity and stability to compensate for the irregularities of society. How else could the insane escape the cares and anxieties of business, family, religion and politics? Hospitals were the proper place for the insane" (Rothman, 1971:133). Beginning in the 1950s, due to a combination of legal, political, economic, and professional forces of change, American society adopted a much different approach to the treatment of those with psychological disorders.

From the early 1950s to the early 1990s between 80 and 90 percent of patients previously cared for by county and state mental hospitals were released into the community or transferred to alternate facilities. Patients' rights advocates and the federal courts played an integral role in transforming the system of care for people with psychological disorders. Lawyers, legislators, mental health professionals, and scholars continue to debate the wisdom of the pervasive deinstitutionalization that has occurred.

Although new statutory and case law proved decisive in extending an array of rights to the mentally ill, the impetus for mental health reform did not originate with patients' rights advocates or with the courts. It began with exposés of the abuse and neglect that had become commonplace in underfunded and understaffed mental hospitals with burgeoning patient populations. By the early 1950s writers, journalists, and sociologists had begun to document the deplorable conditions in mental institutions across the nation, and it became clear that some degree of reform was necessary to provide more humane treatment of society's untouchables (Ward, 1946; Deutsch, 1949; Gorman, 1956).

In 1972 Bruce Ennis's *Prisoners of Psychiatry* catalogued numerous terrifying cases of unjustifiable long-term involuntary commitments and the coercion, abuse, neglect, and stigma visited upon patients within mental hospitals. His indictment of the mental institution is as compelling as it is sweeping. From just one of his many conclusions, we can begin to appreciate the growing demand for reform that arose in the 1950s and 1960s:

The real tragedy of the mental hospital system is that few of the patients in the back wards get better, and many of the patients in the front wards get worse. It is now beyond dispute—even among psychiatrists—that prolonged hospitalization is, in itself, antitherapeutic. The patient who has successfully adapted to the structured, authoritarian world of the mental hospital would find it difficult to adapt again to the real world, and that difficulty decreases his chances of ever being discharged. Mental hospitals train people to be dependent, irresponsible, second-class citizens. (Ennis, 1972:215–16)

How did the once highly regarded mental institutions sink to this level of disapprobation? The asylum was once perceived as providing an essential function in modern society by offering a haven for those unable to care for themselves and in need of long-term custodial treatment. Equally important, institutionalizing the mentally ill relieved the community of the burden of coping with and caring for the mentally ill among them. Despite their utility in sheltering the community from the mentally ill, by the 1960s state mental hospitals were in deep fiscal crisis and losing support in the mental health and legal professions.

STATE HOSPITALS IN CRISIS: ECONOMICS, IDEAS, AND PHARMACOLOGY

Fiscal Burdens of Hospitalization

One of the most obvious difficulties associated with state mental hospitals was that they were draining state budgets. At the 1954 National Governors' Conference on Mental Health, when mental hospitals were committing historically high numbers of patients to long-term care, the "representatives of the forty-eight states all agreed that their states would almost certainly go bankrupt unless they did something with the chronically mentally ill other than to continue to support them for life in state hospitals" (Johnson, 1990:40). From the 1950s to the 1980s per capita expenditures for hospitalized patients in long-term care did indeed rise precipitously. "By 1984, the states' direst predictions had come true: in thirty-five years, the annual cost of exactly the same custodial care for one patient had risen from $720 in 1949 to $41,651" (Johnson, 1990:40).

This fiscal crisis gave the states every incentive to discover and take advantage of any alternative means for caring for the mentally ill. During the early 1960s, largely due to growing concern for the poor conditions in mental hospitals, federal government expenditures for personnel, services, and mental health centers began to increase. "During this period of optimism, large numbers of mental patients were released from hospitals into the community without adequate preparation, a network of appropriate services, or consideration of the social costs" (Mechanic, 1989:91).

In effect, state governments succeeded in transferring the costs of caring for discharged mental patients "from state mental health budgets to federally subsidized programs, such as welfare and Medicaid" (Mechanic, 1989:91). The federalization of financial assistance to the mentally ill was made possible by the growth of welfare programs in the 1960s:

Medicare stimulated a dramatic growth of nursing home beds, and Medicaid financed the cost of nursing home residence. This not only gave the states an opportunity to transfer elderly mentally ill and demented patients receiving custodial care in hospitals to an alternative institution but also allowed transfer of significant state costs to the federal budget. . . . Between 1966 and 1980 the yearly rate of deinstitutionalization averaged 6 percent. It could not have been achieved without the expansion of welfare programs. (Mechanic, 1989:98)

These programs provided the financial resources from the federal government to replace the state hospital system.

Social Science Reform

In the 1950s and 1960s psychologists and sociologists were also developing a number of innovative theories about mental illness that tended to support deinstitutionalization. To one degree or another these theories suggested that mentally ill patients would benefit from less isolation from the larger society. Several well-known psychiatrists and sociologists called into question the older methods of custodial treatment. They suggested that state hospitals were part of the problem, worsening rather than improving the condition of the mentally ill. Theorists of deviant behavior such as R.D. Laing and Thomas Szasz questioned the validity of the idea of "mental illness" itself (Laing, 1969; Szasz, 1970). They argued that the categorization of individuals as mentally ill was an authoritarian means of suppressing dissenting and alternative ways of living and experiencing reality. "Szasz attacked orthodox psychiatry because of his commitment to principles derived from nineteenth-century liberalism. . . . R.D. Laing in England developed an equally powerful critique more compatible with the social activism and political radicalism of [the 1960s]" (Grob, 1991:282).

With increasing frequency, then, members of the intellectual elite began to view mental institutions as coercive mechanisms of the dominant social and state order. They wished to substitute a community or milieu therapy for the custodial care that they believed was counterproductive. "Intellectual leaders within the profession actually believed that they could end not only the scourge of mental illness but all social ills, from war to juvenile delinquency, through a new preventive community psychiatry" (Isaac and Armat, 1990:67). Yet in offering the promise of tremendous improvements in the treatment of the mentally ill, reform-minded psychologists and psychiatrists tended toward unrealistic expectations of the degree of psychological well-being they could restore, especially to the most severely mentally disabled patients.

Medical Advances

Many in the mental health professions found great promise in new miracle drugs for treating the mentally ill. Medical advances in the treatment of mental disorders through the introduction of psychotropic drugs such as reserpine and, later, chlorpromazine (or Thorazine), were important catalysts for wholesale institutional reform. These drugs relieved many of the more disruptive symptoms of mentally ill patients (such as hallucinations) and suggested that effective treatment might be possible outside the sanitarium. The discovery of psychotropic drugs contributed indirectly to deinstitutionalization. Although the new medicines were largely untested, they were seized upon prematurely by both fiscal conservatives and civil rights advocates seeking to further their own agendas (Gronfein, 1985:450).

Psychotropic drugs began to be regarded as something of a panacea that allowed reformers to plausibly argue in favor of the release or transfer of patients from the confines of the state hospitals to "less restrictive" care. But in spite of the apparent effectiveness of the wonder drugs at alleviating many of the behavioral pathologies among patients in custodial care, the new medicines did not cure mental illness. Moreover, they could only help patients if they were consistently administered by staff, and, as Ann Johnson remarks, this led to an overreliance on them that put patients at risk in noninstitutional settings:

The ability of the new drugs to alter ward atmosphere, unarguably a major achievement in and of itself, came to be proof of their efficacy and justification for their further use. With time, unfortunately, psychotropic medications' low cost, availability, and ease of administration helped them become the treatment of choice—the sole treatment of choice in far too many cases. (Johnson, 1990:46)

A pervasive overconfidence in the effectiveness of psychotropic drugs thus contributed to a false sense of security about the potential success of deinstitutionalization.

Alleged pharmacological breakthroughs in treatment in turn contributed to the idea of community or milieu therapy. "Drug therapy would make patients amenable to milieu therapy; a more humane institutional environment would facilitate the release of large numbers of patients into the community; and an extensive network of local services would in turn assist the reintegration of patients into society and oversee, if necessary, their varied medical, economic, occupational, and social needs" (Grob, 1991:156). This climate of optimism helped to create the conditions under which it seemed sensible to begin releasing large numbers of patients with psychological disorders into the community. In the mid-1960s state mental hospitals, which had gradually begun to release patients in the 1950s, accelerated the process in a climate of optimism about the future welfare of mental patients.

Executive Leadership

As the impetus for reform grew across the nation, President John F. Kennedy took a special interest in the prospects for reforming mental health care. Kennedy played an active role in shifting the emphasis of treatment away from state hospitals toward community care. In his 1963 message to Congress he expressed the following goals for mental health policy:

If we launch a broad new mental health program now, it will be possible in a decade or two to reduce the number of new patients now in custodial care by 50% or more. Many more mentally ill can be helped to remain in their own homes without hardship to themselves or their families. Central to a new mental health program is comprehensive community care. (Kennedy, 1983:166)

It was not by accident that the Kennedy administration all but ignored the state mental hospitals as possible recipients of federal aid. As James Cameron points out, "[M]any key figures in the new administration had a profound distrust of state governments born out of the controversies of the civil rights movement and state and local resistance to the implementation of welfare programs" (Cameron, 1989:130). As a result, the legislation that the Kennedy administration proposed was heavily weighted in favor of federally funded local community health center construction and preventive mental health care.

Legislation

A number of important pieces of federal and state legislation, the National Mental Health Act in 1946, the Mental Health Study Act in 1955, the Community Mental Health Centers Act in 1963, and California's Lanterman-Petris-Short Act in 1969, facilitated the transition from custodial care of the mentally ill to the community-oriented system of the new era. The National Mental Health Act of 1946 provided crucial funding for outpatient treatment programs. "Under its provisions the federal government provided grants to states to support existing outpatient facilities and programs or to establish new ones. The ultimate goal . . . was to have one outpatient facility for each 100,000 persons" (Grob, 1991:168). This legislation and a minimal amount of federal grant money had a remarkable impact on the growth of mental health clinics. "Before 1948 more than half of all states had no clinics; by 1949 all but five states had one or more. Six years later there were about 1,234 outpatient psychiatric clinics, of which about two-thirds were state supported or aided" (Grob, 1991:168). The intent of those emphasizing community outpatient clinics in the late 1940s was not to abolish the state hospital system, but merely to reform and supplement its services.

From the mid-1950s throughout the 1960s criticism of the state hospital system, combined with fiscal burdens and medical advances, created a climate more conducive to dramatic change. In 1955 Congress passed the Mental Health Study Act, which created the Joint Commission on Mental Illness and Health to study and report on the status of the mental health care system. "A report of that commission argued for the expansion of community mental health centers and a scaling back of the state mental hospital system. The report was generally well-received and eventually led, under the leadership of the Kennedy administration, to the passage of the Community Mental Health Centers Act of 1963" (Kiesler and Sibulkin, 1987:36).

In 1969 California passed the Lanterman-Petris-Short Act to make commitment more difficult to accomplish. "The law made criteria for involuntary commitment more stringent and created financial incentives to stimulate local government to provide alternative care to the large state institutions" (Mechanic, 1989:222). The law was considered a great victory for advocates of community mental health, but it was not the unequivocal success many had hoped for. As one commentator observed, the "new statute was successful in reducing the amount and duration of hospitalization, but many mentally ill patients did not get adequate community-care services, and others were dealt with through the criminal justice system" (Mechanic, 1989:222). The statute would serve as a model of reform for the public interest attorneys who became involved in mental health care reform and litigation.

If Lanterman-Petris-Short could be considered the Magna Carta of mental health legislation, the Community Mental Health Centers Act represented the crowning achievement of substantive mental health policy reform. The Community Mental Health Centers Act provided the pivotal legislation in transforming the mental health care system. It involved what Dowell and Ciarlo describe as a "radical restructuring of the primary locus of public mental health care and, to a lesser extent, a restructuring of the techniques of mental health services delivery" (Dowell and Ciarlo, 1989:195).

The Community Mental Health Centers Act was a decisive break with the past approach to mental health. "As with other social reform efforts of the 1960s, the federal government would use its vast power to spend in order to influence the delivery of social welfare services" (Cameron, 1989:130). Unfortunately, as a result of the prevailing critical view of the state hospital system, the Kennedy administration and Congress discounted the potential benefits of coordinating new services with the existing network of state hospitals. As we shall see, the structure of rights that advocates have erected with the help of the courts has also made it more difficult for many patients with psychological disorders to receive care either from community mental health facilities or state hospitals.

MAKING IT HARDER TO COMMIT: MENTAL HEALTH LAW AND PUBLIC POLICY

By the 1960s, then, the asylum was considered "antitherapeutic"—corrosive of the very psychological well-being that it should have been helping to restore. Following a steady course of reform, throughout the 1960s and 1970s the mental health system was completely overhauled, yet thirty years later it is commonly acknowledged that mental health reform has failed to live up to some very basic expectations. We need only consider a few commentaries discussing the array of problems that continue to bedevil the system:

Unquestionably, the mental health system is terribly fragmented. (Johnson, 1990:252)

[A]s the pace of deinstitutionalization accelerated sharply in the 1970s, CMHCs [community mental health clinics] devoted proportionately *less* of their attention to state hospital patients. . . . Between 1970 and 1975 the proportion of those suffering from schizophrenia at CMHCs declined from 15% to 10% and the proportion suffering from depression from 20% to 13%. In those same years, the proportion treated suffering from no mental disorder at all more than quadrupled, going from 5% to 22%. (Isaac and Armat, 1990:96)

[S]uccessful litigation and legal reform had spawned a host of "second-generation" issues . . . a dramatic decline in the number of patients residing in large public hospitals; an increase in the number of chronically mentally ill persons who were poor, uninsured, or underinsured; a burgeoning homeless population; the transinstitutionalization of mentally ill patients from public hospitals to other institutions including nursing homes, jails, and temporary shelters; a critical shortage of adequate community-based mental health care and related social services; escalating costs of all services at a time of increased pressures to control expenditures; and continued human prejudice against and fear of mentally disabled persons among the general public. (Keilitz, 1989:365)

Given the long list of grievances against the current system of mental health care, why was wholesale deinstitutionalization considered the most beneficial solution to the perceived problems of existing institutional care of people with psychological disorders? Why was it executed so poorly? What role did the courts play in the demise of the old system, and what did the legal system contribute to the development of a new mental health care system—a system with a new set of seemingly intractable problems and unintended consequences? In order to answer these questions, we need to understand how litigation influenced the outcome of mental health care reform. The judiciary's orientation to civil commitment and custodial care changed dramatically in the 1970s.

The process of committing someone to a mental hospital had traditionally been governed by a few commonly employed principles throughout the United States. The first principle governing state intervention in commitment proceedings is known as *parens patriae*. The state becomes the caregiver for individuals deemed incapable of taking care of themselves. A second source of power "derives from the police power accorded the state. For individuals found to be dangerous to themselves or others, the state has the power to order commitment as a means of protecting the individual and others in society" (Rubin, 1978:34). These long-accepted grants of authority to the states came under attack in the 1960s as social scientists and civil rights lawyers questioned the reliability of designations of mental illness and its boundaries. Broadly speaking, the goal was to open up this process to more careful judicial scrutiny and subject the states to more procedural uniformity.

The Patients' Rights Advocates

Beginning in the 1940s and culminating in the establishment of the ACLU's Mental Health Law Project in 1968, public law advocates, strongly influenced by new theories, and in accord with their own interests in broadening civil rights, took up the cause of institutionalized patients, arguing that they were being routinely denied their constitutional rights by being removed from society. The rights of the mentally ill were so drastically curtailed behind the closed doors of state and county hospitals, they argued, that commitment was tantamount to criminal incarceration in the penitentiary. Moreover, the greater cruelty of institutionalization stemmed from the fact that unlike individuals who were punished for crime, the mentally ill were blameless and random victims of genetic and/or environmental depravity.

Still others took up the cause of patients from the standpoint of their right to quality treatment and care. For example, Morton Birnbaum wrote an influential article in the *American Bar Association Journal* in 1960 in which he made a case for the right to treatment for mental patients that became an important basis for subsequent legal rights (Birnbaum, 1960). When public interest lawyers later used Birnbaum's right-to-treatment principle as a "battering ram" to force deinstitutionalization, Birnbaum became disenchanted and shifted his reform efforts, unsuccessfully, toward making state mental hospital patients under the age of sixty-five eligible for Medicaid (Isaac and Armat, 1990:120). Birnbaum was interested in securing effective treatment for patients in mental institutions, while the ACLU remained committed to abolishing mental institutions altogether.

Civil rights lawyers, advancing the cause of patients' rights throughout the 1960s and 1970s, relied upon the controversial theories of critics such as Szasz, Laing, and Grofman. The new theories "gave the authority of psychiatry to anti-psychiatry" (Isaac and Armat, 1990:27). The ACLU's project on the rights of the mentally ill played a particularly important role in the reforms of the 1960s and 1970s. "[P]rodded by radical psychiatrist Thomas Szasz . . . [t]he ACLU had established the Committee on the Rights of the Mentally Ill in 1945 and had drafted a model commitment statute" (Walker, 1990:309). The ACLU position was clearly opposed to involuntary commitment in all but the most severe cases of mental illness. "Even then, it pressed for more formal hearings to determine this dangerousness" (Walker, 1990:309). The formation of the Mental Health Law Project (MHLP) in 1968 was critical to the success of patients' rights litigation. Much of the litigation pursued in the 1970s and 1980s was sponsored by MHLP lawyers (Appelbaum, 1994).

Challenging the Medical Model of Mental Illness

One of the primary objectives of the ACLU was to challenge the nineteenth-century notion that mental illness, like other physiological afflictions, could be treated and cured. The introductory chapter of the ACLU's handbook of mental patients' rights prefaces a discussion of the medical model with the admonition that "[m]any state mental hospitals are functionally indistinguishable from prisons" (Ennis and Emery, 1978:22). The authors go on to describe the medical model's origins in the early nineteenth century:

At that point in history, mental disorders were believed to be caused by a turbulent society, disordered family life, and, in some instances, oppressive religious indoctrination. Yet despite the presumed social causes, doctors asserted that mental disorder was a physical "disease" like any other. They claimed that the brain reacted to social and economic stress in the same way the liver reacts to excessive consumption of alcohol. . . .

   Because of the prevalence of the medical model . . . psychiatrists—and to a lesser extent psychologists—have been given, or have assumed, enormous power in the mental health system. Although such laws are increasingly being declared unconstitutional, many states authorize any two physicians to invoke the power of the state to compel the involuntary hospitalization and treatment of any individual whom they believe requires such care. . . . Mental health professionals are given this enormous power because of the incorrect assumption that involuntary hospitalization and treatment involve only medical issues. (Ennis and Emery, 1978:23–24)

The presumption is that the mental institution is an antiquated abomination supported by a cadre of "superintendents of the asylums" whose "real function" is to act as "quasipolice, as agents of society, enforcing societal norms of behavior, and facilitating the removal from society of persons whose behavior causes fear, disgust, embarrassment, annoyance, inconvenience, pity, or guilt" (Ennis and Emery, 1978:25). The medical model is thus a myth that serves the purpose of authoritative societal control of behavior.

   The ACLU's position was itself highly exaggerated. State mental hospitals were in need of reform, but the goal of the Mental Health Law Project was to shut the hospitals down, not reform them. As David Mechanic, a noted authority on mental health law, cautions, "Improving due process encourages a more responsible stance from both physicians and the courts, but it hardly solves the problem of coping with many difficult dilemmas that some mentally ill persons present for themselves, their families, and community members" (Mechanic, 1989:224). To simply close the hospitals would serve the interests of a relatively small number of persons who were victimized by their time spent in hospitals. More important, closure served the interests of public interest lawyers and fiscally conservative state legislatures. Many potential beneficiaries of longer-term care who were released or were unable to enter state hospitals because the laws became more restrictive were left to fend for themselves or were foisted upon other institutions such as rest homes and the criminal justice system.

LANDMARK CASES

   Key court rulings established precedents that favored deinstitutionalization. The two most important precedents involved constraining involuntary commitment and establishing the right to treatment as a threshold below which state hospitals could not fall. Combined with reform legislation, these legal rights extended to mental patients effectively ended the era of state mental hospital care.

Constraining Involuntary Commitment

The primary target of the legal advocates for the mentally ill was the practice of involuntary commitment. Reformers focused primarily on lobbying Congress to pass legislation and on constitutional litigation in the federal courts. Several critical cases litigated by the Mental Health Law Project began to establish a new line of precedent that would transform the process of classifying, placing, and treating the mentally ill. In extending fundamental rights to mental patients, the Supreme Court sanctioned, among other things, the right of mental patients to a precommitment hearing, appeal hearings, the right to treatment, the right to refuse treatment, the dangerousness standard, and the least-restrictive-means-of-care standard. These were all procedural restrictions on the commitment process.

The influence of anti-psychiatry reformers on the court cases was only indirect but remained a decisive factor. "Anti-psychiatric theories became the basis for judicial decisions by way of law journal articles that rested upon their assumptions. Indeed, anti-psychiatry so dominated the perspective of articles on mental illness in law journals in the 1970s that it was rare to find an article with a different viewpoint" (Isaac and Armat, 1990:113). In this way the more radical critique of the mental health system filtered into the new jurisprudence of patients' rights by way of the law journals and public interest litigation. The risk to personal liberty that hospitalization presented was readily apparent. The legal advocates of mental health reform, attuned to the ongoing procedural rights revolution, regarded commitment and treatment by doctors as just the type of discretionary state action that needed to be challenged. Thus the procedural rights umbrella was extended to mental patients and would now be wielded against their would-be benefactors in the psychiatric profession.

One of the earliest cases bearing on the rights of mental patients was *Rouse v. Cameron* (1966). *Rouse* represented a breakthrough for patients' rights advocates in spite of the fact that the judge ruled for the plaintiff on statutory rather than constitutional grounds. The case invited further litigation because the ruling suggested the existence of a constitutionally based right to treatment for involuntarily committed patients. In fact, this case laid the foundation for a later Alabama Supreme Court case, *Wyatt v. Stickney* (discussed later), which would affirm a general patient right to treatment.

Several other early cases began to incorporate procedural rights that were beginning to be extended to the criminally accused into involuntary commitment cases. In *Baxstrom v. Herold* (1966) the Supreme Court ruled that a prisoner could not be held beyond the expiration of a criminal sentence simply because he was deemed mentally ill. Baxstrom, declared mentally ill while serving a criminal sentence, had been confined beyond the term of his sentence. The Court ruled that this violated his equal protection rights. The ruling extended to nearly a thousand psychologically impaired inmates in New York prisons. The case "established a critical precedent for both prisoners' and patients' rights" (French, 1987:502).

Lake v. Cameron (1966) applied a ruling from *Shelton v. Tucker* (1960), a criminal case, to mental patients. In *Shelton* the Supreme Court ruled that "even though the government purpose be legitimate and substantial, that purpose cannot be pursued by means that broadly stifle fundamental personal liberties when the end can be more narrowly achieved" (364 U.S. 479, 488). Thus the application of fundamental rights jurisprudence to commitment proceedings meant that the courts would apply strict scrutiny and require states to show a compelling government interest and demonstrate that the means were narrowly tailored to the desired end of the proceeding. This had a substantially limiting impact on civil commitment procedures for the mentally ill. Now "a patient could not be involuntarily hospitalized if an alternative that infringed less on his right to liberty (a community placement) could be found" (Peele et al., 1984:264).

In a second landmark case, *Lessard v. Schmidt* (1972), involving a woman involuntarily committed to a mental hospital, the Milwaukee Legal Services advocates representing Lessard demanded that Wisconsin's commitment laws afford the mentally ill the same legal protections available to the criminal suspect: "effective and timely notice of the 'charges' against him; mandatory notice of right to a jury trial; a right to appointed counsel; a right to remain silent; a right of counsel to be present at psychiatric interviews to guarantee the patient understood the privilege of proof beyond a reasonable doubt" (Isaac and Armat, 1990:126). The district-court opinion found civil commitment to constitute a "massive curtailment of liberty" that required the legal protections demanded by the plaintiffs. On appeal the Supreme Court further clarified the ruling, establishing that a court would now have to determine that the patients were in imminent danger of harming others or themselves before allowing them to be committed for a period longer than seventy-two hours. The impact of this case is noted by one commentator who concluded that "*Lessard* dispensed with the historic standard for civil commitment and substituted a vastly constricted dangerousness requirement. It imported a rigorous set of procedures from criminal law that went far beyond those imposed during any previous period of reform. *Lessard* reflected the ethos of its era" (Appelbaum, 1994:217).

The Right to Treatment

Perhaps the most important victory for the deinstitutionalization movement was achieved in *Wyatt v. Stickney* (1971). In this case Alabama District Judge Frank Johnson established the "right-to-treatment" precedent. As one author characterized it, *Wyatt* represented "a backdoor strategy for defeating involuntary hospitalization altogether" (Kapp, 1994:223). Judge Johnson ruled that state budget cuts had resulted in care levels at the state hospital falling below what he considered to be minimal standards. The judge stipulated that patients were entitled by right "to a humane environment; the right to adequate treatment personnel; and the right to individual treatment" (Kiesler and Sibulkin, 1987:39). He accomplished this in a manner familiar in many court-ordered prison-reform cases, by quantifying various conditions of treatment at the Alabama hospital and using them as proxies for the actual quality of patient treatment. Johnson imposed his own standard for the minimum ratio of "psychiatrists, nurses, psychologists, etc., to patients [and] dictated the number of chaplains, messengers, dietitians, and maintenance repairmen needed. He stipulated how often linen had to be changed, how many showers a patient should receive, and what furniture should be in the dayroom" (Isaac and Armat, 1990:130).

While Johnson's actions appeared to establish an administrative regime at the hospital by judicial fiat, there is another side to the case. Herr, Arons, and Wallace reported that the judge was left with little choice. "The *Wyatt* court has allowed state administrators every opportunity to improve conditions on their own. It was only after the state failed in this effort that the court allowed the parties and *amici* to propose the minimum standards which later became law" (Herr, Arons, and Wallace, 1983:50). While it is natural enough to welcome the court's decisive response to some very bad conditions and subsequent administrative inertia, it is also apparent that this line of precedent jeopardized those with psychological problems in different ways. The right-to-treatment precedent contributed to the discharge of large numbers of patients without regard for how they would be subsequently cared for.

Undoubtedly, mental health advocates had a considerable impact on the outcome of this litigation. "More than any other single group, the civil libertarian lawyers have been responsible for changing our laws concerning civil commitment, making it impossible to hospitalize and to treat many of the most severely ill patients" (Isaac and Armat, 1990:13). The courts were this receptive to the patients' rights advocates, in part, because the parallels to civil rights and criminal law were so striking. Thus they greatly facilitated widespread deinstitutionalization, despite the fact that the fledgling community health care system could not possibly care for the most seriously ill patients. The short-term outcome was precisely what the patients' rights advocates desired. In retrospect, the outcome was less favorable to patients' interests than anyone could have imagined. The triumph of the patients' rights movement helped to improve the treatment of many patients, but it also produced systemic failures of a different type and magnitude.

CONSEQUENCES OF DEINSTITUTIONALIZATION

The impact of decisions in landmark mental health cases on the mental health care system as a whole was to force state institutions to make numerous and more frequent releases of patients from their hospitals because they lacked the resources to meet the standards that the courts were now enforcing. The courts are not blameworthy for addressing the inadequate standards of care they confronted, but the aggregate impact on mental patients was not what they intended. During the 1970s the patients' rights advocates had their day. Unfortunately, discovery and enforcement of these rights meant that old institutions would have to be scrapped before they could be replaced by more effective alternative care facilities. The state mental hospitals were demonized by the patients' rights advocates, and the courts played into the abolitionists' hands by making it impossible for hospitals to live up to the new constitutional standards. Neither advocates nor the courts ever linked the new constitutional protections to a safety net of alternative institutional care.

Problems began to arise almost immediately, because the untested community-based mental health care system proved inadequate to the needs of discharged mentally ill patients. As Professor of Psychiatry John Talbot remarked, "It was fine for advocates of inpatients to call for treatment and care in the community. Unfortunately, the result was not deinstitutionalization but depopulation of the state hospitals and *transinstitutionalization* into nursing homes and board and care facilities" (Herr, Arons, and Wallace, 1983:xi–xii). The transfer of mental patients to other facilities, the criminal justice system, and the streets can hardly be viewed as beneficial to those patients who still needed care and were not receiving it. Moreover, the burden was also transferred back upon the families of the mentally ill and the larger society, because a class of individuals with treatment needs was now being largely neglected by the mental health care system.

One of the inherent inadequacies of the community care approach is that it very often does not adequately address the chronically mentally ill person's need for hospitalization. As one commentator remarked, these patients "need . . . permission to regress occasionally in the course of treatment and the ability to be rehospitalized at once when they need it. The notion that community-based treatment had to be adequate to the task of keeping even the chronically mentally ill out of the hospital forever has been extraordinarily slow to give way to overwhelming evidence that it cannot be done" (Johnson, 1990:185). Inadequate treatment persisted in spite of the supposed advances of the community mental health clinic.

State Hospital Releases in the 1970s

The dramatic decline in the numbers of patients in mental hospitals from 1970 to 1980 correlate with trends in mental health law and litigation. This was the period of the most intensive litigation establishing more restrictive procedural standards. From 1955 to 1970 resident state hospital populations fell from 559,000 to 338,000. In the decade between 1970 and 1980, however, the decade of the pathbreaking lawsuits to force deinstitutionalization of state mental hospitals, they declined even more precipitously, to 132,000 (Morrissey, 1989:317, table 13-1). The court cases changed the way in which commitment, placement, and treatment were handled. "The right to treatment thrusts have undoubtedly helped some patients get better hospital and community treatment, but the suits have decreased the accessibility of treatment for others. This diminished accessibility has been a contributing factor to homelessness" (Peele et al., 1984:269).

The National Institute of Mental Health reported that in 1955 approximately 559,000 patients were residing in state mental institutions on any given day. By 1992 mentally ill patients under custodial care had declined by more than 80 percent to just over 100,000 patients in residence per diem (Bachrach, 1996; Kiesler and Sibulkin, 1987). The exodus from the mental hospitals proceeded at a rather slow pace until the early 1960s, with only 20 percent occurring before that point. From 1963 to 1975 the rate of deinstitutionalization was much higher, with 50 to 60 percent of patients leaving state mental hospitals during this period (Gronfein, 1985:195). By some estimates "as many as half of the elderly discharged from mental hospitals in the post-1964 years came to nursing homes. Nursing homes played a significant role for relocation of the elderly mentally ill but a small role for younger patients. In 1977, only about 5,500 patients under age 45 and primarily with mental illness were residing in nursing homes" (Mechanic, 1989:101).

Hospital Conditions

There is virtually no question that prior to and during the period of deinstitutionalization conditions in many hospitals were deplorable. Erving Goffman depicted the inherent problems with mental hospitals as stemming from the fact that they were total institutions. "The various enforced activities come under a single rational plan designed to fulfill the official aims of the institution" (Mechanic, 1989:163). Yet Goffman's view has been criticized by others for discounting the benefits of institutional care as perceived by patients. "Many patients in mental hospitals report that hospital restrictions do not bother them, that they appreciate the physical care they are receiving, and that the hospital—despite its restrictions—enhances their freedom rather than restricts it" (Mechanic, 1989:164).

In spite of the efforts of patients' rights advocates to abolish them, state hospital systems continue to provide crucial care for the mentally disabled. Among the reasons most often cited for maintaining state hospitals are the following: their backup role for those who cannot be helped by the community mental health system; their role in protecting the community from the most disorderly and dangerous patients; their utility in providing long-term custodial care for those residents who really need it; and treatment and shelter for shorter-term patients who nevertheless are better served by inpatient services (Morrissey, 1989:330). Probably the most detrimental impact resulting from efforts to reform the mental health care system and abolish state mental hospitals was the creation of a large class of homeless mentally ill who receive little or no care.

The Homeless Mentally Ill

The problem of homelessness in America has been widely publicized by advocates and the media during the past two decades. The link between homelessness and psychological disorders is less well known but nonetheless has been fairly well documented by researchers. The Department of Housing and Urban Development and the Urban Institute has claimed that the number was somewhere between a low estimate of 444,000 and a high of 842,000 in the year 1996 (Burt, 2000:9). Some evidence suggests that these numbers had increased to upwards of 400,000 by the late 1980s (Isaac and Armat, 1990:3). Researchers believe that the proportion of mentally ill persons among this population is upwards of one-third (Cohen and Thompson, 1992; Kiesler, 1991).

Compelling evidence of the prevalence of substance-related, affective, and psychotic disorders of the homeless population suggests that the politicization of the homeless problem by those advocates who seek to advance their cause actually does a disservice to large numbers of homeless individuals, especially those suffering from mental illness. "The very term 'homeless,' which self-proclaimed advocates have employed to define the problem, is a misguided simplification. It implicitly validates Coalition for the Homeless founder Robert Hayes's claim that there is a three-word solution to the crisis: 'Housing, housing, housing' "(Isaac and Armat, 1990:2). The fact that such a large percentage of the homeless do suffer from psychological disorders underscores the futility of approaching the problem from a socioeconomic perspective. "Most studies have found that 30–40% suffer from major mental illness—schizophrenia, manic-depressive illness, and clinical depression" (Isaac and Armat, 1990:4).

Mental illness among the homeless is frequently compounded by various forms of substance abuse. One of the more comprehensive studies of the homeless, conducted in Baltimore by clinicians from Johns Hopkins University Medical School, "found 68% of the men and 31% of the women to be alcoholics, and 22% of the men and 16% of the women drug addicted" (Isaac and Armat, 1990:5).

Deinstitutionalization itself and the much more restrictive procedures for involuntary commitment, emphasis on short-term, outpatient services, and the right to refuse treatment all contributed to the burgeoning homeless population. "The problems began in the late 1960s when patients without close family ties began to be released. . . . [S]ome of the patients were placed in nursing homes and others went to boarding houses, single-room occupancy hotels (SROs) and similar low-income housing" (Torrey, 1988:140). Thus in many respects the reformed legal framework surrounding mental health care policy contributed to an erosion of services for the patients it was intended to benefit.

In order to better understand how this systemic failure occurred, it is helpful to differentiate among various types of persons with psychological disorders to determine which are most susceptible to harm within the community. Members of the homeless mentally ill are typically classified into three major categories: chronically mentally ill, street people, and chronic alcoholics. Most individuals within these groups either refuse to be treated or remain involuntarily isolated from the mental health system as a consequence of the severity of their illness. "A population of major concern to the mental health system, and to the community, are young schizophrenics and other seriously disturbed youths, who are aware of their civil liberties and hostile or indifferent to psychiatric ideologies" (Mechanic, 1989:101–2). These are among the types of persons most in need of inpatient or long-term treatment, but they are most susceptible to harm. "They mix with other street people, constitute a significant minority of the homeless population, and at various points in their life trajectories are hospitalized, jailed, or live on the streets" (Mechanic, 1989:102). They are unlikely to receive adequate treatment because they can so easily disappear into the community. Voluntary admission services leave these individuals on the streets and in the hands of law-enforcement officials.

Community Mental Health Clinics

One of the immediate problems that arose with community mental health clinics (CMHCs) was that there was no provision in the regulation promulgated subsequent to the legislation to establish a "mandatory working relationship between CMHCs and state mental hospitals despite the fact that CMHCs were supposed to assume responsibility for patients from the hospitals" (Torrey, 1988:120). The courts provided no such assurances either. Compounding this problem is the fact that CMHCs are not well disposed to help those patients most in need of treatment:

A common CMHC practice is to hire quasi-professionals at lesser salaries than those needed to retain discipline-specific, licensed clinicians. . . . Staff also often prefer to serve "normal" clients who have adjustment, reaction, or mild neurotic disorders. The result of these trends is that the chronically mentally ill, as a whole, are grossly underserved by CMHCs. (French, 1987:504).

Even the ACLU's 1978 handbook noted the problem of a whole new class of patient being served by the CMHCs. "The community mental health centers in California are being utilized, even overutilized, but by an almost entirely new category of persons—essentially middle-class 'neurotics'—who never were, and never would have been, hospitalized" (Ennis and Emery, 1978:215). Where would the nation's severely mentally ill go for treatment? Indeed, how would they even be identified?

TRANSINSTITUTIONALIZATION OF THE MENTALLY ILL

In 1955 Congress directed the National Institute of Mental Health to appoint a joint commission to "reevaluate the nation's approach to mental illness" (Isaac and Armat, 1990:74). In 1961 the commission's report made multiple recommendations for mental health care reform. President Kennedy seized upon the community mental health plan recommendations, which were intended to complement a system of state hospital care, and envisioned them as the central component of the mental health services of the future. After the 1963 legislation CMHCs proliferated from 104 centers in 1966 responsible for 156,000 patients to 758 centers serving a total of 3.3 million in 1981 (Foley and Sharfstein, 1983:263). By 1991, 672 (89 percent) of the CMHCs that had existed in 1981 were still in operation. Sixty-five had merged and 24 had closed (Hadley and Culhane, 1993:98). Still conforming to their service mandate, "the overwhelming majority of CMHCs provide outpatient, partial and emergency services." Less than 2 percent of CMHCs were classified as residential treatment centers (Hadley and Culhane, 1993:99). In spite of the overwhelming emphasis on emergency, outpatient, and partial care, and the more limited resources available for inpatient and chronic care, CMHCs accounted for a significant but still only relatively small proportion of total patient episodes, about one-third.

CMHCs have not lived up to their expectations for successfully managing and treating the mentally ill. This is particularly true for the category of most severely mentally ill patients. Commenting on the inadequacy of CMHCs in treating the severely mentally ill, Fred W. Becker notes that in spite of evidence of the "effectiveness of intensive support and rehabilitation programs for this category of clients . . . few such programs exist because of their cost" (Becker, 1993:110). The conclusion to be drawn from these acknowledged limitations of CMHCs is that at the very least some alternative to hospital-based care should have been in place before any large-scale deinstitutionalization occurred. Any release of patients should have been accompanied by some kind of coordinated system to ensure continued care, and the expectation that the severely mentally ill could be cared for much more cost-effectively in the community was quite unrealistic.

Mental health reform as advanced by patients' rights advocates and articulated by the courts quite suddenly created a large class of beneficiaries of rights who were at the same time acutely vulnerable to harm in the larger society. The forced exodus of the mentally ill from state hospitals into the community saved many patients from terrible conditions and mistreatment in state institutions, but regrettably, they were subsequently exposed to painful neglect and abuse on the streets. While deinstitutionalization created a sizable population of homeless persons, in many instances the burden was simply transferred to other institutions that were ill equipped to provide necessary care.

Nursing Homes

In a recent article in the *Community Mental Health Journal* one commentator acknowledged that "although state mental hospitals still provide the majority of long term care services for the mentally ill" (now a much smaller number of substantially more dangerous patients), large numbers of patients receive treatment elsewhere. The author noted that "to reduce the number of residents in state mental hospitals, many seriously mentally ill people have been placed in nursing homes in the last two decades" (Becker, 1993:109). This "transinstitutionalization" of mentally ill persons has changed the nature of nursing-home care for the elderly. To begin with, many of those who were released from state mental hospitals were transferred to nursing homes. Many more with psychological disorders end up in nursing homes in lieu of alternative care facilities. Some evidence suggests that these patients receive inadequate treatment in these institutions. Increasing numbers of younger patients with severe psychological disorders have also become nursing home residents (Kiesler and Sibulkin, 1987:129–30).

Police and the Mentally Ill

Because so many individuals with mental illness have been thrust into the larger society, the police have also tended to become "a major mental health resource within the community" (Teplin, 1984:65). One of the persistent consequences of deinstitutionalization, then, has been an increased burden on police, primarily in urban areas, to handle complaints and incidents involving mentally ill persons. Research confirms higher arrest rates among formerly hospitalized mental patients (Stedman et al., 1978, cited in Teplin, 1984:68). Nevertheless, research concerning the disposition of mentally ill persons after arrest suggests that the criminal justice system compensates for the mentally ill through increased reliance on local jails and probation, contingent only on the "assessment of the danger a person poses to the community" (Scheurman and Kobrin, cited in Teplin, 1984:117).

According to one study, nearly 700,000 inmates in detention are considered to have serious psychological disorders (Stedman, Morris, and Dennis, 1995). Research by Stedman and colleagues confirms that contrary to much of the conventional wisdom, not many deinstitutionalized patients were transferred into the prison system. Mental hospital admittees, on the other hand, were much more likely to have a history of involvement with the criminal justice system in 1978 than ten years previously (Stedman et al., 1984:490). Thousands of mentally ill persons on the streets are now handled largely by the criminal justice system. "On any day, almost 200,000 people behind bars—more than 1 in 10 of the total—are known to suffer from schizophrenia, manic depression or major depression, the three most severe mental illnesses. The rate is four times that in the general population" (Butterfield, 1998:A1).

The numbers of the mentally ill processed by the criminal justice system may be growing (Torrey, 1995). Testifying before the House Judiciary Committee in September 2000, Michael F. Hogan, director of the Ohio Department of Mental Health, stated that among "the general population in the United States, only 2.8 percent of adults have a serious and persistent mental illness. Nationally, best estimates are that between 6 and 15 percent of the adults in jails and prisons have a serious mental illness" (Hogan, 2000).

Only one in five of these individuals has been prosecuted for a violent crime. Most persons with mental disorders experience only short-term involvement with law-enforcement agencies and correctional institutions. They are unlikely to receive effective treatment under these conditions, passing through the criminal justice system as fully culpable criminals without being treated or referred to appropriate treatment facilities. Rather than ending up in prison or in mental health care facilities, they are more likely to be returned to the streets. The result is a long-term "revolving-door" experience in which the patient is alternately processed by law enforcement, released, possibly treated in some way by mental health professionals, and returned to the community. The process is frequently repeated over the life of the patient (Cohen and Marcos, 1986). One report noted that it is "common to find persons who have been hospitalized 20 times over a 10-year period. Tragically, there are more persons with mental illness in jails and prisons than there are in state hospitals" (Flory and Friedrich, 1999).

Welfare Programs

One of the most obvious consequences of deinstitutionalization was the shift from state to federal funding of services for the mentally ill population. In fact, after the Community Mental Health Centers Act, the availability of federal money seems to have generated a second wave of discharges from state mental hospitals:

Following passage of the Community Mental Health Centers Act, the configuration of fiscal responsibility for the seriously mentally ill changed dramatically. The first change was a liberalization of rules, which made mentally ill individuals living in the community eligible for federal benefits under the Aid to the Disabled program. . . . At the same time, other federal programs [Medicaid and Medicare] were begun that paid part of the costs for mentally ill patients in nursing homes and in the psychiatric units of general hospitals—but relatively little for such patients in state mental hospitals.

The consequence of these federal programs was to create an overwhelming incentive for states to empty state mental hospitals, where costs were borne almost exclusively by the states, and transfer patients to the psychiatric units of general hospitals, nursing homes, and community living facilities, where costs were borne predominantly by the federal government. (Torrey, 1988:150–51).

Already in fiscal crisis and under attack for inadequate care, state mental hospitals were eager to discharge patients into any alternative care system available. Federal funding made this possible.

Figures reflecting the total increase in spending and the proportion of expenditures for the mentally ill borne by the federal government confirm this trend. In 1963 total expenditures for the seriously mentally ill were only $1 billion, but rose to $17 billion by 1985, "a fourfold increase even after inflation and increased population are taken into account." Moreover, the percentage of federal expenditures shifted from 2 percent in 1963 to 38 percent in 1985, with a concomitant decline in state expenditures from 96 percent to 53 percent (Torrey, 1988:151). In the aggregate, these federal programs funneled money to the mentally ill and relieved the states of their fiscal burden in caring for them (Lerman, 1982). By the early 1980s it was abundantly clear that neither this transfer of fiscal responsibility nor the qualitative reform of mental health care had adequately served the mentally ill population.

NEW DIRECTIONS: COUNTERREFORM AND THE REHNQUIST COURT

Largely due to the widespread perception that mental health reform had failed to deliver what advocates had promised, statutory and case law began to tip the balance again in favor of greater institutional autonomy. Restrictions on involuntary commitment were relaxed somewhat, and a few important rulings began to discourage public law litigation in mental health policy. In the 1980s the courts seemed to recognize that rights-based claims were not securing the best care and treatment for the mentally ill.

As far as patients' rights advocates were concerned, "by the early 1980s, it appeared that the concept of a right to community services was in good currency" (Perlin, 1994). The reality was that civil rights victories in the courts during the 1970s were beginning to have some demonstrably negative impacts on mental health policy. In fact, by the end of the 1970s many states were beginning to modify the more restrictive laws governing involuntary commitment to more easily provide effective care for the mentally ill. Most of these new laws targeted the class of patients who could not be proven dangerous to themselves or others (and hence could not be subjected to involuntary commitment under the more restrictive patients' rights regime), but who nevertheless were deteriorating significantly and were believed to require immediate treatment and preventive care (La Fond and Durham, 1992; Keilitz and Hall, 1985).

Reflecting greater public concern for community safety and the mental health profession's desire to improve treatment, the courts relaxed some standards. Rather than vigorously defending mental patients' rights, judges began to defer more readily to the administrative discretion of mental health professionals. The courts were beginning to acknowledge their own limitations in bringing about institutional reform. "Activist judges came to realize that their ability to change the day-to-day operation of prisons or hospitals was extremely limited and would realistically entail a great deal of time appointing committees, reviewing reports, and holding hearings" (La Fond, 1994:217).

The two leading cases that signaled a return to more deferential judicial review of mental health cases were the *Youngberg* and *Pennhurst* cases. When Congress passed the Developmentally Disabled Assistance and Bill of Rights Act (DD Act) in 1976, it specified that "persons with developmental disabilities have a right to appropriate treatment, services, and habilitation" and that any treatment should be least restrictive of their individual liberties. Rather than upholding an interpretation of the statute that encouraged a continuation of civil rights challenges to institutional practices, in *Youngberg v. Romeo* (1982) the Supreme Court held that "the state had 'considerable discretion in determining the scope and nature of its responsibilities' " (Perlin, 1994:198). In *Youngberg* the Supreme Court indicated that the federal courts should be more deferential to mental health professionals in involuntary commitment proceedings. Justice Blackmun stated:

[T]here certainly is no reason to think judges or juries are better qualified than appropriate professionals in making [treatment decisions]. . . . For these reasons, the decision, if made by a professional, is presumptively valid; liability may be imposed only when the decision by the professional is such a substantial departure from accepted professional judgment that the person responsible actually did not base his decision on such a judgment. (457 U.S. 307, 322–23)

The decision in *Pennhurst State School and Hospital v. Halderman* 451 U.S. 1 (1981) further limited expansion of civil rights under the DD Act by ruling that as a "federal-state grant program" the "Act did not create enforceable rights" (Perlin, 1994:198). Michael Perlin, a critic of the new directions in mental health law, has noted that the "*Pennhurst* decision, for all practical purposes, eviscerated the DD

Act as a potential litigational tool for institutionalized mentally disabled persons" (Perlin, 1994:202). He also notes that "the reaffirmation of the finding in *Youngberg* that there was no general right to community services ended most advocacy efforts to establish such a right. The *Pennhurst* opinion effectively put an end to deinstitutionalization and after-care litigation as a strategy of patients' rights advocates" (Perlin, 1994:202). Perlin's assessment of the outcome of the decisions is essentially correct, though he takes a critical view of the mental health profession. Perlin and others who object to greater administrative discretion question the extent to which mental health personnel can safeguard the civil rights of patients. Nevertheless, an overly legalistic approach to the problem has rather obviously limited the availability of care for many of the severely mentally ill.

Charles Kiesler and Amy Sibulkin identify a number of the benefits of state hospital care for mentally ill patients: ease of care; insurability; controlled environment; and relief of family responsibility (Kiesler and Sibulkin, 1987:184). While the deplorable conditions of mental hospitals in the 1960s and 1970s cannot be overlooked, in championing the deinstitutionalization movement, civil rights advocates appear to have exchanged one set of unacceptable circumstances for another. The mentally ill themselves bore the brunt of this shift in public policy:

As seriously mentally ill individuals who had been living on back wards of mental hospitals for twenty, thirty, or even forty years were hastily marched off to nursing homes or boarding houses, state officials and psychiatric professionals piously extolled the virtues of community living and the advantages of the "least restrictive environment." The fact that most nursing homes offered no psychiatric care and less freedom than state hospitals, and the fact that most boarding houses offered only a television set and a neighborhood inhabited by human piranhas, were discreetly ignored. (Torrey, 1988:153)

The politics of deinstitutionalization was generally facilitated by the fact that fiscally "conservative Republicans saw a way to save money . . . [and] the liberal Democrats saw a way to expand civil rights. The promise of doing good by saving money was irresistible" (Isaac and Armat, 1990:15). As a result of this convergence of political interests, many thousands of mentally ill were left to fend for themselves, without even the limited care that institutions had previously offered.

CONCLUSION: JUDICIAL ACTIVISM AND A LEGACY OF NEGLECT

Undoubtedly, the advance of patients' rights has benefited a number of the mentally ill who were inappropriately confined or received inadequate care within state hospitals. At the same time, a large number of other patients who either left the hospitals and continued to be neglected by the mental health system or were never treated at all because the mental health system shifted so dramatically in favor of voluntary community services were ill served by "reform" of the mental health system. The federal courts, profoundly influenced by the mental health bar's preoccupation with fundamental rights, provided crucial legal foundations that reoriented the process of reform from its original concern with improving the physical and mental health of patients within state mental hospitals toward a more generalized concern for patients' rights. The overriding weakness of this approach was that it almost entirely discounted the more fundamental problems of treatment and survival that many of these individuals confronted on a daily basis.

As one analyst of the courts' role in adjudicating controversies involving the mentally ill astutely observes: "[T]he judiciary perceives decisions as the end-point, and as fixed and final, and the system is not geared to monitoring the changing needs of the mentally ill. In monitoring services for the chronically mentally ill, a review procedure that focuses on the results of the work is needed. Yet the judiciary's appellate review of its own efforts is focused on reviewing process, not results" (Peele et al., 1984:262). In helping resolve a very complex societal problem, the courts extended procedural and constitutional protections to patients that tended to shift the pendulum away from overutilization to underutilization of involuntary commitment, inpatient services, and long-term care.

Legal advocates convinced the courts to follow this course until at least the early 1980s, both for the sake of the patients and the larger society, but it is not clear that the rights principles applied to the mentally ill are particularly meaningful in light of the consequences of the freedom they gained. As we have noted, many patients themselves continue to regard favorably their experiences in reformed state institutions. This is the case because both mental health professionals and patients recognize that in exchange for some limitations on their freedom, hospitals provide patients with the care and stability they need to maintain the highest quality of life possible, given the very serious limitations that their illnesses impose.

In spite of this underlying reality and some important countertrends initiated by the Rehnquist Court, much of the current legal doctrine makes it extremely difficult for mentally ill persons to receive long-term care:

Under these circumstances, streets and shelters are increasingly filled with chronic mentally ill young people, particularly males. Many have never received any more treatment than a few days in a general hospital emergency room. They slide into the long downhill course of chronic schizophrenic illness, often exacerbating their condition by taking the "treatments" readily available on the street—drugs and alcohol. In effect, they have been deprived of any chance for recovery for, as was recognized even in the nineteenth century, treatment in the early, acute stages offers the best hope for arresting serious mental illness. (Isaac and Armat, 1990:11)

One of the more general lessons to be learned from the case of legal reform of the mental health care system is that the new substantive due process has created terrible dislocations and human suffering in the name of fundamental rights.

Undoubtedly, mental health institutions were in need of reform, but the rigidity with which the new rights regime was imposed on the actual delivery of services generated a wave of noninstitutional and spillover consequences that supplanted and in many cases even compounded the institutional failures of the past mental health care system. We have seen from mental health reform and other institutional-reform efforts that judicial activism can have harmful unintended consequences in spite of the best-intentioned efforts of civil rights advocates. At root is the fundamental disregard for consequences on the part of advocates. In their efforts to secure a veil of individual rights to protect a diverse array of constituents, public law litigants like the ACLU are overwhelmingly concerned with establishing legal precedents favorable to their client group. They are only very remotely concerned with the consequences of their legal victories. To the extent that the courts have supported civil rights advocates in these efforts, they have perhaps hindered the development of more pragmatic policies that would provide the necessary help to the mentally ill.

Acknowledging the need for social responsibility as well as the protection of individual liberty, Bruce Sales and Daniel Shuman attempt to prescribe a strong dose of legal realism in mental health policy:

Building on this empirical heritage, a new school of thought in mental health law has evolved called therapeutic jurisprudence. . . . Rather than exclusively relying on deontologically driven legal rules, this new movement looks to analyze the consequences of legal rules and incorporate the information in legal decision-making. (Sales and Shuman, 1994:174)

While there may be widespread disagreement in a democracy as to the substance of mental health policy, given the extent to which "deontologically" or "abstractly" derived legal precedent has transformed mental health policy, society may benefit from legal advocates and the judiciary's more careful attention to the unintended consequences of the bulwark of patients' rights they have erected. Undoubtedly, "the law has been playing at the fringe of the enormous tapestry that is mental health care, pulling at individual threads while apparently oblivious to the larger patterns" (Sales and Shuman, 1994:178).

In the late 1980s and 1990s there was some movement away from this neoformalism in contemporary law. To some extent, at least, the more conservative rulings of the federal courts have resulted in a countertrend toward reinstitutionalization of the mentally ill. John La Fond detects a "modest but discernible trend toward expanding the state's authority to commit mentally ill individuals who are not dangerous but considered in need of treatment." La Fond also points out that states are beginning to use the prospect of commitment as a means of achieving "treatment compliance" among noninstitutionalized patients and notes that the courts "have increasingly characterized treatment issues involved in commitment as medical rather than legal" (La Fond, 1994:219). These trends suggest that the courts have begun to return greater autonomy to mental health practitioners and are "less likely to be looking over their shoulders" (La Fond, 1994:220). On balance, it appears that much of what has been achieved by the alleged "conservative backlash" against the excesses of the mental health reform era might have been more easily accomplished had the courts exercised more caution in extending general procedural rights to the intended beneficiaries of the mental health care system.

Chapter 6

The Courts and Criminal Procedure

RIGHTS OF THE ACCUSED, CRIME, AND LAW ENFORCEMENT

Among other amendments to the Constitution, the Fourth, Fifth, and Fourteenth were devised to protect citizens from arbitrary, capricious, and unreasonable governmental injury and/or intrusion in various criminal proceedings. They serve as procedural boundaries between the individual and the state. The judiciary's expansion of individual rights during the Warren Court era resulted in a substantial transformation of the meaning and force of these amendments. During this period the Supreme Court and the lower federal courts strengthened constitutional safeguards against what they deemed unreasonable searches and seizures, prohibited the use of illegally obtained evidence at trial, required that defendants be informed of their rights to counsel and against self-incrimination, established a universal right of criminal defendants to the effective assistance of counsel, and broadened the meaning of cruel and unusual punishment. As in other areas of judicial intervention, critics have charged the courts with overreaching their authority in initiating these important doctrinal shifts in criminal law.

Indeed, the Supreme Court did play a pivotal role in bringing about monumental changes in the criminal justice system during and after the 1960s. Two key cases that we focus on in this chapter drastically altered state criminal trials. *Mapp v. Ohio* required the exclusion of evidence in many cases of warrantless searches, and *Miranda v. Arizona* required law-enforcement officers to inform suspects of their Fifth Amendment rights against self-incrimination. As Lucas Powe notes in his history of the Warren Court, "*Mapp* required half the states to change [their laws]. *Miranda* required *all* the states to change theirs" (Powe, 2000:394). These

two cases resulted in permanent changes to the criminal justice system and complicated the process by which criminals are apprehended, questioned, prosecuted,
and sentenced.

FOURTH AMENDMENT PROTECTION AGAINST UNREASONABLE SEARCH AND SEIZURE AND THE EXCLUSIONARY RULE

The Fourth Amendment states:

The right of the people to be secure in their persons, houses, papers, and effects, against unreasonable searches and seizures, shall not be violated, and no Warrants shall issue, but
upon probable cause, supported by Oath or affirmation, and particularly describing the
place to be searched, and the persons or things to be seized.

In interpreting the search and seizure language of the Fourth Amendment, judges
initially followed the intention of the framers of the Constitution to protect the citizen, in his or her home, from any general and unwarranted intrusion by government officials. What is noticeably absent from the amendment is any mention of a
remedy when a constitutional violation occurs.

The long-standing approach to search and seizure was expressed in an important
early-twentieth-century case, *Weeks v. United States* (1914). The *Weeks* case involved a warrantless search of the plaintiff's home and seizure of many of his personal documents. Because those who conducted the search were federal officers,
the Supreme Court concluded that the action was a clear violation of the Fourth
Amendment right against unreasonable search and seizure. The Court cited the
1886 case of *Boyd v. United States* as precedent. In *Boyd* the Court had concluded
that an invoice taken as evidence without proper warrant was inadmissible, and
that "the inspection by the district attorney of said invoice, when produced in obe-
dience to said notice, and its admission in evidence by the court, were erroneous
and unconstitutional proceedings. We are of opinion, therefore, that the judgment
of the circuit court should be reversed, and the cause remanded, with directions to
award a new trial" (116 U.S. 616, 638). Thus the twentieth-century Supreme Court
judges, interpreting the Fourth Amendment, rejected the English common-law tradition that evidence obtained by any means was admissible in a criminal trial.
Search and seizure required the prior issue of a warrant to the law-enforcement officer, or the courts could go so far as to exclude any illegally obtained evidence
from trial.

Nevertheless, because the Fourth Amendment applies to the federal government
and not to the states, the *Weeks* ruling allowed a dual approach to search and seizure evidence. Unless a state had an exclusionary rule of its own, if state officials
gathered evidence illegally, it could be presented to federal officials and admitted
as evidence in a federal or state criminal trial. Justice Felix Frankfurter referred to
this discrepancy in the law as the "silver platter" exception to the *Weeks* standard
of admissibility of evidence. In *Lustig v. United States* (1949) Frankfurter stated

that "a search is a search by a federal official if he had a hand in it; it is not a search by a federal official if evidence secured by state authorities is turned over to the federal authorities on a silver platter" (338 U.S. 74, 78–79). Thus the *Weeks* doctrine required the exclusion of warrantless search and seizure evidence only in federal cases. States were not required to abide by the standard.

Considering the admissibility of evidence obtained through an illegal search and seizure, the courts were reluctant to draw too broad a protective veil around the defendant in order to deter such behavior. Citizens' rights had to be weighed against the state's interest in establishing guilt and prosecuting criminals.

In *Wolf v. People of the State of Colorado* (1949) the Supreme Court clearly departed from this doctrine, stating that the due process clause of the Fourteenth Amendment did protect citizens from unreasonable search and seizure by state authorities. "The security of one's privacy against arbitrary intrusion by the police—which is at the core of the Fourth Amendment—is basic to a free society. It is therefore implicit in 'the concept of ordered liberty' and as such enforceable against the States through the Due Process Clause" (338 U.S. 25, 27). Nevertheless, the Court refused to mandate the exclusion of evidence as the remedy in such cases. Citing the fact that "most of the English-speaking world does not regard as vital to such protection the exclusion of evidence thus obtained" and the "contrariety of views of the States . . . in the light of the *Weeks* decision," the Court could not find compelling reasons to reject other remedies to deter unreasonable search and seizure (338 U.S. 25, 30–31). The Court thus concluded that "in a prosecution in a State court for a State crime the Fourteenth Amendment does not forbid the admission of evidence obtained by an unreasonable search and seizure" (338 U.S. 25, 33). Until such time as Congress or the state legislatures might act to change the requirement for the states, the Court would leave it up to the states to establish whether an exclusionary rule was the appropriate remedy to a generally acknowledged constitutional violation.

Subsequent cases broadened the scope of the protection and further limited the law-enforcement officer's ability to search or seize property without judicially determined justification and warrant. After the *Wolf* decision a growing number of states adopted the exclusionary rule. The trend is summarized in the majority opinion in *Elkins v. United States* (1960):

Not more than half the states continue totally to adhere to the rule that evidence is freely admissible no matter how it was obtained. Most of the others have adopted the exclusionary rule in its entirety; the rest have adopted it in part. The movement towards the rule of exclusion has been halting but seemingly inexorable. Since the *Wolf* decision one state has switched its position in that direction by legislation, and two others by judicial decision. Another state, uncommitted until 1955, in that year adopted the rule of exclusion. Significantly, most of the exclusionary states which have had to consider the issue have held that evidence obtained by federal officers in a search and seizure unlawful under the Fourth Amendment must be suppressed in a prosecution in the state courts. (364 U.S. 206, 220)

The path of legal change had widened in favor of an extensive application of the exclusionary rule among the states, as well as in federal criminal proceedings, yet as late as 1960 nearly half the states had still not elected to adopt an exclusionary rule. This reflects a long-standing policy debate as to whether incriminating evidence obtained illegally should be suppressed at trial.

Despite a widespread adoption of the exclusionary rule as a deterrent to overzealous search and seizure tactics, the remedy has always created controversy. Critics within the legal profession and law-enforcement officials, while supportive of the Fourth Amendment restriction on unreasonable search and seizure, nonetheless consider the exclusion of evidence to be an extreme remedy to a constitutional violation. Benjamin Cardozo expressed the essence of the dilemma in an opinion he rendered as a judge on the New York Court of Appeals. In *People v. Defore* Cardozo rejected the exclusionary rule for New York State, objecting to the likely consequence of the standard, that a person guilty of a crime would not be convicted solely "because the constable ha[d] blundered" (242 N.Y. 13, 21 [1928]). Considering that with the exception of an involuntary confession, material evidence in a criminal case is generally objectively valid regardless of how it is obtained, to suppress incriminating evidence might well mean that a guilty party goes free on a technicality (Wilkey, 1978).

Mapp v. Ohio: Extending the Exclusionary Rule to the States

A year after the *Elkins* decision the Supreme Court ruled in *Mapp v. Ohio* (1961) that the exclusionary rule should be applied to the states uniformly under the Fourteenth Amendment's due process clause as the only appropriate remedy to illegally obtained evidence. *Mapp* was a monumentally important ruling for the Warren-era extension of the Bill of Rights to the states. Lucas Powe regards the case as "the first of the important Warren Court criminal procedure cases; nothing before it even comes close" (Powe, 2000:198). The Supreme Court rendered a decision in this case that had "national implications because, by its own admission, it was changing the law in half of the states, including New York, then the most populous one" (Powe, 2000:198). The significance of the case was in its requirement that the remedy to illegal search and seizure be the exclusion of evidence at trial.

Justice Tom Clark's majority opinion addressed the concerns of Cardozo but found that the need for an effective remedy to deter the violation exceeded the interests of the state in prosecuting criminals:

There are those who say, as did Justice (then Judge) Cardozo, that, under our constitutional exclusionary doctrine, "[t]he criminal is to go free because the constable has blundered." *People v. Defore,* 242 N.Y. at 21, 150 N.E. at 587. In some cases, this will undoubtedly be the result. But, as was said in *Elkins,* "there is another consideration—the imperative of judicial integrity." 364 U.S. at 222. The criminal goes free, if he must, but it is the law that sets him free. Nothing can destroy a government more quickly than its failure to observe its own laws, or worse, its disregard of the charter of its own existence. (367 U.S. 643, 660)

Thus the majority acknowledged that the remedy would impose a certain burden upon law enforcement, but the Court held that this was necessary to protect the individual's rights in the face of criminal prosecution. The opinion only very vaguely alluded to the nature and extent of the burden it was imposing, reassuring critics that " 'pragmatic evidence of a sort' to the contrary was not wanting. The federal courts themselves have operated under the exclusionary rule of *Weeks* for almost half a century; yet it has not been suggested either that the Federal Bureau of Investigation has thereby been rendered ineffective, or that the administration of criminal justice in the federal courts has thereby been disrupted" (367 U.S. 643, 661). The Court simply did not know what the consequences of this extension of the exclusionary rule would be.

Justice John Marshall Harlan's dissent (joined by Frankfurter and Charles Whittaker) reflected the view that the states might have a legitimate and varied interest in adopting or rejecting the exclusionary rule as a matter of sound law enforcement. Harlan pointed out that the Supreme Court was imposing a particular remedy for a constitutional violation, which in his view ran beyond the boundaries of judicial authority. "[W]hat the Court is now doing is to impose upon the States not only federal substantive standards of 'search and seizure' but also the basic federal remedy for violation of those standards. For I think it entirely clear that the *Weeks* exclusionary rule is but a remedy which, by penalizing past official misconduct, is aimed at deterring such conduct in the future" (367 U.S. 643, 680).

The dissenting opinion underscores the fact that the *Mapp* ruling reflects only one side of a larger controversy in the law with regard to warrantless searches, not an "inexorable" drift in one direction. As Harlan noted, as of 1961 "half of the states still adhere[d] to the common-law non-exclusionary rule" (367 U.S. 643, 681). One school of thought regards warrantless searches as a violation of the Fourth Amendment and views exclusion of the evidence as the only effective method of deterrence. The other school allows certain exceptions to warrantless searches, relying on a reasonableness standard. The former, more restrictive approach to criminal law gained ascendancy throughout the 1960s and 1970s, but more conservative appointees to the Supreme Court have since challenged this trend.

Limiting Application of the Exclusionary Rule

By the early 1980s several members of the Supreme Court were objecting to use of the exclusionary rule in certain types of law-enforcement efforts. The so-called good-faith exception to the exclusionary rule came into use in *United States v. Leon* (1984). In *Leon* the question was whether the exclusionary rule should be applied in cases where clerical errors or oversights invalidated a search warrant and hence tainted the evidence obtained. The majority opinion stated that the "exclusionary rule is designed to deter police misconduct rather than to punish the errors of judges and magistrates" (468 U.S. 897, 916–17). The Court reasoned that if the end of the remedy to unreasonable searches was to deter police misconduct, then any exclusion should be narrowly tailored to that end. Since extension of the exclusionary rule to clerical errors by court officials would have no impact whatever on police misconduct, and as long as the officers acted in good faith in the case, the courts were not to exclude evidence for such technical violations.

Searches Incident to an Arrest and Further Exceptions to the Exclusionary Rule

Another controversy surrounds search and seizure at the time of arrest. There is little dispute in the case law that officials have a right to search the person of someone during an arrest. Judges have differed, however, on the question of how far beyond the person officers are able to search without warrant. In *Trupiano v. United States* (1948) the Court ruled that "in seizing goods and articles, law enforcement agents must secure and use search warrants wherever reasonably practicable" (334 U.S. 699, 705). At the same time, the courts have recognized the importance of balancing Fourth Amendment warrant requirements against the risk of harm, especially lethal danger, to arresting officers.

The "stop and frisk search" is probably the most widely accepted warrantless search. The exception was carefully expounded in *Terry v. Ohio* (1968), where the majority opinion stated that "there must be a narrowly drawn authority to permit a reasonable search for weapons for the protection of the police officer, where he has reason to believe that he is dealing with an armed and dangerous individual, regardless of whether he has probable cause to arrest the individual for a crime. The officer need not be absolutely certain that the individual is armed; the issue is whether a reasonably prudent man in the circumstances would be warranted in the belief that his safety or that of others was in danger" (392 U.S. 1, 31). As the opinion in *Terry* suggests, in the 1960s and 1970s the exceptions to the general warrant requirement were quite narrow.

Following the general trend in search and seizure law, during the 1980s and early 1990s the courts broadened the category of exceptions somewhat. For example, in *Illinois v. Rodriguez* (1990) the Court ruled that if the officer had a reasonable expectation that an exception to the warrant rule applied, a warrantless search might be permissible (497 U.S. 177). In another case, *Maryland v. Buie* (1990), the Court ruled that officers could conduct a "sweep" search of a home during an arrest if there was a reasonable suspicion of danger to the arresting officers (494 U.S. 325).

One of the more recent and important cases bearing on the issue of warrantless search and seizure is *Arizona v. Evans* (1995). In this case the Court ruled that evidence obtained through a search with an invalid arrest warrant was admissible. First, the Court called attention to the distinction between a Fourth Amendment violation and application of the exclusionary rule as the remedy. "[T]he issue of exclusion is separate from whether the Fourth Amendment has been violated, see e.g., *Leon*, supra, at 906, and exclusion is appropriate only if the remedial objectives of the rule are thought most efficaciously served" (514 U.S. 1, 11–12). The case not only contributes to the trend toward good-faith exceptions to the exclusionary rule but also emphasizes the need to consider what impact the exceptional circumstances might have upon general deterrence of illegal searches. Justice Rehnquist reiterated the line of argument from *Illinois v. Krull* (1987) that "the good faith exception applies when an officer conducts a search in objectively reasonable reliance on the constitutionality of a statute that subsequently is declared unconstitutional" (514 U.S. 1, 12). He emphasized that deterrence of "police misconduct" was the overriding consideration in whether to exclude evidence in the case of a warrantless search, stating that "the exclusionary rule was historically designed as a means of deterring police misconduct, not mistakes by court employees" (514 U.S. 1, 12).

The majority opinion also confirmed the *Leon* precedent that since suppressing evidence would have no deterrent impact on clerical error, it would be a counterproductive application of the exclusionary rule. It might actually discourage law-enforcement officials from exercising their authority. "As the trial court in this case stated . . . , 'Excluding the evidence can in no way affect [the officer's] future conduct unless it is to make him less willing to do his duty' " (514 U.S. 1, 13).

At least one recent case, *Florida v. J.L.* (2000), has reaffirmed earlier precedents and has upheld the general restrictions surrounding warrantless searches. The case involved police reliance on an anonymous tip that a juvenile was carrying a concealed firearm. Police subsequently searched the individual and discovered the weapon. In a unanimous ruling the Supreme Court stated that under most circumstances an anonymous tip, without some kind of verification of reliability, did not justify such an invasion of a person's Fourth Amendment rights.

Writing for the majority, Justice Ruth Bader Ginsburg stressed the heightened need for establishing credibility in the case of an anonymous tip. "Unlike a tip from a known informant whose reputation can be assessed and who can be held responsible if her allegations turn out to be fabricated, an anonymous tip alone seldom demonstrates the informant's basis of knowledge or veracity." Given the uncertainty surrounding anonymous tips, the Court ruled that the "reasonable suspicion" standard established in *Terry* could not be applied automatically simply because it was alleged that the suspect was armed. An "automatic firearm exception to our established reliability analysis would rove too far. Such an exception would enable any person seeking to harass another to set in motion an intrusive, embarrassing police search of the targeted person simply by placing an anonymous call falsely reporting the target's unlawful carriage of a gun" (No. 98-1993, March 2000). Thus exceptions remain narrowly tailored to the overall objective of fair and effective law enforcement.

The majority did distinguish the case from those in which public safety concerns were so pressing as to override the general concern for overly intrusive searches. The Court stated that in some instances "the danger alleged in an anonymous tip might be so great as to justify a search even without a showing of reliability," for example, in the case of "a person [allegedly] carrying a bomb." The court also noted a category of exceptions for "public safety officials in quarters where the reasonable expectation of Fourth Amendment privacy is diminished, such as airports . . . and schools" (*Florida v. J.L.*, 98-1993, March 28, 2000). The courts continue to struggle with the boundaries of acceptable search and seizure, but since the *Mapp* ruling the universal remedy for a constitutional violation is the exclusion of evidence from trial.

Deterring Police Misconduct and Consequences of the Exclusionary Remedy

The primary purpose of the exclusionary rule has been to deter the police from ignoring procedure and jeopardizing those who might be unjustly accused and prosecuted as a result. Application of the rule has undoubtedly promoted more uniform methods of law enforcement. The problem is that in protecting the unjustly accused from prosecution and conviction, a significant number of the guilty may go free or more easily plea-bargain because evidence wrongly acquired is excluded at trial. While this point seems intuitively obvious, very little empirical evidence has been collected to evaluate the extent to which universal application of the exclusionary rule impacts crime and law-enforcement practices.

The most recent and most authoritative study to date was conducted by researchers Paul Rubin and Raymond A. Atkins (1999).[1] Employing models from economic analysis of crime and criminal behavior, the authors gathered data from the FBI's Uniform Crime Reports (Becker, 1968; Ehrlich, 1973). Collecting crime statistics from 396 cities, from 1948 through 1969, the authors tested the hypothesis that *Mapp* hampered law enforcement and raised crime levels. Rubin and Atkins noted the following advantages of their data set for assessing the impact of the *Mapp* decision:

If the exclusionary rule changes the behavior of police and alters the probability of apprehension, then the rational choice model predicts an increase in the number of crimes committed. Thus, the police may adhere to the exclusionary rule and commit fewer illegal searches, but an important secondary effect might be fewer crimes investigated, as the police weigh the benefits of investigating a crime against the costs involved. . . . Since police are being forced to use alternatives that are less preferred than search, we would expect the result to be higher crime rates, even if few or even no cases are ultimately lost at trial because of illegally obtained evidence. (Rubin and Atkins, 1999:6–7)

Since the exclusionary rule was in force in some states before the *Mapp* ruling and not in others until after the decision, the researchers were able to use FBI data to evaluate crime rates before and after the ruling went into effect. Analyzing the data from 1958 to 1967, the researchers found that "in jurisdictions forced by the Supreme Court's ruling to exclude evidence, assaults increased by 16.5%, robbery by 7.3%, burglary by 6.0%, larceny by 3.8%, and auto theft by 4.3%. There was also a small but statistically insignificant increase in homicide rates. . . . The empirical findings from this analysis support the main prediction of the economic model of the search warrant process: that forcing states to adopt an exclusionary rule will have a detrimental impact on crime rates" (Rubin and Atkins, 1999:19). Thus the adoption of the exclusionary rule correlated with significant increases in crime rates in many states and localities. Even after controlling for a number of other factors contributing to increased crime, the exclusionary rule still seemed to raise crime rates.

Rubin and Atkins were also able to assess the impact of the 1949 *Wolf* decision. Recall that the *Wolf* ruling allowed the states to bring evidence to trial even if it was tainted by an illegal search or seizure. The researchers were thus interested in ascertaining whether post-*Wolf* crime rates were lower. They concluded that this decision appeared to have a "negative impact on crime," speculating that this was due to the impression among state authorities that federal courts would not challenge state criminal procedure in light of the decision. "We suggest that following *Wolf*, state courts felt more comfortable using unlawfully obtained evidence at trial, and the apparent sanctioning of that behavior by the Supreme Court resulted in slightly lower crime rates" (Rubin and Atkins, 1999:21). The authors also pointed out that crime rates did not spike up temporarily and then return to lower levels. "Following 1962, crime rates began to rise quickly as compared to the crime rates of those cities that already excluded unlawfully obtained evidence, an effect that continued to increase over time" (Rubin and Atkins, 1999:23).

Finally, the authors reported that the impact of *Mapp* may have been masked by the fact that earlier studies focused on larger cities (Nagel, 1965; Comptroller General, 1979; National Institute of Justice, 1983; Davies, 1983). Evaluating the data in smaller cities, they found that increases in crime were greater there than in larger urban areas (Rubin and Atkins, 1999:23–24). The authors themselves were stunned by the magnitude of the increases in crime following the *Mapp* ruling, particularly in smaller metropolitan areas:

Looking at aggregated state data, this decision increased larceny by 3.8%, auto theft by 4%, burglary by 6%, robbery by 7.3% and assault by 16.5%. But these results mask gigantic impacts in smaller cities—where the imposition of the exclusionary rule increased violent crimes by 31% and property crimes by 21%. This compares with a 15% increase in violent crimes in urban cities and only a 3% increase in property crimes in urban cities. These increases in crime rates are a weighty cost attached to each of the Supreme Court's decisions to change criminal procedure. Society may decide the benefits of our new protections are worth these costs, but an informed debate requires that these costs be known and considered. (Rubin and Atkins, 1999:25)

While the findings of this recent study must be viewed with caution because many variables influence crime rates, it appears that the *Mapp* ruling may have contributed significantly to the increased crime rates of the past three decades. It is worth noting that crime rates have recently begun to decline. It may be that more conservative court rulings that have developed exceptions to the exclusionary rule in criminal cases are contributing to the opposite effect. Similar trends are apparent in the history of Fifth Amendment protections against self-incrimination.

FIFTH AMENDMENT PROTECTION FROM
SELF-INCRIMINATION AND PRETRIAL PROCEDURE

The Fifth Amendment states:

No person shall be held to answer for a capital, or otherwise infamous crime, unless on a presentment or indictment of a Grand Jury, except in cases arising in the land or naval forces, or in the Militia, when in actual service in time of War or public danger; nor shall any person be subject for the same offence to be twice put in jeopardy of life or limb; nor shall be compelled in any criminal case to be a witness against himself, nor be deprived of life, liberty, or property, without due process of law; nor shall private property be taken for public use, without just compensation.

The history of Fifth Amendment interpretation suggests that the judiciary has moved in a direction similar to that for the exclusionary rule. The judiciary's long-held approach to establishing whether confessions were admissible in a criminal trial centered on the question of voluntariness. In *Bram v. United States* (1897), after a lengthy discussion of English common law and previous court cases on the subject, the Supreme Court ruled that confessions must be voluntary to be used as evidence in a criminal case. The Court also stated that custodial interrogation was not itself sufficient to establish that a confession was involuntary. Nevertheless, because the potential for coercion was a very real possibility, the trial court should evaluate the circumstances of the interrogation to determine if the confession was, in fact, voluntary:

In this court the general rule that the confession must be free and voluntary, that is, not produced by inducements engendering either hope or fear—is settled by the authorities referred to at the outset. The facts in the particular cases decided in this court, and which have been referred to, manifested so clearly that the confessions were voluntary that no useful purpose can be served by analyzing them. In this court also it has been settled that the mere fact that the confession is made to a police officer, while the accused was under arrest in or out of prison, or was drawn out by his questions, does not necessarily render the confession involuntary; but, as one of the circumstances, such imprisonment or interrogation may be taken into account in determining whether or not the statements of the prisoner were voluntary. (168 U.S. 532, 559)

During the 1960s, in the *Escobedo* and *Miranda* decisions, the Court imposed a universal procedural safeguard against any potential constitutional violations that might result from custodial interrogations. These cases thus extended Fifth Amendment protection against self-incrimination from the trial phase to the pretrial phase of criminal prosecutions.

In *Escobedo v. Illinois* (1964) a man accused of involvement in a murder was questioned before indictment. He was repeatedly denied access to an attorney during this period. The majority opinion of the Supreme Court stressed the coercive nature of interrogation directed "to elicit a confession" and stated that as soon as "the process shifts from investigatory to accusatory—when its focus is on the accused and its purpose is to elicit a confession—our adversary system begins to operate, and, under the circumstances here, the accused must be permitted to consult with his lawyer." Since the accused was not permitted access to legal counsel, "no statement elicited by the police during the interrogation [could] be used against him at a criminal trial" (378 U.S. 478, 492).

The right to counsel was thus extended to pretrial proceedings, and any confessions obtained by the police without advising the suspect of his rights were subject to exclusion at trial. The Court stated, "[R]efusal of a request to engage counsel violates due process not only if the accused is deprived of counsel at trial on the merits, . . . but also if he is deprived of counsel for any part of the pretrial proceedings, provided that he is so prejudiced thereby as to infect his subsequent trial with an absence of 'that fundamental fairness essential to the very concept of justice' " (378 U.S. 478, 491). This was an unprecedented challenge to widely accepted interrogation practices. As Justice Byron White pointed out in the *Escobedo* dissent:

By abandoning the voluntary-involuntary test for admissibility of confessions, the Court seems driven by the notion that it is uncivilized law enforcement to use an accused's own admissions against him at his trial. It attempts to find a home for this new and nebulous rule of due process by attaching it to the right to counsel guaranteed in the federal system by the Sixth Amendment and binding upon the States by virtue of the due process guarantee of the Fourteenth Amendment. (378 U.S. 478, 491)

Justice White's commentary reflects the prior conviction of the courts that ascertaining the voluntariness of a confession on appeal adequately protected a suspect's Fifth Amendment rights. In the 1960s and early 1970s a majority of the Supreme Court was no longer willing to leave the determination of proper interrogation methods to the professionalism of law-enforcement officials.

Although acknowledging that coercive interrogations were by then rare, in *Miranda v. Arizona* (1966) the Court went even further in prescribing a set of guidelines for law enforcement to follow at the pretrial phase of criminal prosecution. The majority opinion stated that the Court was ruling in the case "in order further to explore some facets of the problems thus exposed of applying the privilege against self-incrimination to in-custody interrogation, and to give concrete constitutional guidelines for law enforcement agencies and courts to follow" (384 U.S. 436, 441). The Supreme Court therefore went on to set down the well-known *Miranda* warnings:

As for the procedural safeguards to be employed, unless other fully effective means are devised to inform accused persons of their right of silence and to assure a continuous opportunity to exercise it, the following measures are required. Prior to any questioning, the person must be warned that he has a right to remain silent, that any statement he does make may be used as evidence against him, and that he has a right to the presence of an attorney, either retained or appointed. The defendant may waive effectuation of these rights, provided the waiver is made voluntarily, knowingly and intelligently. If, however, he indicates in any manner and at any stage of the process that he wishes to consult with an attorney before speaking, there can be no questioning. Likewise, if the individual is alone and indicates in any manner that he does not wish to be interrogated, the police may not question him. (384 U.S. 436, 445 [1966]).

An important issue left unresolved by the opinion was whether the *Miranda* warnings were the remedy that the Constitution required for adequate protection of the Fifth Amendment. Could alternative arrest procedures provide the necessary safeguards? For example, if Congress could devise "other fully effective means . . . to inform accused persons," then the Court was implicitly conceding that *Miranda* provided only one remedy among other possible remedies to protect a Fifth Amendment right. It was not long before Congress, concerned about the impact of the new warnings on law enforcement, enacted a measure that seemed to return the whole self-incrimination issue to the prior voluntariness standard.

CONGRESSIONAL RESPONSE TO *MIRANDA*

In the *Miranda* opinion the Supreme Court stated that Congress and the states might promulgate laws and regulations to supersede the *Miranda* warnings. In 1968 Congress enacted new laws governing pretrial questioning. Section 3501, part of Title II of the Omnibus Crime Control and Safe Streets Act, was intended to restore the voluntariness test for the admissibility of a suspect's incriminating statements. Section 3501 reads as follows:

Sec. 3501. Admissibility of confessions
(a) In any criminal prosecution brought by the United States or by the District of Columbia, a confession, as defined in subsection (e) hereof, shall be admissible in evidence if it is voluntarily given. Before such confession is received in evidence, the trial judge shall, out of the presence of the jury, determine any issue as to voluntariness. If the trial judge determines that the confession was voluntarily made it shall be admitted in evidence and the trial judge shall permit the jury to hear relevant evidence on the issue of voluntariness and shall instruct the jury to give such weight to the confession as the jury feels it deserves under all the circumstances.

The statute then goes on to delineate criteria for the judge to use to determine whether the confession was voluntary. Section 3501 lay dormant for nearly thirty years until a few attorneys stirred enough interest in the law to get the attention of the Supreme Court. Justice Scalia, in particular, seemed convinced that the statute might effectively overrule the *Miranda* decision and return the standard for admissibility of confessions to the older voluntariness standard. In a concurring opinion in *Davis v. United States* (1994) Scalia indicated that he thought that the Supreme Court should address this question:

For most of this century, voluntariness *vel non* was the touchstone of admissibility of confessions. See *Miranda v. Arizona*, 384 U.S. 436, 506–507 (1966) (Harlan, J., dissenting). Section 3501 of Title 18 *seems* to provide for that standard in federal criminal prosecutions today. I say "seems" because I do not wish to prejudge any issue of law. I am entirely open to the argument that §3501 does not mean what it appears to say; that it is inapplicable for some other reason; or even that it is unconstitutional. But I will no longer be open to the argument that this Court should continue to ignore the commands of §3501 simply because the Executive declines to insist that we observe them. (512 U.S. 452)

Six years later the Court heard a case that brought the *Miranda* ruling squarely against the subsequent claim of Section 3501. A federal appellate court upheld a conviction based on evidence admitted under the voluntariness standard of Section 3501.

In June 2000, in *Dickerson v. United States*, the Supreme Court ruled on the question of whether Section 3501 was a constitutionally permissible alternative to the warnings required by the *Miranda* ruling. Justice Rehnquist first pointed out that the legislation "in essence makes the admissibility of such statements turn solely on whether they were made voluntarily." The defendant (now petitioner) had "moved to suppress a statement he had made to the Federal Bureau of Investigation, on the ground he had not received '*Miranda* warnings' before being interrogated" (99-5525). On appeal "the Fourth Circuit acknowledged that petitioner had not received *Miranda* warnings, but held that §3501 was satisfied because his statement was voluntary. It concluded that *Miranda* was not a constitutional holding, and that, therefore, Congress could by statute have the final say on the admissibility question." Now, with the choice between *Miranda* and the statute before it, the Supreme Court rejected the lower-court ruling and upheld *Miranda*: "We hold that *Miranda*, being a constitutional decision of this Court, may not be in effect overruled by an Act of Congress, and we decline to overrule *Miranda* ourselves. We therefore hold that *Miranda* and its progeny in this Court govern the admissibility of statements made during custodial interrogation in both state and federal courts" (99-5525).

The disposition of the case turned on the question of "whether Congress has constitutional authority to thus supersede *Miranda*." That, in turn, depended on whether *Miranda* warnings were considered indispensable to a criminal defendant's exercise of Fifth Amendment rights. Although *Miranda* invited legislative action to protect the constitutional right against coerced self-incrimination, it stated that any legislative alternative must be "at least as effective in apprising accused persons of their right of silence and in assuring a continuous opportunity to exercise it." In support of the notion that *Miranda* warnings were a minimal constitutional standard, not merely a prophylactic guide, the Court pointed out that "[t]he *Miranda* opinion itself begins by stating that the Court granted certiorari 'to explore some facets of the problems of applying the privilege against self-incrimination to in-custody interrogation, *and to give concrete constitutional guidelines for law enforcement agencies and courts to follow.*' 384 U.S., at 441–442 (emphasis added). In fact, the majority opinion is replete with statements indicating that the majority thought it was announcing a constitutional rule" (99-5525).

Justice Rehnquist also noted that regardless of the Court's retrospective view of the *Miranda* decision, "*stare decisis* weighs heavily against overruling it now." He argued that because the *Miranda* warnings had become "routine police practice to the point where the warnings have become part of our national culture" and that there was a likelihood that the voluntariness standard would be more difficult "for officers to conform to, and for courts to apply consistently," *Miranda* must be upheld (99-5525).

The voluntariness test relied upon before *Miranda* had resulted in impermissible lapses in the criminal justice system's protection of Fifth Amendment rights:

In *Miranda*, we . . . concluded that the coercion inherent in custodial interrogation blurs the line between voluntary and involuntary statements, and thus heightens the risk that an individual will not be "accorded his privilege under the Fifth Amendment . . . not to be compelled to incriminate himself" *Id.*, at 439. Accordingly, we laid down "concrete constitutional guidelines for law enforcement agencies and courts to follow" *Id.*, at 442. (99-5525)

The Court emphasized that it could not foresee "the potential alternatives for protecting the privilege which might be devised by Congress or the States," and that any legislative solutions would have to be "at least as effective in apprising accused persons of their right of silence and in assuring a continuous opportunity to exercise it *Id.*, at 442" (99-5525).

Justices Scalia and Thomas dissented from the decision, arguing that because of the many exceptions made by the courts in Fifth Amendment controversies, both standards were really still in effect simultaneously. Scalia contended that *Miranda* had never actually replaced the voluntariness test. "Under the current regime, which the Court today retains in its entirety, courts are frequently called upon to undertake *both* inquiries. That is because, as explained earlier, voluntariness remains the *constitutional* standard, and as such continues to govern the admissibility for impeachment purposes of statements taken in violation of *Miranda*" (99-5525). Clearly Scalia believed that the decision usurped the power of Congress to legislate standards for criminal procedure.

He argued further that the majority was in fact confirming *Miranda*'s "extra-constitutional" prophylactic prescription:

Today's judgment converts *Miranda* from a milestone of judicial overreaching into the very Cheops' Pyramid (or perhaps the Sphinx would be a better analogue) of judicial arrogance. In imposing its Court-made code upon the States, the original opinion at least *asserted* that it was demanded by the Constitution. Today's decision does not pretend that it is—and yet *still* asserts the right to impose it against the will of the people's representatives in Congress. (99-5525)

The dissenting opinion expresses a continued opposition to *Miranda*'s constraints on the criminal justice system. Opponents in law enforcement and the courts wish to retain greater flexibility in determining whether incriminating statements should be allowed or suppressed. The question of how much or how little impact the *Miranda* ruling had upon operation of law enforcement was never squarely addressed by the courts.

IMPACT OF THE *MIRANDA* RULING ON CONFESSIONS

Declining Crime-Clearance Rates Following *Miranda*?

As in the case of the exclusionary rule under the Fourth Amendment, few empirical data are available to assess the impact of the *Miranda* decision on the actual operation of the criminal justice system. In an exhaustive review of existing studies, and presenting their own data, Paul Cassell and colleagues have provided the best evidence to date of the impact of *Miranda* on law enforcement objectives and crime.[2] Using FBI crime-clearance data, Cassell and Hayman report that clearance rates for crimes dropped precipitously in the years following *Miranda* and have remained lower ever since that decline. Clearance rates reflect the proportion of crimes considered "solved" by law-enforcement officials. "To clear a crime, police need not actually obtain a conviction, but only determine to their own satisfaction that the crime has been solved" (Cassell and Hayman, 1996:864). The authors of the study report that "violent crime clearance rates were fairly stable from 1950–1965, generally hovering above 60%. They even increased slightly from 1962-1965. Then, in the three years following *Miranda*, the rates fell dramatically—to 55% in 1966, to 51% in 1967, to 47% in 1968. Violent crime clearance rates have hovered around 45% ever since." The authors thus conclude that "contrary to the notion that clearance rates returned to pre-*Miranda* levels, violent crime clearance rates in fact have been permanently depressed since the decision" (Cassell and Fowles, 1998:841).

In a related article Cassell and Hayman have noted the paucity of empirical research on the impact of *Miranda* requirements. In order to furnish relevant data, they conducted an elaborate case study in Salt Lake County, Utah. In 1994 the researchers "gathered information on police questioning and suspects' confessions in a sample of more than 200 cases" (Cassell and Hayman, 1996:841). Among a number of noteworthy findings, the authors reported that "a surprisingly large number of suspects (about 21%) are never questioned, that a substantial fraction of suspects (about 16%) invoke their *Miranda* rights, and that only about 33% of all suspects give confessions" (Cassell and Hayman, 1996:841).

The researchers also attempted to ascertain the frequency with which criminal suspects invoked their *Miranda* rights, "preventing any police questioning." From the screenings they did of a sample of 219 suspects, the researchers found that "about 20% of all suspects invoke their *Miranda* rights." Underscoring the "public policy implications" of their findings, Cassell and Hayman reported that if their figure was representative of the nation as a whole, "then each year approximately 300,000 criminal suspects for FBI index crimes invoke their rights before police questioning" (Cassell and Hayman, 1996:858, 861).

Declining Confession Rates Following *Miranda*

Addressing the question of "how often today suspects confess or otherwise make incriminating statements," Cassell and Hayman reported that "9.5% of the suspects invoked their rights, 33.3% were successfully questioned, 36.1% were questioned unsuccessfully, and 21.0% were not questioned." Comparing these findings with confession rates prior to *Miranda*, the authors estimated that "interrogations were successful, very roughly speaking, in about 55% to 60% of interrogations conducted." Cassell and Hayman thus concluded that since the "33.3% overall success rate (and even our 42.2% questioning success rate) is well below the 55%–60% estimated pre-*Miranda* rate," the findings were "consistent with the hypothesis that Miranda has harmed the confession rate." Comparing success rates with rates in Great Britain and Canada corroborated these findings. These countries do not have *Miranda* requirements, and confession rates there "are in excess of 60%, sometimes substantially so. Comparing such rates to our 33.3% rate also suggests that the American *Miranda* rules have an inhibiting effect on suspects" (Cassell and Hayman, 1996:872).

A Shift toward Less Successful, Noncustodial Interviews

Cassell and Hayman also suggested that law-enforcement officials may more frequently resort to noncustodial interviews since the *Miranda* ruling. Officials are not required to inform suspects of their rights in these situations. Nevertheless, the authors pointed out that "the value of that tactic appears to be mitigated by the lower success rates of non-custodial interviews. Also, the very fact that police have tried to shift suggests, contrary to the view of some defenders of *Miranda*, that interrogating police officers believe the *Miranda* rules are harmful to their efforts" (Cassell and Hayman, 1996:873).

Lower Confession Rates, Lower Conviction Rates, More Plea Bargaining

The researchers also found that "defendants who confessed were more likely to be convicted—and more likely to be convicted of more serious charges—than those who did not" and that defendants "were less likely to receive concessions in plea bargaining." The relationship between confessions and convictions was quite startling. "[W]hen police successfully questioned a suspect, that suspect was likely to be convicted of some charge in 78.9% of the cases; when they unsuccessfully questioned a suspect, that suspect was likely to be convicted in only 49.3% of the cases. The difference in the rates for successful versus unsuccessful questioning is therefore 29.6%." Confession rates also substantially impacted the plea-bargaining process. "Of suspects whom police successfully questioned, 30.6% pled to charges at the same level as initially filed, compared to only 15.4% for suspects invoking *Miranda* rights, 9.4% for suspects questioned unsuccessfully, and 10.8% for suspects not questioned" (Cassell and Hayman, 1996:909–16).

The authors concluded that although their study "presents data on many aspects of police interrogation, it still leaves many questions unanswered. . . . Further research in the area of police interrogation is the only way to illuminate these issues." Cassell and colleagues' exhaustive review of the literature and existing studies on criminal confessions before and after *Miranda*, combined with their case study and FBI clearance-rate data, provide convincing evidence that the Supreme Court's *Miranda* ruling had a significant impact on law-enforcement objectives. The authors conclude that "the general thrust of our study, reviewed in light of other data, seems clear: *Miranda* imposes costs on society by reducing the number of confessions and, consequently, the success of criminal prosecutions" (Cassell and Hayman, 1996:916–23).

CONCLUSION

In Fourth Amendment search and seizure cases, the Supreme Court initially employed a reasonableness standard, allowing evidence to be admitted except where the most egregious violations of a suspect's rights occurred. By the 1940s the courts were excluding evidence in cases where federal officers had obtained it without proper authorization. The courts nevertheless retained a looser standard for the states, allowing them to choose their own remedy to violations of Fourth Amendment rights. In spite of the obvious historical and intuitive distinction between a violation of the Fourth Amendment and the particular remedy imposed for it, in the 1961 *Mapp* ruling the Warren Court designated the exclusionary rule as the only acceptable deterrent to illegal search and seizure. This rule governing Fourth Amendment violations was extended to all of the states through the Fourteenth Amendment.

Similarly, Fifth Amendment jurisprudence began with the somewhat vague notion that incriminating statements were admissible provided that a judge determined them to be voluntary. This standard remained in force from the late nineteenth century until 1966, when it was replaced by the *Miranda* decision. Five years after the *Mapp* ruling the Supreme Court imposed a national requirement that all suspects be informed of their various rights at the time of questioning. These constitute the familiar *Miranda* warnings.

The combination of these changes in Fourth and Fifth Amendment jurisprudence appears to have had some significantly detrimental impacts upon the operation of the criminal justice system. Initial studies tended to discount this possibility, but more recent analysis has yielded contrary evidence. The aggregate impact may have been to substantially increase crime rates nationwide and to make law-enforcement more difficult, more dangerous, and less successful. Rubin and Atkins estimate that following adoption of the exclusionary rule, in smaller urban centers violent crimes increased by as much as 31% and property crimes by 21%. In larger cities the researchers reported a 15% increase in violent crimes and only a 3% increase in property crimes. Cassell and colleagues estimate that as a result of the *Miranda* decision, "each year there are 28,000 fewer convictions for violent crimes, 79,000 fewer for property crimes and 500,000 fewer for other crimes" (Cassell and Fowles, 1998:64). If these statistics can be attributed to court intervention in the criminal justice system, American society is paying a high price for the judiciary's choice of remedies for Fourth and Fifth Amendment violations.

Law-enforcement organizations continue to register considerable opposition to the exclusionary rule and the *Miranda* warnings. For example, following the *Dickerson* ruling, which upheld *Miranda*, the National Association of Police Organizations issued a statement objecting to the decision on the grounds that it would inappropriately exclude voluntary confessions even for minor technical violations of *Miranda*. Executive Director of the National Association of Police Organizations Robert T. Scully stated:

We are very disappointed in the Court's decision. In our view, while clearing up the confusion as to whether *Miranda* was constitutionally compelled, the Court improperly applied the Fifth Amendment to voluntary and freely given statements from a suspect. The Court has applied the Fifth Amendment privilege to good faith police conduct in this case, that technically violated *Miranda* due to some confusion as to when the warnings were required, but which resulted in a voluntary and freely given statement from the defendant. (NAPO, 2000)

The Clinton administration's Justice Department defended the decision, arguing that *Miranda* provided the necessary safeguards against self-incrimination:

> The department said Congress . . . could not constitutionally authorize the use of voluntary confessions when suspects have not been read their so-called *Miranda* rights. . . . U.S. At- torney General Janet Reno said in the 41-page court filing that the *Miranda* decision has come to play a unique and important role by promoting public confidence in the criminal justice system's fairness. "Overruling *Miranda* at this juncture, more than three decades af- ter it was announced and after law enforcement has accommodated to its basic require- ments, would thus tend to undermine public confidence in the fairness of that system," Reno said. . . . Reno conceded that "the public pays a heavy price" when technical violations of *Miranda* result in the suppression of key evidence and criminals go free. But the benefits of *Miranda* include clear guidelines for police officers and increased credibility in the eyes of jurors regarding confessions made after the warning has been given, she said. (Reuters, 1999)

The federal judiciary has undoubtedly had a considerable impact on the disposi- tion of a great many criminal investigations, interrogations, attempts by authorities to obtain evidence, proceedings of criminal trials, plea bargains, and convictions. The most recent research suggests that in fashioning remedies to protect the rights of the accused, the courts may have actually created more favorable conditions for criminal activity, hindered law enforcement, and perhaps compromised the aver- age citizen's chances of remaining free from criminal victimization.

NOTES

1. The researchers reviewed a number of studies showing minimal impact of the exclusionary rule on trial convictions: "Effect of *Mapp v. Ohio* on Police Search and Sei- zure Practices in Narcotics Cases" (1968); S.S. Nagel, "Testing the Effects of Excluding Il- legally Seized Evidence" (1965); D.H. Oaks, "Studying the Exclusionary Rule in Search and Seizure" (1970); J.E. Spiotto, "Search and Seizure: An Empirical Study of the Exclusionary Rule and Its Alternatives" (1972); Bradley Canon, "The Exclusionary Rule: Have Critics Proven That It Doesn't Deter Police?" (1979); and "Criminal Justice in Crisis" (1988). The researchers accept these findings as valid, but contend that the studies do not capture the real-world impact of the exclusionary rule. If the rule acts to deter a significant number of criminal investigations because of the increased procedural burdens and costs, it will result in fewer investigations. Crime rates would then increase as the real and expected costs of criminal activity decline. Since the exclusionary rule's primary influence is upon whether or not a crime investigation is undertaken in the first place, the proportion of crimes solved, being limited to criminal investigations undertaken, would not reflect the impact of the exclusionary rule at all.

2. Cassell (1997) has provided a comprehensive review of studies and data on crime-clearance rates, as well as additional data. The following earlier studies show some decline in crime-clearance rates since the *Miranda* ruling: Seeburger and Wettick, "*Miranda* in Pittsburgh—A Statistical Study" (1967:12, table 1; 13, table 3); and LaFree, "Adversarial and Nonadversarial Justice: A Comparison of Guilty Pleas and Trials" (1985:298–99, table 2).

"National Crime Clearance Rates" are reported in the Uniform Crime Reports, published annually or semiannually since the 1950s (Federal Bureau of Investigation, U.S. Department of Justice, Uniform Crime Reports, Crime in the United States). A collection of crime-clearance rates for 1950 to 1974 can be found in Fox, *Forecasting Crime Data: An Econometric Analysis* (1978:83–86, table A-1).

The most widely cited study suggesting that *Miranda* had little impact on crime-clearance rates is that of Stephen J. Schulhofer, "*Miranda*'s Practical Effect: Substantial Benefits and Vanishingly Small Social Costs" (1996); also see Stephen J. Schulhofer, "Bashing *Miranda* Is Unjustified—and Harmful" (1997). The main thrust of Schulhofer's argument is that the increasing crime rate, outstripping the resources of law enforcement, accounts for the decline in clearance rates in the 1960s. Controlling for this, Cassell still finds a residual impact of more than 7 percent.

A number of surveys of police officers at the time of the *Miranda* decision demonstrated that officers nearly uniformly reported greater difficulty in obtaining confessions after the *Miranda* warnings were required. See Stephens, Flanders, and Canon, "Law Enforcement and the Supreme Court: Police Perceptions of the *Miranda* Requirements" (1972); Stephens, *The Supreme Court and Confessions of Guilt* (1973); Wolfstone, "*Miranda*—A Survey of Its Impact" (1971); and Witt, "Non-Coercive Interrogation and the Administration of Criminal Justice: The Impact of *Miranda* on Police Effectuality" (1973).

Chapter 7

Courts, Voting Rights, and the Consequences of Racial Redistricting

By virtually any numerical measure the Voting Rights Act (VRA) can be considered a resounding success in advancing the civil rights movement. The law had a major impact on the number of blacks elected to state legislatures and Congress. Following passage of the Voting Rights Act of 1965, the number of black officeholders in the South increased dramatically. In 1965 "only 3 blacks were state legislators in the eleven states of the Old Confederacy; by 1985 that number had increased to 176—almost 10 percent of the legislative seats" (Handley and Grofman, 1994:336). Enforcement of the VRA and the judiciary's interpretation of its provisions, particularly its acceptance of the 1982 amendments, had a substantial influence over the type of political representation that blacks would achieve. As we shall see, a number of scholars suggest that numerical gains may have come at the expense of substantive representation. Before turning to these issues, we must provide an account of the VRA itself and the judiciary's role in mediating voting rights controversies in court.

The Voting Rights Act of 1965, which enforced the voting franchise for black Americans in the South, was probably the most significant and toughest legislation of the civil rights era. President Lyndon Johnson, speaking at a Howard University commencement ceremony in 1965, alluded to a fundamental shift in his administration's orientation toward civil rights laws and their enforcement. Johnson inaugurated what he described as "the next and more profound stage of the battle for civil rights. We seek not just freedom but opportunity—not just legal equity but human ability—not just equality as a right and a theory but equality as a fact and as a result" (quoted in Graham, 1990:174). In pushing for a strong voting rights law to secure the black voting franchise in the South, Johnson was well aware of the

South's long-standing opposition to African American civil rights. Prior to passage of the Voting Rights Act of 1965 black voter registration in the South was only a fraction of what it should have been.

After the Thirteenth, Fourteenth, and Fifteenth Amendments were passed in the decade following the Civil War, white supremacists in the South devised numerous ways to deny blacks access to the ballot. The success of this systematic discrimination is reflected in the registration statistics for blacks. "In 1940 black voters in the South were estimated at a maximum of 151,000, about 3 percent of voting-age blacks in the region" (Davidson, 1992:12). Black voter registration had begun to increase substantially in the South throughout the 1940s and 1950s, largely as a result of the Supreme Court's prohibition against white primaries in *Smith v. Allwright* (1944). "By 1947, three years after *Smith*, [black voter registration] had increased to 595,000 and in 1956 to 1,238,038—still a mere 25 percent of voting-age blacks compared with 60 percent of whites who were registered" (Davidson, 1992:12). Blacks were clearly making substantial gains before passage of the Voting Rights Act, but progress was hampered by a variety of discriminatory practices continued by Southern white supremacists.

THE VOTING RIGHTS ACT OF 1965

The Voting Rights Act of 1965 was passed in order to ensure that the Fifteenth Amendment would have the force and effect in the South that it was originally intended to have. The 1965 law was not the first federal attempt to remedy electoral discrimination:

Legislation adopted in 1957, 1960, and 1964 had gradually expanded the authority of the Attorney General to seek injunctive relief against racial voting discrimination and of the federal courts to provide relief. Litigation under these statutes had, however, been largely ineffectual. In considering the 1965 statute, Congress concluded that case-by-case litigation had failed to enforce compliance with the Fifteenth Amendment because it had proved too slow, too expensive, and too cumbersome, and because a decree outlawing a discriminatory practice could easily be circumvented simply by adopting a different method of discrimination. (Farber, Eskridge, and Frickey, 1993:215)

All along, many Southern officials had subverted the Fifteenth Amendment and had continued to prevent blacks from voting by a number of insidious methods.

Minority vote dilution, limiting minority voting through various prerequisites for voter registration, had been used by white supremacists to nullify black voter strength since the end of the Civil War. Taking aim at this problem, Section 4 of the legislation targeted Southern states "through a triggering formula, which made the act applicable to those states or counties that used some form of literacy test, good moral character test, or related devices as a prerequisite for voting, and in which less than 50 percent of the voting-age population was registered by November 1, 1964 or less than 50 percent actually voted in the 1964, presidential election" (Foster, 1985:67).

Section 2: Vote Dilution

The statutory remedy to the persistent practices resulting in minority vote dilution was laid out in Section 2 of the Voting Rights Act of 1965. Section 2 prohibits states and political subdivisions from using any standards, practices, or procedures that abridge the right to vote of any member of a protected class of racial and ethnic minorities. In 1982 Congress amended Section 2 to clarify that it "would not require a finding of intent" in Section 2 vote dilution claims. Rather than requiring a showing of discriminatory purpose on the part of the government body implementing the challenged electoral practice, a plaintiff could prevail simply by showing that the "totality of circumstances" revealed that "the political processes leading to nomination or election . . . are not equally open in that [blacks] have less opportunity than other members of the electorate to participate in the political process and to elect representatives of their choice." The legislative history of the amendment sets out a lengthy, nonexhaustive list of factors to be considered under the "totality of circumstances," referred to commonly as the "Senate factors" (Engstrom, 1985:35).

Section 5: Preclearance Provisions

Section 5 was devised to ensure federal oversight of electoral apportionment. It froze all voting laws in voting districts where the VRA was applicable pursuant to Section 4 "pending federal approval of proposed changes. . . . The proposed changes would be precleared, jurisdiction by jurisdiction, after federal scrutiny of the particular facts only if the changes did 'not have the purpose and . . . [would] not have the effect of denying or abridging the right to vote on account of race or color" (Davidson, 1992:19). This section was included to prohibit by law any measures that would deliberately obstruct or complicate black registration and voting in the South. Enforcement was placed in the hands of the Department of Justice, the attorney general, and the District of Columbia District Court in order to prevent Southern judges from subverting the purpose of the law (Cunningham, 2001; Graham, 1990:169).

In the first few days after passage of the VRA the Department of Justice began the offensive: DOJ lawyers filed suit in the federal courts in Alabama, Georgia, Mississippi, Texas, and Virginia to eliminate poll taxes (August 7–10, 1965). Similarly, literacy tests were suspended in Alabama, Georgia, Louisiana, Mississippi, North Carolina, and South Carolina (August 7, 1965). On August 9, 1965, Attorney General Katzenbach activated Section 4 by dispatching 45 federal voting examiners . . . into nine designated counties and parishes in Alabama, Louisiana, and Mississippi (Ball, Krane, and Lauth, 1982:51). The black voter registration drive that ensued after passage of the VRA was impressive, both in terms of the rate of registration and the sheer numbers of blacks who registered. In less than three weeks "27,385 blacks in Alabama, Louisiana, and Mississippi had been registered. . . . In Mississippi . . . black voter registration increased from 6.7 percent before the act to 59.8 percent in 1967" (Grofman, 1990:21). In the eleven Southern states studied by Alt the overall increase in voting-age black registration was from

43.1 percent in 1964 to 62 percent in 1968 (Alt, 1994:374, table 12.1). The Federal Election Commission (FEC) reported in 1999 that black voter turnout in federal elections since 1972 has generally fluctuated between 35 percent in non-presidential-election years and 56 percent in presidential-election years. White turnout has fairly consistently averaged about 10 points higher, fluctuating between 46 percent and 64 percent, respectively. Black voter registration, expressed as a percentage of those eligible to vote, has also fluctuated somewhat but remains in the range of 58 to 66 percent since 1980. The comparable white voter registration is only 4 to 6 points higher than for blacks—between 64 and 70 percent since 1980 (Federal Election Commission, 1998).

The 1982 Amendments to the Voting Rights Act

The Voting Rights Act of 1965 was amended in 1982. The amendments were intended to address and further clarify the nature of remedies to minority vote dilution in winner-take-all electoral systems. As one observer noted, Congress intended "to clear statutory language surrounding the *purpose* and *intent* prong of Section 2. The amendment provides that proof of discriminatory *purpose* or *intent* was not required under a Section 2 claim" (Center for Voting and Democracy, 2000). Kevin Hill underscores the importance of the 1982 amendments for the election of black legislators in the South: "The 1982 amendments . . . [were] used to create 12 new majority black districts in 1992. As a result of negotiations and court battles between the various state legislatures and the Justice Department, 12 new majority black districts were created in 1992: 1 each in Virginia, South Carolina, Louisiana, Alabama, and Texas; 2 each in North Carolina and Georgia; and 3 in Florida" (Hill, 1995:385).

THE VOTING RIGHTS ACT AND THE SUPREME COURT

As we have pointed out, for years before the federal legislation took effect, Southern states had employed a variety of means for preventing blacks from voting and getting elected. Through the redistricting process districts were gerrymandered by election commissions "so that black voters would not make up more than a third of the voters in each district." Another method was to substitute at-large elections for smaller districts where black candidates might be elected by black majorities (Davidson, 1992:24). It was up to the federal agencies charged with implementing the Voting Rights Act, and the federal courts, to ensure that the South did not adopt new measures to deny or dilute the black vote. The Supreme Court played a crucial role in the advancement of voting rights for blacks, both before and after the breakthrough civil rights legislation. As noted earlier, *Smith v. Allwright* (1944) outlawed the white primary, but counties in the South that had previously relied on multiple-district (smaller, more numerous districts) voting responded by returning to at-large elections. This ensured white majorities and predictably prevented black candidates from being elected to office.

Continuing on the path of civil rights advancement, in *Gomillion v. Lightfoot* (1960) the Supreme Court ruled that a racially motivated gerrymander in Tuskegee, Alabama, violated the Fifteenth Amendment by purposely discriminating against black voters. Justice Frankfurter argued that in spite of the political nature of the state action and the deference that legislative bodies normally deserve, racial gerrymandering violated African Americans' Fifteenth Amendment rights. "When a State exercises power wholly within the domain of state interest, it is insulated from federal judicial review. But such insulation is not carried over when state power is used as an instrument for circumventing a federally protected right" (364 U.S. 339, 348). The court intervened in this redistricting case only because it found enough evidence of purposeful discrimination.

A year after passage of the VRA the Supreme Court decided *South Carolina v. Katzenbach* (1966), the test case for the tough enforcement provisions of the new civil rights law. The Court upheld both Section 2 and Section 5 of the VRA as constitutional. Writing for the majority, Chief Justice Earl Warren agreed that while it was "an uncommon exercise of Congressional power, as South Carolina contends, . . . the Court has recognized that exceptional conditions can justify legislative measures not otherwise appropriate" (383 U.S. 301, 334–35). The Court recognized the extraordinary federal power that would be brought to bear on Southern states, but given their defiance of constitutional protections extended to blacks by the Fifteenth Amendment, federal government intrusion was deemed necessary to ensure equal protection of the black voting franchise. In the same year the Court in *Harper v. Virginia Board of Elections* (1966) overruled a 1937 decision and declared that poll taxes violated the Constitution.

Three years later *Allen v. State Board of Elections* (1969) activated Section 5 of the VRA. Previously, Section 5 had seldom been used: The Justice Department, in the three and one-half years between passage of the act and the *Allen* decision, had objected to only six proposed changes in election procedures in covered jurisdictions, and none of these had concerned vote dilution. In the three and one-half years following *Allen* there were 118 objections, of which 88 involved dilution schemes. These included attempts to replace single-member-district systems with multimember ones, to replace plurality rules by majority-vote requirements, to create numbered-place systems and staggered terms, and to annex disproportionately white suburbs. A tally at the end of 1989 revealed that the Department of Justice objected to 2,335 proposed changes under Section 5 (Davidson, 1992:29).

In her controversial work *Whose Votes Count?* Abigail Thernstrom points out the central difficulty with the *Allen* decision: "*Allen* marked a radical change in the meaning of the act: the majority opinion had found a Fourteenth Amendment right to protection from vote dilution in a statute that rested unequivocally on the Fifteenth Amendment" (Thernstrom, 1987:25). This broad reading of Section 5 and its entanglement with the Warren Court's newly conceived "one-person, one-vote" theory of representation explains why Section 5 litigation proliferated to the extent that it did after *Allen*.

The decision gave the courts the authority to make substantive determinations about how effective black votes needed to be in any redistricting scheme. This was a crucial step toward judicially mandated majority-minority districts, and as implementation progressed, "holding public office came to be viewed as critical to the larger civil rights goal" (Thernstrom, 1987:30). Throughout the 1970s the Supreme Court became the primary institution determining the conditions that constituted discriminatory election practices and the nature of the remedies.

From "Totality of Circumstances" to "Racially Polarized Voting"

In *White v. Regester* (1973) the Supreme Court ruled that discriminatory gerrymandering could be inferred from the "totality of the circumstances" surrounding the particular practices in dispute. The Court was not particularly clear what these were, but subsequent lower court decisions delineated a number of circumstances—a laundry list. The fundamental problems were not solved, however. What consistent standard could any court apply to decide whether black votes were diluted? The answer was really none; the lower courts simply made subjective, intuitive judgments and justified them with the veneer of the *White* precedent.

No intent standard was imposed as part of the totality of the circumstances until the Supreme Court attempted to impose an alternative to the laundry-list approach in *Mobile v. Bolden* (1980). The Court arrived at an intent standard by applying a precedent from *Washington v. Davis* (1976), an affirmative-action case involving an employment exam for police officers. In that case Justice White essentially held that "disproportionate racial consequences" of a "statute or ordinance having neutral purposes" did not constitute a violation of equal protection under the Constitution. This precedent imposed a burden of proof on plaintiffs to show discriminatory intent in order to enforce Section 2 of the VRA.

In the *Mobile* case the Court ruled that election districting plans merely having some discriminatory effect are beyond Section 2 protection:

It may be that Negro candidates have been defeated, but that fact alone does not work a constitutional deprivation. . . . [T]he District Court and the Court of Appeals supported their conclusion by drawing upon the substantial history of official racial discrimination in Alabama. But past discrimination cannot, in the manner of original sin, condemn governmental action that is not itself unlawful. The ultimate question remains whether a discriminatory intent has been proved in a given case. More distant instances of official discrimination in other cases are of limited help in resolving that question. (446 U.S. 55, 75 [1980])

A discriminatory-intent standard was apparently what Congress had in mind when it passed the Voting Rights Act. The language of Section 2 was not viewed as problematic by members of Congress and was widely considered to be a restatement of the Fifteenth Amendment. But after seven years of the discriminatory-results approach originating with *White*, the *Mobile* ruling amounted to a reversal of precedent.

In spite of the setback, civil rights groups continued to win cases under the new standard: "Voting rights attorneys marshaled the assistance of historians and social scientists in an effort to demonstrate the presence of discriminatory motives at the time electoral arrangements were adopted, or to justify an inference that certain arrangements had been maintained subsequently for the purpose of diluting minority voting strength" (Foster, 1985:33). Courts that wished to find vote dilution could rely on the "totality-of-circumstances" standard and then simply rule that there was sufficient evidence of discriminatory intent (Thernstrom, 1987:76). Some analysts have argued that the *Mobile* precedent was a costly defeat to minority voting rights advocacy. Davidson and Grofman argue that because "the evidentiary standard laid down in *Bolden* was seen as virtually impossible to satisfy without 'smoking gun' evidence of intentional discrimination, constitutional challenges to at-large elections virtually came to a halt" (Davidson and Grofman, 1994:382). The academic dispute over the impact of the new intent standard was resolved by statute soon after the decision.

Reacting to the *Mobile* ruling, civil rights advocates launched an ultimately successful lobbying effort for a statutory codification of a results standard for minority redistricting. Two years after the decision, registering strong objections to the intent standard for minority vote dilution claims, Congress amended the VRA to explicitly prohibit discriminatory impact for any reason. Section 2 was amended as follows: "No voting qualification or prerequisite to voting or standard, practice or procedure shall be imposed or applied by any State or political subdivision in a manner which *results* in a denial or abridgement of the right of any citizen of the United States to vote on account of race or color" (Farber, Eskridge, and Frickey, 1993:233). The legislative record left little latitude for future misinterpretation by the Court. The courts were directed "to focus on the discriminatory effects that electoral arrangements might have on minority voting power, not on the discriminatory intent of those who devised the electoral arrangements" (Grofman, 1990:120).

The Court's Interpretation of Section 2 after the 1982 Amendments to the VRA

Five years after the 1982 amendment was enacted, the Supreme Court's first ruling on the amendment settled the matter. In *Thornburg v. Gingles* (1986) the Court ruled that racially polarized voting, defined as "blacks voting as a bloc one way, whites voting as a bloc the opposite way and in sufficient numbers in an at-large system to defeat black candidates," was a sufficient cause to infer minority vote dilution. A finding of such "polarized voting would be sufficient grounds for a court to order replacement of the at-large system and the creation of an appropriate number of majority-minority districts" (Scarrow, 1994:6). The totality-of-circumstances standard, "a grab bag of factors whose exact relevance to a vote dilution claim is very much left to the vagaries of the trial court," was effectively replaced by a more "clearly specified set of conditions sufficient to prove a voting rights violation" (Grofman, 1992:226).

The Court not only jettisoned the intent standard but greatly simplified the plaintiff's task of demonstrating minority vote dilution. The problem was that nobody had ever thoughtfully debated whether the creation of majority-minority districts was the best way to implement the Voting Rights Act, or if minority voter influence was better spread around in majority white districts. The courts simply said that the solution would be majority-minority districts. In the area of reapportionment generally, the Court had never taken such a bold step.

Nonracial Gerrymandering Cases: The Political Thicket Thickens?

Writing in 1971, Robert Dixon observed that the "Court still characterizes reapportionment cases as mere right-to-vote cases, and focuses on something called individual voter weight, which is measured solely by the equality of district populations" (Dixon, 1971:18). In other words, beyond this simplistic application of the "one-person, one-vote" principle required by the Warren Court's *Baker v. Carr* (1962) and *Reynolds v. Sims* (1964) decisions, the Court avoided the nonracial gerrymandering question throughout the 1970s and early 1980s. As Justice White pointed out in *Gaffney v. Cummings* (1973):

What is done in so arranging for elections, or to achieve political ends or allocate political power, is not wholly exempt from judicial scrutiny under the 14th Amendment. . . . multimember districts may be vulnerable, if racial or political groups have been fenced out of the political process and their voting strength invidiously minimized. Beyond this we have not ventured far or attempted the impossible task of extirpating politics from what are the essentially political processes of the sovereign States. (412 U.S. 735, 754)

This restraintist jurisprudence seemed to hold sway until 1986, when in *Davis v. Bandemer* the Supreme Court potentially cast a much wider net over reapportionment. Political scientist and reapportionment expert Bernard Grofman has stated that "*Davis v. Bandemer* is potentially the most important redistricting case since *Reynolds v. Sims* . . . because it opens to judicial review the only aspect of redistricting that had been seemingly immune from judicial scrutiny, the intentional partisan gerrymander" (Grofman, 1990:3). Yet in spite of opening the door to judicial intervention in partisan reapportionment cases, the Court has been reluctant to actually cast out gerrymandered voting plans as unconstitutional. In the *Davis* case itself some of the Indiana reapportionment plan appeared "especially . . . egregious," but the Supreme Court did not strike it down (Grofman, 1990:5).

While the Supreme Court has now formally penetrated this traditional haven from judicial review, for tactical reasons it has not strayed far into that political thicket. Nevertheless, the emphasis in *Davis* follows the racial-minority pattern in further extending rights to political groups, not just to individual citizens. Political scientist Bruce Cain cautions that since "both the *Davis v. Bandemer* and *Thornburg v. Gingles* cases shift the representational emphasis away from formal individual equality and toward compensating group representation, I would expect that middle America, to the extent that it is aware of these cases, is less enthusiastic about the Court's current views on representation than MALDEF [Mexican American Legal Defense and Education Fund] or the NAACP are" (Grofman, 1990:131). While the Supreme Court has shifted ground somewhat in the more recent minority voting rights cases, it is still reluctant to relinquish its guardianship of discrete and insular minorities in favor of a more race-neutral application of equal protection principles.

VOTING RIGHTS CASES IN THE 1990s

Based on the 1982 Voting Rights Act Amendments and the favorable precedent established in *Gingles*, it appeared that redistricting to maximize the number of minority voting districts would become a reality after the 1990 census. "In the aftermath of the 1990 census, the Justice Department under President George Bush pressed states to maximize the number of majority-black districts. The effort to meet this demand and preserve the turf of white incumbents led to numerous oddly shaped, serpentine districts that are now the focus of litigation nationwide" (Biskupic, 1996:A4). In fact, this racial gerrymandering continued to occur in the early 1990s, but the Supreme Court again shifted to a position that was somewhat more critical of racial redistricting in 1993.

As in other areas of judicial intervention, the shifting ideological composition of the Supreme Court has influenced recent rulings in voting rights cases, possibly forecasting greater deference to states and localities in drawing electoral districts. Paralleling some of the rulings and precedents in affirmative-action cases, the Court has struck down race-conscious gerrymandering, arguing that it violates equal protection principles. In *Shaw v. Reno* (1993) the Supreme Court ruled that electoral districts in North Carolina, which had been redrawn as majority-minority districts to ensure that black representatives would be elected, were presumptively unconstitutional. Justice O'Connor, the swing vote on the sharply divided Court, argued that since the appellants had challenged a "reapportionment scheme" on the grounds that it was "so irrational on its face that it [could] be understood only as an effort to segregate voters into separate voting districts because of their race," the district court was required to "determine whether the North Carolina plan [was] narrowly tailored to further a compelling governmental interest" (509 U.S. 630, 656). She also expressed a concern that racial gerrymandering was counterproductive to the goal of eradicating racial discrimination:

A reapportionment plan that includes in one district individuals who belong to the same race, but who are otherwise widely separated by geographical and political boundaries, and who may have little in common with one another but the color of their skin, bears an uncomfortable resemblance to political apartheid. It reinforces the perception that members of the same racial group—regardless of their age, education, economic status, or the community in which they live—think alike, share the same political interests, and will prefer the same candidates at the polls. We have rejected such perceptions elsewhere as impermissible racial stereotypes. . . . By perpetuating such notions, a racial gerrymander may exacerbate the very patterns of racial bloc voting that majority-minority districting is sometimes said to counteract.

The message that such districting sends to elected representatives is equally pernicious. When a district obviously is created solely to effectuate the perceived common interests of one racial group, elected officials are more likely to believe that their primary obligation is to represent only the members of that group, rather than their constituency as a whole. This is altogether antithetical to our system of representative democracy. (509 U.S. 630, 645–46)

The *Shaw* decision's apparent repudiation of cases upholding racial gerrymandering created considerable turmoil as Southern electoral districts were redrawn after the 1990 census, but subsequent cases suggest that *Shaw* is limited to the most egregious instances of racial gerrymandering.

Districts redrawn under the supervision of the Justice Department were challenged in lower federal courts, and some redistricting was found to be unconstitutional in Texas, Louisiana, and Georgia. In the first Georgia case, *Miller v. Johnson* (1995), the Supreme Court affirmed the lower-court finding that Georgia's Eleventh Congressional District was unconstitutionally redrawn. In *Miller* the Court found that to use race as the predominant factor in reapportionment violated the equal protection clause of the Fourteenth Amendment. But Georgia had essentially conceded creating a black-majority congressional district on the basis of race alone. That made it an easier plan to strike down under the *Shaw* precedent. In a separate concurring opinion Justice O'Connor stated that she "understood the new court standard to be a 'demanding one' for challengers of race-conscious districts to meet, applying 'only to extreme instances of gerrymandering' in which the state has relied on race in 'substantial disregard of customary and traditional districting practices' " (Greenhouse, 1999:A16). So it was not a foregone conclusion that the courts would begin striking down redistricting plans promoting majority-minority districts.

In *Abrams v. Johnson* (1997), a second case resulting from Georgia redistricting efforts, the Supreme Court ruled that Georgia's creation of three black-majority districts in 1992 was also the result of unconstitutional racial gerrymandering. The Court struck down the redistricting plans and upheld the district court's reversion to the single black-majority district in place since 1982. In doing so, the Court specifically stated that Justice Department efforts to coerce the state to maximize the number of black-majority districts were tainted with racial considerations. Justice Anthony Kennedy stated in the majority opinion:

The considerable evidence of Justice Department pressure on Georgia to create the maximum number of majority black districts, leading the state legislature to act based on an overriding concern with race, disturbed any sound basis for the trial court to defer to the 1991 plan; the unconstitutional predominance of race in the 1992 plan's provenance of the Second and Eleventh Districts caused them to be improper departure points; and the proposals for either two or three majority black districts in plans urged in the remedy phase of this litigation were flawed by evidence of predominant racial motive in their design. Thus, the trial court acted well within its discretion in deciding it could not draw two majority black districts without engaging in racial gerrymandering. (117 S. Ct. 1925 [1997])

The case established that any overt attempts to maximize the number of minority districts would be declared unconstitutional. As long as no elimination of existing minority districts occurred (a "no-retrogression" standard), states could not be pressured to create additional majority-minority districts. In addition, the Justice

Department was clearly rebuked for what the Court characterized as overzealous enforcement efforts.

The Louisiana case, *Reno v. Bossier Parish School Board* (1997) also involved important issues: the different standards applied to redistricting plans under Section 2 and Section 5 of the Voting Rights Act. In 1993 the Department of Justice rejected a redistricting plan creating one majority-minority district because the NAACP had offered an alternative providing for two such districts. The district court had upheld the Department of Justice's denial, but the appellate court had reversed the decision, ruling that the voting plan did not have a discriminatory purpose or retrogressive result. Accordingly, the Louisiana district was thus entitled to preclearance from the Department of Justice for the one-district plan.

Writing for the majority, Justice O'Connor made it clear that a possible Section 2 violation of the VRA on the grounds that minority voting strength was diluted was not sufficient to establish discriminatory intent, or a Section 5 violation of the VRA. The benchmark to establish a Section 5 violation was whether the plan resulted in a retrogression of minority voting in the district. Since the plan did not, the district court erred in upholding the Justice Department's claim. The decision left open the question of whether a Section 2 vote dilution violation had occurred and how that would ultimately bear on the resolution of whether an intent to discriminate, under Section 5 or otherwise, was evident. Justice O'Connor wrote, "We have previously observed that a jurisdiction's single decision to choose a redistricting plan that has a dilutive impact does not, without more, suffice to establish that the jurisdiction acted with a discriminatory purpose" (520 U.S. 471).

The implication of the decision was that "DOJ may not deny pre-clearance solely because the new voting plan fails to maximize the number of minority voting districts. Instead, the DOJ may block a proposed voting plan only if it manifests a discriminatory intent to 'retrogress.' In practice, this means that so long as a new districting plan maintains the existing number of minority voting districts, it will receive pre-clearance" (Center for Individual Rights, 1997). The Supreme Court's review of racially gerrymandered districts has generally targeted only the most obvious cases and has left considerable latitude to most states and localities in their redistricting efforts (Cunningham, 2001). This observation is borne out by the most recent decision revisiting North Carolina redistricting.

Pursuant to the *Shaw* decision, a federal district court for North Carolina reexamined the districts in question in the case and held them to be constitutional. The appeals court overruled the district court, and the case again reached the Supreme Court. In *Hunt v. Cromartie* (1999) the Court ruled that redistricting cases would not be dismissed summarily simply because race was a factor in redistricting. Writing for the majority, Justice Thomas stated, "Laws classifying citizens based on race are constitutionally suspect and must be strictly scrutinized. A facially neutral law warrants such scrutiny if it can be proved that the law was motivated by a racial purpose or object, *Miller v. Johnson*, 515 U.S. 900, 913, or is unexplainable on grounds other than race" (98-85).

Justice Thomas noted the complexity of determining the legislature's intent in redistricting and established a precedent of substantive review of evidence before any judgment could be rendered. "The task of assessing a jurisdiction's motivation . . . is not a simple matter; on the contrary, it is an inherently complex endeavor, one requiring the trial court to perform a 'sensitive inquiry into such circumstantial and direct evidence of intent as may be available.' *Arlington Heights, supra,* at 266" (98-85). The majority opinion conceded that the redistricting plan appeared to be an impermissible instance of racial gerrymandering but reversed the appellate court's decision because it had summarily ruled against the North Carolina redistricting plan. "Viewed *in toto* . . . evidence tends to support an inference that the State drew its district lines with an impermissible racial motive. . . . Summary judgment, however, is appropriate only where there is no genuine issue of material fact and the moving party is entitled to judgment as a matter of law" (98-85). The Court was careful to avoid any suggestion that a heightened level of scrutiny would mean that the burden of proof had shifted to the state or locality. Unconstitutional racial gerrymandering would have to be proven by the plaintiffs according to the *Gingles* standards of compactness, extent of polarization, or racial-bloc voting.

CONSEQUENCES OF REDISTRICTING TO CREATE MAJORITY-MINORITY DISTRICTS

Though the Supreme Court has clearly been indispensable to the legitimation of majority-minority districts, critics have argued that fragmentation along racial lines remains one of the dangers of this approach. "By conferring a benefit on groups (i.e., a constitutional right to representation), the VRA may actually be creating an incentive for people to think along group lines, thereby unwittingly encouraging potentially destabilizing factionalism and group conflict" (Grofman, 1990:133). Of course, there are alternative outcomes. Bruce Cain contends that "the effects of incentives for factionalism stemming from a remedial voting rights policy seem relatively weak and, in any event, must be balanced against the need to bolster minority voices in a society in which the majority has numerous advantages" (Cain, 1992:271). Whether voting rights policy contributes to greater conflict in racial politics or benefits minorities without exacting too high a price is a perplexing and important issue for future analysis (Peterson, 1995). Certainly the judiciary has played a major role in arbitrating the implementation of voting rights reforms and bears some responsibility, whatever the outcome.

Although these issues generally remain in dispute, a number of studies have examined some of the possible adverse consequences of racial redistricting for black political participation. At least two important consequences have been identified by researchers. One is that racial redistricting may reduce party competition within the districts themselves. The other is that the creation of majority-minority districts tends to favor more conservative candidates in surrounding districts.

Reduced Party Competition

One important and potentially injurious consequence of creating majority-minority districts, as opposed to leaving minority votes diffused throughout a number of districts, is that the practice will tend to limit intradistrict party competition. Blacks and Hispanics tend to vote heavily Democratic, so majority-minority districts concentrate overwhelming minority Democratic support, diminishing two-party competition within these and other districts. Thus, although more minority candidates are elected to office, the political party that the minority electorate overwhelmingly identifies with (the Democrats), probably loses power. Conversely, minorities have less influence on the positions and policies of Republican candidates because Republicans do not need to compete for the minority vote in their districts.

The lack of "intra-district party competition" within majority-minority districts actually "removes the incentive for minority group citizens to participate in voting. . . . Studies have thus shown that voter turnout has decreased in many majority-minority Congressional districts" (Scarrow, 1994:11). It is ironic indeed if the VRA has been implemented in such a way that many minority voters choose not to vote simply because they feel that it will not make enough of a difference in their newly won districts.

Proportional Gains, Substantive Losses in Minority Redistricting

Ironically, increasing the proportional representation of blacks in legislatures may also dilute substantive minority voting strength in another sense. Though this issue is rarely discussed by its proponents, racial redistricting tends to "bleach" surrounding districts, further isolating black constituencies and black representatives. In his 1997 study of African American representation in Congress, Kenny Whitby discusses this possible impact:

If the overall goal is to increase the level of substantive representation for African-Americans, then the creation of the greatest number of majority-black districts might undermine that objective. . . . [A]djusting district boundary lines to accommodate more blacks necessitates "bleaching" adjoining districts, thus making them more conservative and more Republican. The key question becomes: Does the creation of more majority-black districts decrease the overall level of policy responsiveness from white representatives? (Whitby, 1997:120)

Whitby suggests that while blacks are gaining in numerical representation, they may become more isolated politically as a result. Racial redistricting to benefit blacks may create similar polarization of voting and thus diminish the potential of African American representatives to build coalitions across racial lines and to represent blacks as effectively as possible on nonracial issues. Other research tends to answer Whitby's question in the affirmative.

A 1996 study of racial redistricting found that the optimal levels of black population for maximizing substantive representation of black interests was slightly below 50 percent, not the 65 percent or greater majorities usually created in racially gerrymandered districts. In creating majority-minority districts "there may be a trade-off between increasing the number of minority officeholders and enacting legislation that furthers the interests of the minority community." The researchers reported that "outside of the South, dividing minority voters equally across districts maximizes substantive representation; inside the South the optimal scheme creates concentrated districts on the order of 47% black voting-age population. In addition, minority candidates may have a substantial chance of being elected from districts with less than 50% minority voters" (Cameron, Epstein, and O'Halloran, 1996:187). If this is true, then majority-black voting districts, created with the intention of ensuring proportional black representation in Congress or state legislative bodies, are unnecessarily diluting minority voting strength in other districts. Redistricting eliminates black electoral influence in these districts and may provide no appreciable gain in political influence in the overwhelmingly black districts created.

These findings were challenged for methodological weaknesses by David Lublin. Lublin charged that Cameron and colleagues' analysis ignored "the effect of the presence of Latinos on the election of African Americans. In addition, they do not consider that racial redistricting not only changes the aggregation of seats into votes but also indirectly boosts the Republican share of votes and seats" (Lublin, 1999b:183). Responding to Lublin, Cameron and his colleagues took these new issues into account, reevaluated their data, and found that the previous conclusions remained valid:

Subjecting these claims to direct empirical examination, we find that our previous results are unaltered by the inclusion of Latino voters in our estimates of equal opportunity, and that incumbency advantage cannot fully explain the recent victories of minority candidates in the South. Neither do the critiques of our results regarding substantive representation stand up to systematic analysis: Evidence at both the state level and over time confirms our conclusion that districts on the order of 45% black voting-age population maximize the expected number of votes for minority-supported legislation. (Epstein and O'Halloran, 1999:190)

Carol Swain, another expert on the impact of racial gerrymandering on minority representation, has also observed negative policy consequences following the creation of majority-minority districts. Swain argues that surrounding districts became more conservative and less supportive of policies favored by African Americans after the 1994 election. "Black politicians gained safer seats in a hostile Congress where many now consider themselves under siege. With the Republican capture of the House of Representatives, all but two of the African American representatives in Congress have become minority members of the minority party. African Americans lost 3 chairmanships of full committees and 17 chairmanships of subcommittees as well as other important leadership posts" (Swain, 1995:84).

Swain points out that this practice of racial redistricting seems to have been actively embraced by Republicans as a means for gaining seats in Congress. In the early 1990s the Republican National Committee "combined redistricting with its outreach program to minorities" (Swain, 1993:205). This was a direct result of the recognition by Republican Party officials that the creation of majority-minority districts draws Democratic votes away from other districts. Swain points out that substantive black representation in Congress can be enhanced by other means than racial redistricting: through increased black representation from predominantly white districts and through white representation of black interests (Swain, 1993:207–11). These are strategies that would be advanced by savvy Democrats against the Republican Party.

Another researcher, Kevin Hill, drew similar conclusions from his study of the impact of minority redistricting in the 1992 elections. Hill found "that almost half of the nine districts swinging Republican in the South in 1992 did so because they lost significant numbers of blacks. In the end, the link between the rising fortunes of blacks and Republicans as a result of redistricting is unmistakable" (Hill, 1995:401). Ironically, these studies suggest that it is the Democrats who are losing influence in Congress as a result of racial redistricting. Their ideological bias in favor of proportional representation costs them a significant measure of partisan electoral influence.

Given the rather obvious political incentives for Republicans to support racial redistricting, is it realistic to think that conservative Republican judges are politically motivated in applying strict scrutiny to redistricting cases? Racial redistricting may well have contributed to greater numbers of Republican electoral victories. If that is the case, ideologically motivated judges would be inclined to remain silent or side with advocates of proportional representation. It thus seems quite likely that more conservative rulings that restrict the creation of majority-minority districts, stem from a genuine disagreement with past interpretations of the equal protection clause that allowed redistricting along racial lines.

WHAT HAPPENS WHEN RACIAL GERRYMANDERING DECLINES?

Several studies also suggest that when deliberate attempts to create majority-minority districts decline or are struck down by courts, African Americans do not typically lose their seats. In these districts white "crossover" voters are contributing to the election of significant numbers of African American candidates. In the wake of Supreme Court decisions more hostile to racial redistricting, many observers expected a substantial decline in black electoral success. "Supporters of deliberate racial gerrymandering typically denounced the decisions as likely to produce a permanent decimation of the Congressional Black Caucus (with his usual self- restraint, the Rev. Jesse Jackson predicted an 'ethnic cleansing' of Congress)" (Democratic Leadership Council, 1996). The underlying assumption is usually that racial voting is entirely polarized. Aside from the fact that the Supreme Court's challenge to racial redistricting was not as great a threat as many had supposed, in many elections white voters were simply not as polarized as many commentators initially predicted. "If the first post-*Miller* election is any indication, it turns out the country does not have to choose between racially divisive gerrymandering or gross under-representation of African Americans. Although the courts forced reductions in the minority population percentages of black incumbents in four states (Florida, Georgia, Louisiana, and Texas), all of the affected incumbents won re-election (one, Cleo Fields of Louisiana, chose not to run)" (Democratic Leadership Council, 1996).

In a 1996 issue of the *American Prospect* featuring a number of articles addressing minority elections after the *Shaw* ruling, Jamin B. Raskin warned that "[w]hite voters and losing Republican candidates have now filed suit against integrated House districts in California, Florida, Georgia, Illinois, Louisiana, Texas, North Carolina, and Virginia. Dozens more state and local legislative districts hang on a thread. . . . If the new district lines are repudiated by the Court, the South could lose all 17 of its black representatives, setting the region back politically to 1970, when the southern delegation was lily-white" (Raskin, 1996:17–18).

Pildes (1996), Raskin (1996), and Swain (1996) obviously did not anticipate that whites would vote for black candidates in the numbers they did, nor did they expect them to be responsive to issues of importance among minority voters. In many cases these fears turned out to be highly exaggerated. "To be sure, the Court's invalidation of racially gerrymandered Congressional districts in North Carolina, Florida, Texas, Georgia and Louisiana has given rise to cries of 'unprecedented judicial activism,' disregard of historical discrimination, 'a return to the days of all-white government,' and wholesale dismantling of majority-minority districts. But those cries have been necessarily tempered by the fact that blacks and other minorities have achieved electoral success in growing numbers" (Griffith, 1998:835).

The following report highlights a number of instances across the country where African American candidates were elected in majority white districts:

(1) In Georgia, after Congresswoman Cynthia McKinney's 12th District was redrawn following *Miller*, McKinney complained of impending "extinction," but was reelected with a solid crossover vote from white voters in her 65% white district.

(2) Georgia Congressman Sanford Bishop ran and won in a 35% black district.

(3) In Texas, Sheila Jackson Lee and Eddie Bernice Johnson were both elected to Congress from majority white districts.

(4) In Indiana, black Democrat Julia Carson was elected to Congress from a 69% white district.

(5) In Oklahoma, Congressman J.C. Watts, a black Republican, was elected from an overwhelmingly white district, and before him, Andrew Young, Allan Wheat, Ron Dellums, Harold Ford and Gary Franks were elected to the House of Representatives from majority-white districts.

(6) Illinois Senator Carol Moseley-Braun and Virginia Governor Douglas Wilder were both elected from majority white state electorates.

(7) Mississippi has witnessed the election of Reuben Anderson and Fred Banks to the state Supreme Court, both receiving substantial support from white voters. (Griffith, 1998:884)

In some instances, black-majority districts have also elected white representatives. This occurred in a Chicago ward in 1999. "The boundaries of Chicago's 18th

Ward had previously been racially gerrymandered into a complex, elongated, and strange shape in order to encompass as many black voters as possible . . . [but] voters re-elected a white Irish alderman" (Jeter, 1999:A3).

In April 1999 an Ohio appellate court upheld the constitutionality of the state's at-large election system for judges. In the district-court the judge had written a lengthy opinion documenting a long history of nonracial factors determining election practices. "[Judge] Smith said the countywide system is 'based solely on geography and not on population or the racial composition of the population' and many factors, such as incumbency, party affiliation, endorsements and name recognition, override race in determining who is elected." The judge also provided a long list of blacks "who ha[d] been elected to state, city and county offices in at-large elections, including 11 of 18 black candidates who sought judgeships in Franklin County from 1977 to 1996" (Bradshaw, 1999).

Reports of minority electoral successes in city elections cast further doubt on more cynical predictions that a decline in racial redistricting would result in a substantial loss of black officeholders. Black candidates in these elections have also been helped by racial crossover voting:

Indeed, cross-racial voting shouldn't be so surprising anymore. Not only are white candidates faring well in majority-black cities—the success of Martin O'Malley, the Baltimore "white man" left unnamed in the *Post* and *Times* headlines, follows on the heels of Jerry Brown's victory in Oakland—but black candidates are having success in majority-white cities as well. Majority-white Denver and plurality-white Dallas and Houston have all reelected or are about to reelect African American mayors. Just as encouraging is the fact that black mayors in majority-black cities are doing increasingly well with white voters: in heavily African American New Orleans, for instance, black incumbent Marc Morial was reelected in 1998 with 43 percent of the white vote, almost five times more than his earlier tally. Clearly, the dynamics of urban politics are changing—and in encouraging ways. (Siegel, 1999)

THE PROBLEM OF MINORITY REPRESENTATION

In discussing the success of black representatives in majority-white districts, Carol Swain emphasizes that the candidates were able to balance the interests of both white and black Democratic constituents. "To be successful, black representatives will have to . . . find common ground between the races and emphasize that commonality. Such decisions need not hurt black representation" (Swain, 1993:141). Reports of substantial numbers of newly elected black officials and the reelection of many black incumbents certainly cast doubt on claims that racial gerrymandering is necessary to secure African American political representation.

Even outspoken advocates of majority-minority districts, such as Pildes and Raskin, concede that racial gerrymandering "probably hurts the Democratic party," but they continue to advocate the practice, arguing that it is "necessary if black officeholders are going to be elected in greater than token numbers" (Pildes, 1996:16). Responding to Pildes and Raskin's challenge, Carol Swain points out that more and more whites are voting for black candidates in districts where the population of black voters is less than 50 percent. "Before the race-conscious districting of the 1990s, 40 percent of the blacks in Congress were elected from nonblack districts—either majority-white districts or those where the combined minority population exceeded 50 percent" (Swain, 1996:18).

Swain noted that in 1996 "11 black incumbents represent districts that have nonblack majorities and eight represent districts where the black voting-age population is barely in the majority. . . . Given lower black registration and turnout levels, some of the representatives of nonblack and barely black districts have majority-white electorates on election day. Still, black officeholders are getting re-elected" (Swain, 1996:18). If anything, these reports suggest that racial gerrymandering may well jeopardize minority interests and future prospects for their substantive representation in Congress and state legislatures.

The Supreme Court is not unaware of the potential problem for minority representation that is created by racial gerrymandering. In *Shaw v. Reno* Justice Sandra Day O'Connor stated that in a racially gerrymandered district "elected officials are more likely to believe that their primary obligation is to represent only members of that group rather than the constituency as a whole. This is altogether antithetical to our system of representative democracy" (509 U.S. 630, 646). A number of those who support majority-minority districts believe that the American electoral system, because it is a winner-take-all system, undermines the goal of representation itself. Lani Guinier's response to O'Connor is that

[i]f you're a loser in a district, no matter how that district is aggregated, you didn't choose where you are voting, it's being chosen for you by the incumbent politicians who are drawing these lines. . . . You're not getting to exercise choice, you're just getting to exercise a sense of belonging. The bottom line is, what the Supreme Court is telling us is not about race, it's about democracy, and they are telling us, we really don't believe in having a full democracy in which the voters are encouraged to participate, to mobilize, to organize. What we believe in is having the appearance of a democracy. (quoted in Lu, 1997:9)

Guinier's commentary suggests very strongly that those who advocate racial gerrymandering to get more African Americans elected are actually strongly opposed to the American electoral system writ large. They would prefer a system in which each racial, ethnic, gender, and religious group (as well as others) received a proportionate share of legislative seats. Many commentators believe that this kind of system might tend to splinter society into conflicting factions and interest groups. At present, proportional representation does not appear to be the type of democratic representation that a majority of Americans understand and accept.

CONCLUSION: A CONSERVATIVE COURT AND THE UNCERTAIN FUTURE OF RACIAL REDISTRICTING

While evidence of the consequences is sketchy and conclusions can only be tentatively drawn, we can say with relative certainty that racial redistricting has succeeded in ensuring a higher level of proportional representation of African Americans in state legislatures and Congress. The practical political consequences of this policy remain in dispute, but several studies suggest what seems to be a likely outcome. When black votes are drawn into supermajority districts (with black populations exceeding 60 or 70 percent) to ensure black electoral seats in legislative bodies, blacks lose influence in surrounding districts. Why else would Republicans support a practice that consolidated Democratic votes? Republicans find it easier to elect Republican candidates in surrounding districts. This is a direct result of the political practice of racial gerrymandering, which the courts endorsed during the 1970s and 1980s.

The courts have only recently begun to question the practice and to render decisions making racial redistricting more difficult. These decisions are generally rendered by slim majorities. The Supreme Court is not categorically opposed to racial redistricting, and it is by no means clear that racial redistricting will always be opposed by the Court in the future. Ironically, if racial redistricting continues, black political influence will likely be diluted to some extent. Republicans and non–African Americans will likely be less responsive to issues important to African Americans. It will also appear to many black voters, in spite of mounting evidence to the contrary, that black interests require black representation.

Apart from adverse political consequences, this is hardly what advocates of civil rights causes had expected or hoped for. Remedial policies influencing racial representation are likely to harden the color line in America by accentuating racial differences and institutionalizing racial division. To the extent that they have played a role in reviewing and accepting these practices as constitutional, the courts have contributed to the reorientation of civil rights objectives from assimilation and integration to proportional representation and racial division. In voting rights controversies equal protection has come to mean one thing for black voters and something else for whites. As in the case of affirmative action, judicial intervention in the implementation of the VRA has also contributed to the adoption and preservation of policies that run counter to what a majority of Americans would probably perceive as a consistent interpretation of equal protection rights across racial lines.

Conclusion: The Courts and Institutional Reform

RECAPITULATION AND ANALYSIS

Historical fluctuations in judicial power are at least partly attributable to the malleability of American jurisprudence. By Robert Bork's account the "theoretical emptiness at its center makes law, particularly constitutional law, unstable, a ship with a great deal of sail but a very shallow keel, vulnerable to the winds of intellectual or moral fashion. . . . This weakness in the law's intellectual structure may be exploited by new theories of moral relativism and egalitarianism" (Bork, 1984:6). The difficulty was perhaps less obvious at the founding, when Alexander Hamilton characterized the judiciary as the "weakest of the three departments of power" (Hamilton, Madison, and Jay, 1961, 79). To a great extent, the societal consensus rooted in the Enlightenment natural rights tradition militated against any significant advance of legal relativism and an activist judiciary. For much of the nineteenth century the Supreme Court could rely on textual reference to the Constitution and a jurisprudence of "original intent." A much broader consensus existed among citizens and jurists alike about what the Constitution meant and what rights it was designed to protect as a social contract. Extending Bork's analogy, if American jurisprudence is like a ship, for most of the nineteenth century the winds carried it in only one direction that was familiar to most Americans. By the end of the nineteenth century the consensus had begun to break down.

The changing political economy of the late nineteenth and early twentieth centuries challenged traditional understandings of the rights and responsibilities of American citizenship. Populist and progressive reformers attacked the laissez-faire ideology of industrialists as unjust, immoral, and antidemocratic. New theories of politics, law, and social justice began to emerge within the legal and scholarly communities. National and state governments began to grow apace with an industrializing economy in order to balance corporate and public interests. Fighting a rearguard action against progressive politics, the judiciary slipped from its restraintist moorings, no longer able to rely on original-intent jurisprudence to protect certain property rights. The initial response of the "old men" on the Supreme Court to the progressive agenda was to manufacture a defense of economic interests, then under attack, through normative interpretations of the commerce clause and the Fourteenth Amendment's due process clause. As the Court attempted to protect economic interests against progressive reformers, the conflict with majoritarian political forces eventually overwhelmed it. The Court returned to a more deferential jurisprudence in economic affairs. Yet, transformed by Franklin Roosevelt's appointments (albeit not as quickly as Roosevelt desired), the New Deal Supreme Court simultaneously espoused the more progressive sensibilities of the era.

Though the Court avoided controversy by receding to a generally perfunctory role in review of federal and state economic regulation, philosophically it had shifted profoundly away from the legal formalism of the nineteenth century. Accordingly, the Hughes Court laid out a general guideline for judicial activism against state power in 1937 in the *Carolene Products* footnote. This was later the theoretical edifice upon which the Warren Court built an entire industry for civil rights and civil liberties advocates. Justice Robert Jackson clearly believed that the door was ajar for future judicial statecraft even as he defended the 1937 decisions upholding the New Deal. Jackson declared, "No doubt another day will find one of its tasks to be correction of mistakes that time will reveal in this structure in which we now take pride. As one who knows well the workmen and the work of this generation, I bespeak the right of the future to undo our work when it no longer serves acceptably" (quoted in Schwartz, 1993:245). In principle, then, the Court had freed itself to command a potentially vast policy-making power in applying the Bill of Rights to the states.

Beginning in the 1950s, following the *Carolene Products* construction, the Warren Court reasserted the Court's independent political authority within the modern welfare state on behalf of the individual and "discrete and insular minorities." As Bernard Schwartz has written in his history of the Supreme Court, "Judicial restraint was to prove inadequate to meet the needs of the society during the second half of the century. Starting with the accession of Chief Justice Warren, the Court was once again to assume a primary role in the constitutional structure" (Schwartz, 1993:245). Were these changes legitimate exercises of judicial power, or, as Bork and others have suggested, were the courts asserting only thinly veiled judicial will against elected officials under a mere pretense of constitutional adjudication?

The Wilsonian understanding of the Constitution as a "living document" requiring episodic reconstruction to keep pace with the times provided a crucial underpinning for the Warren Court's substantive due process and equal protection rulings (Jacobsohn, 1986; Wolfe, 1986). In fact, in step with Woodrow Wilson's highly critical view of the "natural rights" tradition, Justice William Brennan, per-

haps the most ardent advocate of the modern rights revolution, has explicitly defended his activism on the bench in Wilsonian terms. "The genius of the
Constitution rests not in any static meaning it might have had in a world that is
dead and gone, but in the adaptability of its great principles to cope with current
problems and current needs" (Lasser, 1992:558). Though a critical foundation had
been laid by the progressive justices of the New Deal, the activist rulings of the
Warren Court, particularly with respect to "fundamental rights" and "discrete and
insular minorities," brought the twentieth-century rights revolution to fruition.

Following the activist lead of the Warren Court and the fundamental rights emphasis of influential advocacy groups within the legal profession since at least the
early 1960s, public interest lawyers and federal judges have transformed an array
of social policies during several decades. Beginning in the 1980s, ideological conservatism and a jurisprudence of judicial restraint have prompted courts to moderate previous reforms in all of the policy areas we have reviewed. Nevertheless,
neither critics nor proponents of these countertrends generally acknowledge the
substantial empirical evidence suggesting that reform efforts frequently caused severe institutional upheavals and harmful consequences, not only to third parties
but also in many respects to the intended beneficiaries themselves. Because lawyers and judges are primarily concerned with constitutional and statutory interpretation, rights claims, and the application of precedent to particular cases, the
literature tends to focus on the precedents and politics surrounding important rulings. The long-term implications of past judicial intervention are only beginning to
come to light.

A recurrent problem with the judiciary's extension of fundamental rights to the
institutions we have studied is that when courts intervene, they do not merely point
out a constitutional or statutory violation that must be corrected. They typically
dictate a detailed set of remedies to address the issue. This type of intervention has
generated a notoriously rigid approach to institutional reform. The judiciary was
not designed to legislate or to execute the laws, only to interpret their meaning. It
lacks the accountability required of a policy-making body. Judges are only accountable to the public under the most rare and extreme circumstances.

Yet in the wake of elaborate court orders, prisons, mental hospitals, schools, police departments, and corporations must all continue to balance individual rights
against group or societal interests. Unfortunately, judges do not have the expertise,
the time, or the inclination to make the kind of long-term incremental adjustments
that may be critical to institutional stability and progress. That is why court-ordered remedies rarely work as planned and have so many unanticipated consequences. Moreover, as we have seen, modification or reversal of court rulings
adversely impacting social and political institutions generally takes years.

FROM EXPOUNDING PRINCIPLES OF JUSTICE TO
FASHIONING REMEDIES

The courts have moved well beyond what Alexander Bickel described as the
discovery of principles of justice in expanding the rights universe. In attempting to

deal with vexing social and institutional evils, they have imposed remedies that have had a profound impact on American society. The courts have created a moral expectation that these remedies are the only defensible instruments of change. Following landmark cases, institutional reforms frequently proceed in a climate of scandal. The discovery of constitutional violations has usually meant that remedies fashioned by the courts are more extreme, and the unintended consequences more lasting and pervasive. As a result, other governmental actors may be deprived of the opportunity to address problems after public debate and the deliberations of accountable representatives.

Busing

In the case of busing the courts took an aggressive role in the enforcement of the *Brown* decision, specifying that schools must be desegregated with all deliberate speed. To further this end, the courts sanctioned, and the school systems and the public largely accepted, forced busing as the predominant method of achieving racial integration. The overall impact of busing was quite mixed, if not a complete failure. Schools in the South, where the problem of de jure segregation originated, rather quickly desegregated. In the North school busing brought intense conflict, and large numbers of middle-class whites removed their children from public schools under busing orders.

Rather than halt white flight by imposing interdistrict remedies, the courts refrained, leaving the suburban schools to white, middle-class students and relegating the majority of lower-income blacks to inner-city schools, where problems associated with the underclass (for example, drugs, crime, and violence) remain a serious problem. There is little evidence to suggest that black academic achievement improved as a result of integration efforts. Busing has foundered on the rock of residential segregation. A number of busing decrees have been abandoned because they have not produced the desired result, in spite of strenuous efforts, social turmoil, and expense. In many school districts forced busing remains one of the means of achieving school integration, and in these districts courts continue to oversee busing activities. Whatever the merits of busing to achieve racial balance, there is little question that the failed busing strategy seriously and negatively impacted many of our major cities at the cost of millions of dollars and the destruction of many genuine ethnic communities.

Affirmative Action

In the case of affirmative action, rather than prohibiting any form of race-based discrimination, by interpreting Title VII of the Civil Rights Act in a way that directly contradicted the stated intentions of the law, the Supreme Court redefined affirmative action to favor goals, quotas, and timetables for achieving some degree of proportional representation in employment. In the late 1970s "reverse-discrimination" cases began to challenge the ascendancy of this preferential treatment approach. The courts distinguished among variations of affirmative action,

prohibiting hiring quotas and minority set-asides as general remedies to past discrimination, but accepting diversity as a legitimate goal in hiring and education
policies.

The Supreme Court's dissensus in the *Bakke* decision reflected fundamental differences among jurists about how to interpret the equal protection clause and the
Civil Rights Act. Still, in the case of minority set-asides, particularly in the *Metro
Broadcasting* ruling, the Court could still find a majority to support some forms of
preferential treatment. By the early 1990s, in spite of some more liberal appointments by the Clinton administration, the consensus seemed to have shifted in favor
of race-neutral hiring and education policies. Nevertheless, the Court's previously
favorable position on voluntary affirmative-action practices in the private sector
remained intact. The Clinton administration itself took steps to mitigate the impact
of the *Adarand* case (which set a precedent that would prohibit any affirmative-action policies relying on racial classifications).

In the past forty years African Americans have seen their status in American society improve dramatically. Court decisions most certainly have contributed to
that shift. However, we think that it would have occurred (without some of the negative features accompanying it) if the Court had been more modest in exercising its
authority. Affirmative action may have helped some blacks, but the evidence suggests that it has also contributed to racial polarization. It may well be leading us to
a society in which considerations of merit are largely replaced by ethnic and racial
quotas for a wide variety of ethnic groups with possibly quite negative consequences.

Prisons

Prison reform is often regarded as one of the best examples of successful court
intervention. Most commentators agree that prisons were in need of reform, but
whether the courts raised important issues and whether they properly and effectively intervened are two very distinct questions. The first thing we can say about
prison reform is that it generated a huge volume of litigation, so much that Congress created an office of magistrates to mediate due process disputes within prisons. Thus, due to the amount of litigation that ensued, judicial reform resulted in an
institutional overload problem. Was the huge increase in litigation justified?

In many states prison conditions were thought to be so bad that the costs of federal court intervention were considered justifiable, yet some of the consequences
were not beneficial. In a number of states, Texas in particular, prison reform has
very definitely resulted in a diminution of officer authority and morale, an increase
in inmate violence, and a dramatic decline in institutional autonomy. Protracted
litigation and the appointment of a special master to administer prison reform also
resulted in a large number of high-level administrators leaving the Texas prison
system. Other states experienced less dramatic upheavals, but the process of reform nearly always affected these same aspects of administration. Studies of state
financial costs in implementing court-ordered reforms are varied. Some show sig-

nificant budget increases, while others conclude that expenditures fluctuated more in accord with general fiscal trends.

The most general conclusion we can draw from an evaluation of court intervention in prison reform is that the "totality-of-circumstances" or "conditions" judgments, such as the one imposed in Alabama, are extremely difficult to implement successfully. Critics of intervention, who are nonetheless partly sympathetic with the courts, sometimes argue that a more incremental approach is necessary in order to avoid the worst institutional upheavals. Yet when the courts apply the language of constitutional rights, arousing the intense moral indignation of a new class of victims and their advocates, it becomes extremely difficult for courts to contain the scope of conflict.

Deinstitutionalization

In the case of the deinstitutionalization of the mentally ill, Congress and state legislatures initially played a predominant role in reform. By the early 1970s, however, the courts were ruling in favor of patients' rights advocates and declared a new constellation of rights applicable to the mentally ill. A number of these rights were procedural guarantees carried over from criminal defendant cases. Others, such as the right to treatment or the right to refuse treatment, were newly discovered rights peculiar to institutionalized patients.

The consequences of the deinstitutionalization that took place as a result of the new legal standards were complex and interrelated. Primarily as a result of legislation, the community mental health clinic became the preeminent new health service institution for those with psychological disorders. The immediate problem, which persists to this day, was that people with serious affective disorders were not willing or capable of voluntarily seeking community services. As a result of the convergence of state fiscal burdens, a professional climate more hostile to the state mental hospital, and case law making civil commitment much more difficult, the severely mentally disabled were dumped on the streets or transferred to nursing homes and other institutions that were ill equipped to care for them. The advances in rights achieved on behalf of these less fortunate persons have greatly contributed to the creation of a large number of homeless and severely mentally ill who are not being treated.

It is true that conditions in mental hospitals in the past were bad, and some people were placed in them against their will when they should not have been. However, one can hardly maintain that the situation is better today than it would have been with the slow but more steady progress that would have occurred through legislative and institutional reforms alone.

Rights of the Accused

In the 1960s the rules pertaining to admissibility of evidence in criminal trials changed dramatically to better protect the rights of the accused. In Fourth Amendment search and seizure cases, in spite of the obvious historical and intuitive distinction between a violation of the Fourth Amendment and the particular remedy imposed for it, the Warren Court, in *Mapp*, designated the exclusionary rule as the only acceptable deterrent to illegal search and seizure. Even though the rule was employed by only half the states at the time of the decision, the Supreme Court extended the exclusionary rule to all of the states through the Fourteenth Amendment.

Similarly, Fifth Amendment jurisprudence began with the somewhat vague notion that incriminating statements were admissible according to a voluntariness standard. If a judge determined that a confession or incriminating statements were made voluntarily, they could be admitted as evidence in a criminal trial. This long-standing practice was outlawed by the *Miranda* decision. The Supreme Court imposed a national requirement that all suspects be informed of their various rights at the time of questioning. These constitute the familiar *Miranda* warnings. The combination of these changes in Fourth and Fifth Amendment jurisprudence seem to have had significantly detrimental impacts upon the operation of the criminal justice system.

Voting Rights

It is practically beyond dispute that racial redistricting has succeeded in ensuring a higher level of proportional representation of African Americans in state legislatures and Congress. This is far from an ideal outcome from the standpoint of substantive black political interests. Instead of allowing black voter influence to remain more evenly spread out across a larger number of voting districts, racial redistricting has overconcentrated black voters in majority-black districts. Several studies suggest that as a result, in surrounding districts larger numbers of white Republicans are elected. Arguably, blacks have suffered a diminution in their influence as members of a broad-based Democratic electoral coalition. Much evidence suggests that Republican candidates have benefited most from racial redistricting. Whatever else might be said, if black voter interests are best represented by Democrats, maximizing the number of minority districts has diluted black voter strength by polarizing the electorate, a problem that racial redistricting was supposed to remedy.

There are other areas, not covered in this study, in which court decisions pointed the way to public policy changes the results of which have been decidedly negative. Public policies that require formal hearings before students can be expelled or suspended and that reject various dress codes have certainly contributed, as Abigail Thernstrom demonstrates, to the disorder that has come to characterize many public schools. In turn, disorder has had a distinctly negative impact upon what can be taught and learned (Thernstrom, 1999).

THE LANGUAGE OF RIGHTS

The problem that arises largely as a consequence of the fundamental law and individual rights tradition in American political culture is that public policy, now crafted in part by the courts, tends to be conceived and defended in terms of rights. The language of rights has always laid an exceptionally powerful claim against any government action in America. The legal profession has been steeped in the rights tradition since before the Revolutionary War. The problem for contemporary America is that there is so much government action, in contrast to little more than a century ago, that rights have now been grossly distorted in their application to modern institutions.

It is no accident that the most vociferous institutional reformers have been various advocacy groups spawned by the American Civil Liberties Union. During the New Deal a majority inside and outside government viewed the accountability of executive authority, flowing from a president or governor downward throughout federal or state agencies, as a sufficient safeguard against abuses of power. In the 1960s intellectuals, legislators, public interest advocates, and many members of the legal profession began to challenge this executive-dominated institutional authority. Many of these critics turned to the courts, because through the power of judicial review they believed that they could strengthen and expand the bulwark of individual rights, more effectively safeguarding the individual from modern executive power. Judges became more receptive to these arguments as they perceived the reluctance of legislative majorities and executive institutions to carry on the reforms that advocates and their victims demanded under the aegis of constitutional rights. The ACLU emerged as the preeminent public law firm, working to secure a host of civil rights guarantees on many institutional fronts. Utilizing class-action lawsuits, seeking out the most advantageous test cases, avoiding more cautious state courts, and targeting sympathetic federal judges, the ACLU and its various specialists were successful in advancing just the kind of causes that civil libertarians loved, administrators hated, and the rest of society would bear the cost of for years to come. The judiciary itself has suffered from the civil rights crusades. The courts in many cases reached a point of institutional overload as public law litigation mushroomed into a massive enterprise.

The courts have become a forum in which interest groups wishing to circumvent legislative bodies, where their interests face greater opposition, can at times greatly enhance their influence over public policy. In the process society forfeits a considerable measure of flexibility in influencing the incentives of individuals to behave in ways that are, for example, conducive to good public order and safety or contribute to a robust economy. As social and economic conditions inevitably change, policy making is hampered by claims of those who are asserting their rights. Instead of resting on a broad societal consensus, a successful advancement of rights becomes a matter of organization, tactics, and continuous litigation. Rather than being resolved through a more democratic process that is responsive to the claims of society on individual behavior, many of the leading controversial issues of the day have been settled by the courts and substantially influenced by advocacy-group notions of individual rights. What does this portend for the future integrity of liberal institutions and the structure of political power in American society?

No doubt the language of rights has provided an essential catalyst for institutional change. For some time now the growing rights industry has attempted to orient court rulings toward substantive readings of relevant legislation and attendant administrative responsibilities of the government that are favorable to their particular agenda or that of their constituents. In the process the courts have forced social and economic institutions to give way to the imperatives of a more robust concept of equality, both individual and collective. Whatever advantages institutions may have conferred on the individual and society, they are viewed as only secondary considerations, that is, if they are weighed at all. All too often, it seems, the courts have favored politically determined rights, which in the long run may be inadequate to the task of balancing individual freedoms with the collective interests of society. Ultimately, these newly conceived rights may prove more vulnerable to the whims and passions of conflicting elites in American society than the liberal institutions they have formidably challenged.

LEGAL REALISM AND THE RETURN OF SUBSTANTIVE DUE PROCESS

Legal realism emerged at the turn of the twentieth century as a challenge to the nineteenth-century formalism that progressive and, later, New Deal lawyers and judges would not accept as socially responsible. They believed that the inequities and complexities of modern industrial economic organization and the new, more active role of the regulatory state required a jurisprudence that would improve the lot of the average citizen. By the early 1930s the substantive due process that the "nine old men" of the *Lochner* era had clung to could no longer preserve a dying political regime that majoritarian pressures were overwhelmingly rejecting.

But legal realism's claim ran much deeper than the shifting of constitutional principles to keep up with the times. It changed the very objective of legal analysis from one of applying rules and precedents in law to one of furthering progressive social and political agendas. As the modern American state grew in tandem with the economy, Progressive Era regulatory agencies, such as the Federal Trade Commission and the Interstate Commerce Commission, were joined by a host of new agencies during and after the New Deal. Legal realism transformed the process and the substance of adjudication as the courts interpreted and applied this growing body of administrative law. Empirical study had a much greater authority in the legal profession during the New Deal than ever before, and social science continues to fuel judicial activism today.

By the 1960s and 1970s judicial deference to executive agencies was being questioned by a new generation of lawyers and judges in a political environment that was undergoing dramatic change. For the most part, political reforms in Congress and within the Democratic Party and generational and structural changes within the media, other elite professions, interest groups, and, to a great extent, a growing proportion of the general public tended to legitimate these changes within the American legal culture. Michael Kammen has described the transformation of American law by the legal profession as a "rediscovery" of the Bill of Rights:

A generation ago . . . the Bill of Rights was "rediscovered" and became fully binding upon the states. That process and the reorientation that it required in American thinking must be considered nothing less than a sea-change in U.S. constitutionalism. During the 1950s, '60s and '70s, constitutionalism in the minds of many Americans came to be coextensive with a rigorous application of the Bill of Rights. (Kammen, 1986:389)

The disturbing aspect of his characterization and that of many others who are sympathetic to this "sea-change" in American law is that it expresses no concern for the actual process that brought this about. Nor do Kammen and others seem concerned about the consequences of the new jurisprudence for the various publics involved with the institutions being reformed.

As long as the rights universe is expanding and the Constitution is becoming more egalitarian and democratic, most of these observers are satisfied. When others criticize the judiciary for resurrecting substantive due process in the name of fundamental rights, for misinterpreting statutes, for mishandling institutional reform, and for overestimating its institutional capacity, they are frequently dismissed as conservative, neoconservative, or perhaps simply right-wing ideologues intent on revising the Constitution to curtail many of America's civil rights and liberties. In defense of modern advances in rights, apologists for an activist judiciary have thus sought to elevate the judiciary above the very democratic control that they suppose the courts are securing for us all in the name of the Bill of Rights. When judges render more conservative rulings (at least partly, if covertly, in recognition of the failures of judicial intervention), these judges are often charged with politicizing the courts and making them more antidemocratic than ever.

AMERICAN POLITICAL CULTURE AND JUDICIAL ACTIVISM

American political culture, perhaps more than that of any other advanced industrial nation, exhibits a profound mistrust of bureaucracy and bureaucrats. The political reforms of the rights revolution of the 1960s and 1970s reflected that exceptional characteristic, bringing to the surface a strong undercurrent of antipathy to the New Deal reliance on executive leadership. At the same time, the public is, more than ever, disinclined to trust legislative institutions to resolve political conflict. Following some long-term political and juridical trends, the judiciary has thus assumed a substantially greater share of authority in contemporary policy making.

Arguably, the rise of a modern American bureaucratic state has granted certain situational advantages to federal courts that have extended judicial authority beyond Progressive Era and New Deal expectations. In numerous areas of public policy the courts have proved decisive in initiating, redirecting, or outright carrying on the reform of long-standing institutions. Prior to the rights revolution courts would have been responsible only for mediating conflict according to much narrower matters of law. Under the contemporary, rights-dominated regime the courts have in varying degrees assumed many of the responsibilities of governance itself through the particular remedies they have imposed. The problem is not that they have become antimajoritarian in doing so. They have always been so. That is the inherent danger of the institution, of statutory interpretation, and of judicial review itself. The more immediate problem is that the courts have assumed so much administrative power in "rediscovering" the Bill of Rights.

In making his wager in favor of judicial review and extensive judicial power, Alexander Hamilton never supposed that that power could be entrusted to some kind of systemic or professionally derived benevolence. Its legitimacy would always have to be safeguarded by political struggle. Historically, one of the greatest powers the courts have possessed is the power to enshrine important aspects of the lexicon of democratic majorities in the language of constitutional rights. Even within the constraints imposed by the ultimate majoritarian control society possesses against the naked abuse of judicial power, we have seen that the federal courts can pose a great danger to groups within the majority and even among the intended beneficiaries of rights bestowed.

It is no less apparent that the courts have jeopardized the judiciary's authority in the American political system. In many respects they have reached a point of institutional overload. Moreover, the oscillation from activism to restraint in adjudicating controversial political issues (at least partly a response to burgeoning caseloads and a perception that the courts are straining their institutional capacity) gives the impression that the courts have politicized rights—perhaps obscuring the nation's sense of what remains and what is no longer fundamental about the American Constitution.

Americans have generally regarded the political system as an arena in which the populace debates and explores public moral issues. In that way they clarify and implement their evolving understanding of the public good. In recent years we seem to have moved increasingly in the direction of expecting such issues to be decided not by the people but by judges. Whatever the positive elements of such a shift, it has certainly reduced the role of the citizens in discussing, debating, and deciding many of the issues that affect them, weakening, we believe, the democratic order. In the long run that may be the most deleterious consequence of the judicial activism of the past four to five decades.

Federal judges have secured for themselves a strategically vital role in brokering long-term advantages and disadvantages for entire classes of individuals within an increasingly impenetrable rights-based regime. By invoking statutory or constitutional interpretation, court rulings can confer a status of legitimacy upon untested or outright misguided policies that makes them much more difficult to reshape and correct. Whether they are prodded by trends in the legal profession, interest-group litigants, or their own moral or ideological inclinations, judges will eventually be called to account for their policy making. That is the price of power in America.

Cases

Bibliography

AELE Law Library of Case Summaries: Corrections Law for Jails, Prisons, and Detention Facilities. 1998. "Overcrowding." Park Ridge, IL: AELE Law Enforcement Legal Center. http://www.aele.org/jc83.html (September 24, 2001).

Alt, James. 1994. "The Impact of the Voting Rights Act on Black and White Voter Registration in the South." In Chandler Davidson and Bernard Grofman, eds., *Quiet Revolution in the South: The Impact of the Voting Rights Act, 1965–1990*. Princeton, NJ: Princeton University Press, pp. 351–77.

Appelbaum, Paul S. 1994. *Almost a Revolution: Mental Health Law and the Limits of Change*. New York: Oxford University Press.

Armor, David. 1995. *Forced Justice: School Desegregation and the Law*. New York: Oxford University Press.

Atkins, Burton, and Henry Glick, eds. 1972. *Prisons, Protest, and Politics*. Englewood Cliffs, NJ: Prentice-Hall.

Bachrach, L.L. 1996. "The State of the State Mental Health Hospital." *Psychiatric Services*, 47:1071–78.

"Back Where It All Began: School Desegregation." 1994. *Economist,* May 28, p. 29.

Bailyn, Bernard. 1967. *The Ideological Origins of the American Revolution*. Cambridge, MA: Belknap Press of Harvard University Press.

Ball, Howard, Dale Krane, and Thomas P. Lauth. 1982. *Compromised Compliance: Implementation of the 1965 Voting Rights Act*. Westport, CT: Greenwood Press.

Bandow, Doug. 1987. "The Conservative Judicial Agenda: A Critique." In James Dorn and Henry Manne, eds., *Economic Liberties and the Judiciary*. Fairfax, VA: George Mason University Press, pp. 257–78.

Becker, Fred W. 1993. "The Politics of Closing State Mental Hospitals: A Case of Increasing Policy Gridlock." *Community Mental Health Journal*, 29, no. 2:103–14.

Becker, Gary S. 1968. "Crime and Punishment: An Economic Approach." *Journal of Political Economy,* 76:169–217.

Bell, Barry. 1986. "Prisoners' Rights, Institutional Needs, and the Burger Court." *Virginia Law Review,* 72:161–93.

Bell, Derrick ed. 1980. *Shades of Brown: New Perspectives on School Desegregation.* New York: Teachers College Press.

Belz, Herman. 1991. *Equality Transformed.* New Brunswick, NJ: Transaction Publishers.

Berger, Raoul. 1977. *Government by Judiciary: The Transformation of the Fourteenth Amendment.* Cambridge, MA: Harvard University Press.

Bickel, Alexander. 1962. *The Least Dangerous Branch.* Indianapolis: Bobbs-Merrill.

Birnbaum, Morton. 1960. "The Right to Treatment." *American Bar Association Journal,* 46:499–503.

Biskupic, Joan. 1996. "Justices Revisit Issue of Minority Voting Districts." *Washington Post,* December 10, p. A4.

Biskupic, Joan. 1999. "N.C. Redistricting Gets Another Chance; High Court Says Hard Evidence of Racial Gerrymandering Must Be Presented." *Washington Post,* May 18, p. A8.

Blumrosen, Alfred W. 1994. "The Law Transmission System and the Southern Jurisprudence of Employment Discrimination." In Paul Burstein, ed., *Equal Employment Opportunity: Labor Market Discrimination and Public Policy.* New York: Aldine De Gruyter, pp. 231–46.

Bodenhamer, David, and James Ely, Jr., eds. 1993. *The Bill of Rights in Modern America: After 200 Years.* Bloomington: Indiana University Press.

Bolick, Clint. 1996. *The Affirmative Action Fraud: Can We Restore the American Civil Rights Vision?* Washington, DC: Cato Institute.

Bork, Robert. 1984. *Tradition and Morality in Constitutional Law.* Washington, DC: American Enterprise Institute.

Bork, Robert. 1990. *The Tempting of America: The Political Seduction of the Law.* New York: Free Press.

Bork, Robert. 1996. *Slouching towards Gomorrah: Modern Liberalism and American Decline.* New York: HarperCollins.

Bowen, William G., and Derek Bok. 1998. *The Shape of the River: Long-Term Consequences of Considering Race in College and University Admissions.* Princeton, NJ: Princeton University Press.

Braddock, Jomills Henry. 1985. "School Desegregation and Black Assimilation." *Journal of Social Issues,* 41, no. 3:9–22.

Bradshaw, James. 1999. "Court Will Not Allow Racial Gerrymandering." *Columbus Dispatch,* April 14. http://www.archive.net/special/gerrymander_3.htm.

Breyer, Stephen. 1982. *Regulation and Its Reform.* Cambridge, MA: Harvard University Press.

Brimelow, Peter, and Leslie Spencer. 1993. "When Quotas Replace Merit, Everybody Suffers." *Forbes,* February 15, pp. 80–102.

"Brown 40 Years On." 1994. *Economist,* May 28, p. 15.

Bureau of Justice Statistics. 1994. http://mojo.calyx.net/, 1.

Burt, Martha. 2000. *America's Homeless II: Population and Services.* Washington, DC: Urban Institute, pp. 1–15.

"But Some Are More Equal than Others: Affirmative Action." 1995. *Economist,* April 15, pp. 21–23.

Butterfield, Fox. 1998. "Prisons Replace Hospitals for the Nation's Mentally Ill." *New York Times*, March 5, p. Al.

Cain, Bruce. 1992. "Voting Rights and Democratic Theory: Toward a Color-Blind Society." In Bernard Grofman and Chandler Davidson, eds., *Controversies in Minority Voting: The Voting Rights Act in Perspective*. Washington, DC: Brookings Institution, pp. 261–77.

Calabresi, Steven. 1996. "Out of Order." *Policy Review*, 79 (September/October). http://www.policyreview.org/sept96/cal.html (September 24, 2001).

Caldeira, Gregory. 1986. "Neither the Purse nor the Sword: Dynamics of Public Confidence in the Supreme Court." *American Political Science Review,* 80, no. 4 (December): 1209–26.

Caldeira, Gregory A., and John R. Wright. 1995. "Lobbying for Justice: The Rise of Organized Conflict in the Politics of Federal Judgeships." In Lee Epstein, ed., *Contemplating Courts*. Washington, DC: CQ Press, pp. 44–71.

Cameron, Charles, David Epstein, and Sharyn O'Halloran. 1996. "Do Majority-Minority Districts Maximize Substantive Black Representation in Congress?" *American Political Science Review*, 90, no. 4:794–812.

Cameron, James. 1989. "A National Community Mental Health Program: Policy Initiation and Progress." In David Rochefort, ed., *Handbook on Mental Health Policy in the United States*. New York: Greenwood Press, pp. 121–42.

Campbell, J.R., C.M. Hombo, and J. Mazzeo. 2000. *NAEP 1999 Trends in Academic Progress: Three Decades of Student Performance*. NCES 2000-469. Washington, DC: U.S. Department of Education, Office of Educational Research and Improvement, National Center for Education Statistics.

Canon, Bradley. 1974. "Is the Exclusionary Rule in Failing Health? Some New Data and a Plea against a Precipitous Conclusion." *Kentucky Law Journal*, 62:681.

Canon, Bradley. 1979. "The Exclusionary Rule: Have Critics Proven That It Doesn't Deter Police?" *Judicature*, 62:398–403.

Carter, Robert, Daniel Glaser, and Leslie T. Wilkins. 1985. *Correctional Institutions*. 3rd ed. New York: Harper and Row.

Cassell, Paul G. 1996. "*Miranda'* s Social Costs: An Empirical Reassessment." *Northwestern University Law Review,* 90:391. Lexis-Nexis Academic Universe.

Cassell, Paul G. 1997. "*Miranda*'s 'Negligible' Effect on Law Enforcement." *Harvard Journal of Law and Public Policy*, 20 (Winter):327–46.

Cassell, Paul G., and Richard Fowles. 1998. "Handcuffing the Cops? A Thirty-Year Perspective on *Miranda*'s Harmful Effects on Law Enforcement." *Stanford Law Review*, 50 (April):1055–1145. Lexis-Nexis Academic Universe.

Cassell, Paul G., and Bret S. Hayman. 1996. "Police Interrogation in the 1990s: An Empirical Study of the Effects of *Miranda*." *UCLA Law Review,* 43 (February):839–931. Lexis-Nexis Academic Universe.

Center for Individual Rights. 1997. "Supreme Court Rebuffs Clinton Justice Department Campaign to Racially Gerrymander Local Voting Districts." Center for Individual Rights, May 12. http://www.adversity.net/special/gerrymander_3.htm (September 19, 2001).

Center for Voting and Democracy. 2000. "Voting Rights." August 23. http://www.igc.apc.org/cvd/issues/race/index.html (September 25, 2001).

Champion, Dean. 1988. "Some Recent Trends in Civil Litigation by Federal and State Prison Inmates." *Federal Probation*, September, pp. 43–47.

Chapman, James P., and Eric Dorkin. 1998. *Federal Court Prison Litigation Project Revised Handbook.* 8th ed. Chicago: Illinois Institute for Community Law.

Chase, William. 1982. *The American Law School and the Rise of Administrative Government.* Madison: University of Wisconsin Press.

Chemerinsky, Erwin. 1995. "Race and the Supreme Court." *Trial,* October, pp. 86–88.

Chesler, Mark, Joseph Sanders, and Debra Kalmuss. 1988. *Social Science in Court: Mobilizing Experts in the School Desegregation Cases.* Madison: University of Wisconsin Press.

Chilton, Bradley Stewart. 1991. *Prisons under the Gavel: The Federal Court Takeover of Georgia Prisons.* Columbus: Ohio State University Press.

Choper, Jesse. 1980. *Judicial Review and the National Political Process.* Chicago: University of Chicago Press.

Clark, W.A.V. 1987. "School Desegregation and White Flight: A Reexamination and Case Study." *Social Science Research,* 16:211–28.

Cohen, C.I., and K.S. Thompson. 1992. "Homeless Mentally Ill or Mentally Ill Homeless?" *American Journal of Psychiatry,* 149:816–23.

Cohen, Carl. 1995. *Naked Racial Preference.* Lanham, MD: Madison Books.

Cohen, N.L., and L.R. Marcos. 1986. "Psychiatric Care of the Homeless Mentally Ill." *Psychiatric Annals,* 16, no. 12:729–32.

Cole, Richard, and Jack Call. 1992. "When Courts Find Jail and Prison Overcrowding Unconstitutional." *Federal Probation,* March, pp. 29–39.

Coleman, James S., et al. 1966. *Equality of Educational Opportunity.* Washington, DC: U.S. Dept. of Health, Education, and Welfare, Office of Education.

Comptroller General. 1979. "Impact of the Exclusionary Rule on Federal Criminal Prosecutions." B-171019.

Cooper, Phillip. 1988. *Hard Judicial Choices: Federal District Court Judges and State and Local Officials.* New York: Oxford University Press.

Crain, R., and R. Mahard. 1982. *Desegregation Plans That Raise Black Achievement: A Review of the Research.* Santa Monica: RAND Corporation.

"Criminal Justice in Crisis." 1988. ABA Special Committee on Criminal Justice in a Free Society, November. http://www.druglibrary.org/special/king/cjic.htm (September 27, 2001).

Cripe, Clair A. 1990. "Courts, Corrections, and the Constitution: A Practitioner's View." In John DiIulio, Jr., ed. *Courts, Corrections, and the Constitution: The Impact of Judicial Intervention on Prisons and Jails.* New York: Oxford University Press, pp. 268–86.

Cunningham, Maurice. 2001. *Maximization, Whatever the Cost: Race, Redistricting, and the Department of Justice.* Westport, CT: Praeger Publishers.

Cushman, Barry. 1998. *Rethinking the New Deal Court: The Structure of a Constitutional Revolution.* New York: Oxford University Press.

Dahl, Robert. 1957. "Decision-Making in a Democracy: The Supreme Court as a National Policy-Maker." *Journal of Public Law,* 6:279–95.

Dale, Charles, ed. 1995. "Compilation and Overview of Federal Laws and Regulations Establishing Affirmative Action Goals or Other Preference Based on Race, Gender, or Ethnicity." Congressional Research Service, February 17.

Davidson, Chandler. 1992. "The Voting Rights Act: A Brief History." In Bernard Grofman and Chandler Davidson, eds., *Controversies in Minority Voting: The Voting Rights Act in Perspective.* Washington, DC: Brookings Institution, pp. 7–51.

Davidson, Chandler, and Bernard Grofman. 1994. "The Voting Rights Act and the Second Reconstruction." In Chandler Davidson and Bernard Grofman, eds., *Quiet Revolution in the South: The Impact of the Voting Rights Act, 1965–1990*. Princeton, NJ: Princeton University Press, pp. 378–87.

Davies, T.Y. 1983. "A Hard Look at What We Know (and Still Need to Learn) about the 'Costs' of the Exclusionary Rule: The NIJ Study and Other Studies of 'Lost' Arrests." *American Bar Foundation Research Journal*, 3:611–90.

Davis, F. James. 1965. "The Effects of a Freeway Displacement on Racial Housing Segregation in a Northern City." *Phylon*, 26, no. 3 (Fall):209–15.

Dawson, Michael. 1994. *Behind the Mule: Race and Class in African-American Politics*. Princeton, NJ: Princeton University Press.

Democratic Leadership Council. 1996. "Good News on Race and Redistricting." *Update*, Tuesday, December 3. http://www.ndol.org/ndol_ci.cfm?contentid=2537&kaid==127&subid=176 (September 19, 2001).

Dentler, R.A. 1990. "Conclusions from a National Study." In N. Estes, D.U. Levine, and D.R. Waldrip, eds., *Magnet Schools: Recent Developments and Perspectives*. Austin: Morgan Printing and Publishing.

Detlefsen, Robert. 1995. "Affirmative Action and Business Deregulation: On the Reagan Administration's Failure to Revise Executive Order No. 11246." In James Riddlesperger, Jr., and Donald Jackson, eds., *Presidential Leadership and Civil Rights Policy*. Westport, CT: Greenwood Press, pp. 59–70.

Deutsch, Albert. 1949. *The Mentally Ill in America*. 2nd ed. New York: Columbia University Press.

DiIulio, John, Jr. 1987a. *Governing Prisons: A Comparative Study of Correctional Management*. New York: Free Press.

DiIulio, John, Jr. 1987b. "Prison Discipline and Prison Reform." *Public Interest*, 89 (Fall):71–90.

DiIulio, John, Jr. 1990. "Conclusion: What Judges Can Do to Improve Prisons and Jails." In John DiIulio, Jr., ed., *Courts, Corrections, and the Constitution: The Impact of Judicial Intervention on Prisons and Jails*. New York: Oxford University Press, pp. 287–322.

Dimond, Paul. 1985. *Beyond Busing: Inside the Challenge to Urban Segregation*. Ann Arbor: University of Michigan Press.

Dixon, Robert G. 1971. "The Court, the People, and 'One Man, One Vote.' " In Nelson Polsby, ed., *Reapportionment in the 1970s*. Berkeley: University of California Press, pp. 1–55.

Dometrius, Nelson, and Lee Sigelman. 1984. "Assessing Progress toward Affirmative Action Goals in State and Local Government: A New Benchmark." *Public Administration Review* (May/June):241–246.

Donohue, John, III, and James Heckman. 1991. "Continuous versus Episodic Change: The Impact of Civil Rights Policy on the Economic Status of Blacks." *Journal of Economic Literature*, 29 (December):1603–43.

Donohue, William. 1985. *The Politics of the American Civil Liberties Union*. New Brunswick, NJ: Transaction Books.

Donohue, William. 1994. *Twilight of Liberty: The Legacy of the ACLU*. New Brunswick, NJ: Transaction Publishers.

Dorn, James, and Henry Manne, eds. 1987. *Economic Liberties and the Judiciary*. Fairfax, VA: George Mason University Press.

Dowell, David, and James Ciarlo. 1989. "An Evaluative Overview of the Community Mental Health Centers Program." In David Rochefort, ed., *Handbook on Mental Health Policy in the United States.* Westport, CT: Greenwood Press, pp. 195–236.

Downs, Anthony. 1970. *Urban Problems and Prospects.* Chicago: Markham.

Drake, Willie Avon, and Robert D. Holsworth. 1996. *Affirmative Action and the Stalled Quest for Black Progress.* Urbana: University of Illinois Press.

Durham, M., and John La Fond. 1985. "The Empirical Consequences and Policy Implications of Broadening the Statutory Criteria for Civil Commitment." *Yale Law and Policy Review,* 3:395–446.

Dworkin, Ronald. 1993. *Life's Dominion: An Argument about Abortion, Euthanasia, and Individual Freedom.* New York: Alfred Knopf.

Eastland, Terry. 1996. *Ending Affirmative Action: The Case for Color-Blind Justice.* New York: Basic Books.

Edley, Christopher, Jr. 1990. *Administrative Law: Rethinking Judicial Control of Bureaucracy.* New Haven, CT: Yale University Press.

Edley, Christopher, Jr. 1996. *Not All Black and White: Affirmative Action, Race, and American Values.* New York: Hill and Wang.

Edwards, John. 1995. *When Race Counts: The Morality of Racial Preference in Britain and America.* London: Routledge.

"Effect of *Mapp v. Ohio* on Police Search and Seizure Practices in Narcotics Cases." 1968. *Columbia Journal of Law and Social Problems,* 4:87.

Ehrlich, Isaac. 1973. "Participation in Illegitimate Activities: An Economic Analysis." *Journal of Political Economy,* 81, no. 3:521–565.

Ekland-Olson, Sheldon, and Steve Martin. 1988. "Organizational Compliance with Court-Ordered Reform." *Law and Society Review,* 22:359–83.

Ely, John Hart. 1980. *Democracy and Distrust: A Theory of Judicial Review.* Cambridge, MA: Harvard University Press.

Empirical Research on Affirmative Action and Anti-Discrimination. 1995. "Empirical Research on Affirmative Action." July 19. http://clinton2.nara.gov/WH/EOP/OP-/html/aa/aa03.html (September 19, 2001).

Engel, Kathleen, and Stanley Rothman. 1983. "The Paradox of Prison Reform." *Public Interest,* 73 (Fall):91–105.

Engstrom, John. 1985. "Racial Vote Dilution: The Concept and the Court." In Lorn Foster, ed., *The Voting Rights Act: Consequences and Implications.* New York: Praeger Scientific, pp. 13–43.

Ennis, Bruce. 1972. *Prisoners of Psychiatry: Mental Patients, Psychiatrists, and the Law.* New York: Harcourt Brace Jovanovich.

Ennis, Bruce, and Richard Emery. 1978. *The Rights of Mental Patients: The Revised Edition of the Basic ACLU Guide to a Mental Patient's Rights.* New York: Avon Books.

Epstein, David, and Sharyn O'Halloran. 1999. "A Social Science Approach to Race, Redistricting, and Representation." *American Political Science Review* 93 (March):187–91.

Epstein, Lee. 1985. *Conservatives in Court.* Knoxville: University of Tennessee Press.

Epstein, Richard. 1992. *Forbidden Grounds: The Case against Employment Discrimination Laws.* Cambridge, MA: Harvard University Press.

Eyler, Janet, Valerie J. Cook, and Leslie E. Ward. 1983. "Resegregation: Segregation within Desegregated Schools." In Christine Rossell and Willis Hawley, eds., *The*

Consequences of School Desegregation. Philadelphia: Temple University Press, pp. 126–62.

Farber, Daniel, William N. Eskridge, Jr., and Philip P. Frickey. 1993. *Cases and Materials on Constitutional Law: Themes for the Constitution's Third Century.* St. Paul: West Publishing Company.

Farley, Reynolds, and Clarence Wurdock. 1977. *Can Governmental Policies Integrate Public Schools?* Ann Arbor: Population Studies Center, University of Michigan.

Federal Election Commission. 1998. "Voter Registration and Turnout in Federal Elections by Race/Ethnicity, 1972–1996." December 8. http://www.fec.gov/pages/Raceto.htm (September 19, 2001).

Feeley, Malcolm M., and Roger A. Hanson. 1990. "The Impact of Judicial Intervention on Prisons and Jails: A Framework for Analysis and a Review of the Literature." In John DiIulio, Jr., ed., *Courts, Corrections, and the Constitution: The Impact of Judicial Intervention on Prisons and Jails.* New York: Oxford University Press, pp. 12–46.

Feeley, Malcolm M., and Edward L. Rubin. 1998. Judicial Policy Making and the Modern State: How the Courts Reformed America's Prisons. Cambridge: Cambridge University Press.

Ferguson, Ronald F. 1998. "Teachers' Perceptions and Expectations and the Black-White Test Score Gap." In Christopher Jencks and Meredith Phillips, eds., *The Black-White Test Score Gap.* Washington, DC: Brookings Institution Press, pp. 273–317.

Fetner, Gerald. 1982. *Ordered Liberty: Legal Reform in the Twentieth Century.* New York: Alfred A. Knopf.

Fieweger, Michael. 1993. "Consent Decrees in Prison and Jail Reform—Relaxed Standard of Review for Government Motions to Modify Consent Decrees." *Journal of Criminal Law and Criminology* 83:1024–54.

Fish, Peter. 1973. *The Politics of Federal Judicial Administration.* Princeton, NJ: Princeton University Press.

Fisher, Anne B. 1985. "Businessmen Like to Hire by the Numbers." *Fortune,* September 16, pp. 26ff.

Fisher, Anne B. 1994. "Businessmen Like to Hire by the Numbers." In Paul Burstein, ed., *Equal Employment Opportunity: Labor Market Discrimination and Public Policy.* New York: Aldine De Gruyter, pp. 269–79.

Fisher, William, III, Morton J. Horwitz, and Thomas Reed, eds. 1993. *American Legal Realism.* New York: Oxford University Press.

Fletcher, William. 1982. "The Discretionary Constitution: Institutional Remedies and Judicial Legitimacy." *Yale Law Journal,* 91 (March):635–97.

Flory, Curtis, and Rose Marie Friedrich. 1999. "Half a Million Liberated from Institutions to Community Settings without Provision for Long-Term Care." The Treatment Advocacy Center. Originally appeared in *Catalyst,* 1, no. 2 (November/December 1999). http://www.psychlaws.org/HospitalClosure/Flory.htm (May 22, 2002).

Foley, Henry A., and Steven S. Sharfstein. 1983. *Madness and Government: Who Cares for the Mentally Ill?* Washington, DC: American Psychiatric Press.

Foster, Lorn, ed. 1985. *The Voting Rights Act: Consequences and Implications.* New York: Praeger Scientific.

Fox, James Alan. 1978. *Forecasting Crime Data: An Econometric Analysis.* Lexington, MA: Lexington Books.

Franklin, John, and Alfred Moss, Jr. 1994. *From Slavery to Freedom: A History of African Americans.* 7th ed. New York: McGraw-Hill.

Freeman, Richard. 1973. "Changes in the Labor Market for Black Americans, 1948–72." *Brookings Papers on Economic Activity,* volume 1, pp. 67–120.

French, L. 1987. "Victimization of the Mentally Ill: An Unintended Consequence of Deinstitutionalization." *Journal of the National Association of Social Workers,* 32 (November–December):502–5.

Friedelbaum, Stanley. 1994. *The Rehnquist Court: In Pursuit of Judicial Conservatism.* Westport, CT: Greenwood Press.

Gambitta, Richard A.L., Marlynn L. May, and James C. Foster, eds. 1981. *Governing through Courts.* Beverly Hills, CA: Sage Publications.

Gans, Herbert. 1969. *The Levittowners.* New York: Vintage.

Garcia, Luis T., Nancy Erskine, Kathy Hawn, and Susanne R. Casmay. 1981. "The Effect of Affirmative Action on Attributions about Minority Group Members." *Journal of Personality,* 49:427–37.

Garrow, David. 1988. "The Federal Courts and School Desegregation in the 1970s." *Law and Society Review,* 21, no. 5:879–84.

Gates, Henry Louis. 1992. "Pluralism and Its Discontents." *Profession 92,* Modern Language Association, pp. 35–38.

Gerard, Harold, and Norman Miller. 1975. *School Desegregation: A Long-Term Study.* New York: Plenum Press.

Gerber, Scott Douglas. 1995. *To Secure These Rights: The Declaration of Independence and Constitutional Interpretation.* New York: New York University Press.

Goffman, Erving. 1963. *Stigma: Notes on the Management of Spoiled Identity.* Englewood Cliffs, NJ: Prentice-Hall.

Goldberg, George. 1984. *Reconsecrating America.* Grand Rapids, MI: Eardmans Publishing Co.

Goldwin, Robert, and William A. Schambra, eds.1985. *How Does the Constitution Secure Rights?* Washington, DC: American Enterprise Institute.

Goldwin, Robert, William A. Schambra, Art Kaufman, eds. 1987. *Constitutional Controversies.* Washington, DC: American Enterprise Institute.

Gorman, Mike. 1956. *Every Other Bed.* Cleveland: World Publishing Co.

Graglia, Lino. 1976. *Disaster by Decree: The Supreme Court Decisions on Race and the Schools.* Ithaca, NY: Cornell University Press.

Graham, Hugh. 1990. *The Civil Rights Era: Origins and Development of National Policy, 1960–1972.* New York: Oxford University Press.

Graham, Hugh. 1992. "The Origins of Affirmative Action: Civil Rights and the Regulatory State." *Annals of the American Academy of Political and Social Science,* 523 (September):50–62.

Greene, Kathanne. 1989. *Affirmative Action and Principles of Justice.* Westport, CT: Greenwood Press.

Greenhouse, Linda. 1999. "High Court Takes Case on Districts and Rights." *New York Times,* January 23, p. A16.

Griffith, Benjamin. 1998. "Implementing the Race-Predominant Standard for State and Local Government Redistricting Plans." *Stetson Law Review,* 27, no. 3 (Winter):835. http://www.lexisnexis.com/universe.

Grissmer, David, Ann Flanagan, and Stephanie Williamson. 1998. "Why Did the Black-White Score Gap Narrow in the 1970s and 1980s?" In Christopher Jencks and

Meredith Phillips, eds., *The Black-White Test Score Gap*. Washington, DC: Brookings Institution Press, pp. 182–228.

Grob, Gerald. 1991. *From Asylum to Community: Mental Health Policy in Modern America*. Princeton, NJ: Princeton University Press.

Grofman, Bernard. 1992. "Expert Witness Testimony and the Evolution of Voting Rights Case Law." In Bernard Grofman and Chandler Davidson, eds., *Controversies in Minority Voting: The Voting Rights Act in Perspective*. Washington, DC: Brookings Institution, pp. 197–229.

Grofman, Bernard, ed. 1990. *Political Gerrymandering and the Courts*. New York: Agathon Press.

Grofman, Bernard, and Chandler Davidson, eds. 1992. *Controversies in Minority Voting: The Voting Rights Act in Perspective*. Washington, DC: Brookings Institution.

Gronfein, William. 1985. "Incentives and Intentions in Mental Health Policy: A Comparison of the Medicaid and Community Mental Health Programs." *Journal of Health and Social Behavior*, 192–206.

Gronfein, William. 1985. "Psychotropic Drugs and the Origins of Deinstitutionalization." *Social Problems*, 32 (June): 437–54.

Gunther, Gerald. 1981. *Cases and Materials on Individual Rights in Constitutional Law*. 3rd ed. Mineola, NY: Foundation Press.

Gunther, Gerald. 1994. *Learned Hand: The Man and the Judge*. New York: Knopf.

Haas, Kenneth C. 1982. "The Comparative Study of State and Federal Judicial Behavior Revisited." *Journal of Politics*, 44 (August):721–46.

Hadley, T.R., and D.P. Culhane. 1993. "The Status of CMHC's Ten Years into Block Grant Financing." *Community Mental Health Journal*, 29, no. 2:95–102.

Hamilton, Alexander, James Madison, and John Jay. 1961. *The Federalist Papers*. New York: Mentor Books.

Handley, Lisa, and Bernard Grofman. 1994. "The Impact of the Voting Rights Act on Minority Representation: Black Officeholding in Southern State Legislatures and Congressional Delegations." In Chandler Davidson and Bernard Grofman, eds., *Quiet Revolution in the South: The Impact of the Voting Rights Act, 1965–1990*. Princeton, NJ: Princeton University Press, pp. 335–50.

Hanson, Roger, and Henry Daley. 1995. "Challenging the Conditions of Prisons and Jails: A Report on Section 1983 Litigation." *Bureau of Justice Statistics* U.S. Doc. J29.26 C35 (January): 1–48.

Harriman, Linda, and Jeffrey Straussman. 1983. "Do Judges Determine Budget Decisions? Federal Court Decisions in Prison Reform and State Spending for Corrections." *Public Administration Review*, (July/August):343–51.

Harris, M. Kay, and Dudley Spiller, Jr. 1977. *After Decision: Implementation of Judicial Decrees in Correctional Settings*. Washington, DC: U.S. Department of Justice, October.

Harris, Richard, and Sidney Milkis, eds. 1989. *Remaking American Politics*. Boulder, CO: Westview Press.

Harvard Law Review. 1986. "The Modification of Consent Decrees in Institutional Reform Litigation." *Harvard Law Review*, 99:1020–39.

Haycock, Kati. 2001. "Helping All Students Achieve: Closing the Achievement Gap." *Educational Leadership*, 58, no. 6 (March). http://www.ascd.org/reading-room/edlead/0103/haycock.html.

Heckman, James. 1989. "The Impact of Government on the Economic Status of Black Americans." In Steven Shulman and William Darity, Jr., eds., *The Question of Discrimination: Racial Inequality in the U.S. Labor Market.* Middletown, CT: Wesleyan University Press, pp. 50–80.

Herr, Stanley S., Stephen Arons, and Richard E. Wallace, Jr. 1983. *Legal Rights and Mental-Health Care.* Lexington, MA: D.C. Heath and Company.

Hickok, Eugene, and Gary McDowell. 1993. *Justice vs. Law: Courts and Politics in American Society.* New York: Free Press.

Hill, Herbert. 1989. "Black Labor and Affirmative Action: An Historical Perspective." In Steven Shulman and William Darity, Jr., eds., *The Question of Discrimination: Racial Inequality in the U.S. Labor Market.* Middletown, CT: Wesleyan University Press, pp. 190–267.

Hill, Kevin A. 1995. "Congressional Redistricting: Does the Creation of Majority Black Districts Aid Republicans?" *Journal of Politics,* 57, no. 2 (May): 384–401.

Hirschkop, Philip J., Nancy Crisman, and Michael A. Milleman. 1972. "Litigating an Affirmative Prisoners' Rights Action." In "Symposium: Sentencing and Corrections." *American Criminal Law Review,* 11 (Fall):35–64.

Hochschild, Jennifer. 1984. The New American Dilemma: Liberal Democracy and School Desegregation. New Haven, CT: Yale University Press.

Hogan, Michael F. 2000. Director, Ohio Department of Mental Health. Testimony. House Committee on the Judiciary, September 21. http://www.house.gov/judiciary/hoga0921.htm.

Holmes, Oliver Wendell. 1993. "The Common Law." 1881. In William Fisher III, Morton J. Horwitz, and Thomas Reed, eds., *American Legal Realism.* New York: Oxford University Press, p. 9.

Holmes, Steven A. 1995. "U.S. Issues New, Strict Tests for Affirmative Action Plans." *New York Times,* June 29, pp. A1, A16.

Horan, Dennis, Edward R. Grant, and Paige C. Cunningham, eds. 1987. *Abortion and the Constitution: Reversing Roe v. Wade through the Courts.* Washington, DC: Georgetown University Press.

Horowitz, Donald. 1977. *The Courts and Social Policy.* Washington, DC: Brookings Institution.

Horwitz, Morton J. 1992. *The Transformation of American Law, 1870–1960: The Crisis of Legal Orthodoxy.* New York: Oxford University Press.

Huber, Peter. 1988. *Liability: The Legal Revolution and Its Consequences.* New York: Basic Books.

Huff, C. Ronald. 1980. "The Discovery of Prisoners' Rights: A Sociological Analysis." In Geoffrey P. Alpert, ed., *Legal Rights of Prisoners.* Beverly Hills, CA: Sage Publications, pp. 47–65.

Hula, Richard. 1984. "Housing Market Effects of Public School Desegregation: The Case of Dallas, Texas." *Urban Affairs Quarterly,* 19, no. 3 (March):409–23.

Hurst, Blake. 1995. "Runaway Judge." *The American Enterprise,* (May–June):52–56.

Isaac, Rael, and Virginia Armat. 1990. *Madness in the Streets: How Psychiatry and the Law Abandoned the Mentally Ill.* New York: Free Press.

Jacobs, James B. 1977. *Stateville: The Penitentiary in Mass Society.* Chicago: University of Chicago Press.

Jacobs, James B. 1983. *New Perspectives on Prisons and Imprisonment.* Ithaca, NY: Cornell University Press.

Jacobsohn, Gary. 1986. *The Supreme Court and the Decline of Constitutional Aspiration.* Totowa, NJ: Rowman and Littlefield.

Jargowsky, Paul A., and Mary Jo Bane. 1991. "Ghetto Poverty in the United States, 1970–1980." In Christopher Jencks and Paul Peterson, eds., *The Urban Underclass.* Washington, DC: Brookings Institution, pp. 235–73.

Jencks, Christopher, and Paul Peterson, eds. 1991. *The Urban Underclass.* Washington, DC: Brookings Institution.

Jencks, Christopher, and Meredith Phillips, eds. 1998. *The Black-White Test Score Gap.* Washington, DC: Brookings Institution.

Jeter, Jon. 1999. "Racial Gerrymandering Fails in Windy City." *Washington Post,* February 27, p. A3.

Johnson, Ann Braden. 1990. *Out of Bedlam: The Truth about Deinstitutionalization.* New York: Basic Books.

Johnson, Charles, and Bradley Canon. 1984. *Judicial Policies: Implementation and Impact.* Washington, DC: Congressional Quarterly Press.

Johnson, John. 1981. *American Legal Culture, 1908–1940.* Westport, CT: Greenwood Press.

Johnston, Robert C., and Debra Viadero. 2000. "Unmet Promise: Raising Minority Achievement" *Education Week on the Web,* March 15. http://www.edweek.org/ew/ewstory.cfm?slug=27gapintro.h19 (September 19, 2001).

Kahn, Ronald. 1994. *The Supreme Court and Constitutional Theory, 1953–1993.* Lawrence: University Press of Kansas.

Kalman, Laura. 1996. *The Strange Career of Legal Liberalism.* New Haven, CT: Yale University Press.

Kammen, Michael. 1986. *A Machine That Would Go of Itself: The Constitution in American Culture.* New York: Alfred Knopf.

Kapp, Marshall. 1994. "Treatment and Refusal Rights in Mental Health: Therapeutic Justice and Clinical Accommodation." *American Journal of Orthopsychiatry,* 64:223–34.

Katyal, Neal. 1995. "Why Affirmative Action in Higher Education Is Safe in the Courts." *Journal of Blacks in Higher Education,* (Autumn):83–89.

Kauffman, Kelsey. 1988. *Prison Officers and Their World.* Cambridge, MA: Harvard University Press.

Kaufman, Irving. 1981. "Prison Reform: A View from the Bench." *American Bar Association Journal,* 67 (November):1470–71.

Kaus, Mickey. 1992. *The End of Equality.* New York: Basic Books.

Keilitz, I. 1989. "Legal Issues in Mental Health Care: Current Perspectives." In David Rochefort, ed., *Handbook on Mental Health Policy in the United States.* Westport, CT: Greenwood Press, pp. 363–84.

Keilitz, I., and T. Hall. 1985. "State Statutes Governing Involuntary Outpatient Civil Commitment." *Mental and Physical Disability Law Reporter,* 9:378–400.

Kennedy, John F. 1983. "Message from the President of the United States Relative to Mental Illness and Mental Retardation." 88th Congress, 1st Session, House of Representatives, Document No. 58. 1963. In Henry A. Foley and Steven S. Sharfstein, *Madness and Government: Who Cares for the Mentally Ill?* Washington, DC: American Psychiatric Press, appendix A, pp. 163–76.

Kerwin, Cornelius. 1994. *Rulemaking: How Government Agencies Write Law and Make Policy.* Washington, DC: Congressional Quarterly Press.

Kiesler, Charles. 1991. "Homelessness and Public Policy Priorities." *American Psychologist,* 46:1245–52.

Kiesler, Charles, and Amy Sibulkin. 1987. *Mental Hospitalization: Myths and Facts about a National Crisis.* Newbury Park, CA: Sage Publications.

Kinnamon, Jon M. 1985. "Judicial Oversight of Discretion in the Prison System." In Carl F. Pinkele and William C. Louthan, eds., *Discretion, Justice, and Democracy: A Public Policy Perspective.* Ames: Iowa State University Press, pp. 71–80.

Kozol, Jonathan. 1991. *Savage Inequalities: Children in America's Schools.* New York: Crown Publishing Co.

Kravitz, David, et al., eds. 1997. "Effects of AAP on Non Target Group Members' Perceptions of Target Group Members, and on Relations between Parties." *Affirmative Action: A Review of Psychological and Behavioral Research.* http://www.siop.org/Afirm-Act/siopsaartoc.htm (September 19, 2001).

Kull, Andrew. 1992. *The Color-Blind Constitution.* Cambridge, MA: Harvard University Press.

La Fond, John. 1994. "Law and the Delivery of Involuntary Mental Health Services." *American Journal of Orthopsychiatry,* 64 (April):209–22.

La Fond, John, and M.I. Durham. 1992. *Back to the Asylum: The Future of Mental Health Law and Policy in the United States.* New York: Oxford University Press.

LaFree, Gary D. 1985. "Adversarial and Nonadversarial Justice: A Comparison of Guilty Pleas and Trials." *Criminology,* 23:289–312.

Laing, R.D. 1969. *The Divided Self.* New York: Pantheon.

Lamb, H. Richard, ed. 1984. *The Homeless Mentally Ill: A Task Force Report of the American Psychiatric Association.* Washington, DC: American Psychiatric Association.

Landis, James. 1987. "The Administrative Process." In Walter Gellhorn, Clark Byse, Peter L. Straus, Todd Rakoff, and Roy A. Schotland, eds., *Administrative Law: Cases and Comments.* 8th ed. Vol. 1. University Casebook Series. Mineola, NY: Foundation Press, pp. 3–7.

Lasser, William. 1988. *The Limits of Judicial Power: The Supreme Court in American Politics.* Chapel Hill: University of North Carolina Press.

Lasser, William. 1992. *Perspectives on American Government.* Lexington, MA: D.C. Heath and Company.

Leeke, William D. 1980. "The Negotiated Settlement: Prisoners' Rights in Action." In Geoffrey Alpert, ed., *Legal Rights of Prisoners.* Beverly Hills, CA: Sage Publications, pp. 113–27.

Legomsky, Stephen. 1987. *Immigration and the Judiciary: Law and Politics in Britain and America.* New York: Oxford University Press.

Lemov, Penelope. 1993. "Taking Your Prison Back from the Feds." *Governing,* (January):22–23.

Leonard, Jonathan. 1991. "The Impact of Affirmative Action on Employment." In Russell Nieli, ed., *Racial Preference and Racial Justice: The New Affirmative Action Controversy.* Washington, DC: Ethics and Public Policy Center, pp. 493–98.

Lerman, Paul. 1982. *Deinstitutionalization and the Welfare State.* New Brunswick, NJ: Rutgers University Press.

Lipset, Seymour Martin. 1995. "Two Americas, Two Systems: Whites, Blacks, and the Debate over Affirmative Action." *New Democrat,* May/June. http://www.ndol.org/ndol_ci.cfm?contentid=2438&kaid=102&subid=229 (September 19, 2001).

Litan, Robert, and Clifford Winston, eds. 1988. *Liability: Perspectives and Policy.* Washington, DC: Brookings Institution.

Loury, Glenn. 1992. "Incentive Effects of Affirmative Action." *Annals of the American Academy of Political and Social Science,* 523 (September):19–29.

Loury, Glenn. 1997. "The Conservative Line on Race." *Atlantic Monthly,* (November):144–54.

Lu, Cathy. 1997. "The Geography of Race in Elections: Color-Blindness and Redistricting." *Human Rights,* 4 (Fall):6–9.

Lublin, David. 1999a. *The Paradox of Representation: Racial Gerrymandering and Minority Interests in Congress.* Princeton, NJ: Princeton University Press.

Lublin, David. 1999b. "Racial Redistricting and African-American Representation: A Critique of 'Do Majority-Minority Districts Maximize Substantive Black Representation in Congress?' " *American Political Science Review,* 93 (March):183–86.

Lynch, Frederick. 1989. *Invisible Victims: White Males and the Crisis of Affirmative Action.* Westport, CT: Greenwood Press.

MacDonald, Heather. 1993. "The Diversity Industry: Cashing In on Affirmative Action." *New Republic,* (July 5):22–25.

Magnet, Myron. 1993. *The Dream and the Nightmare: The Sixties' Legacy to the Underclass.* New York: William Morrow and Co.

Mansfield, Harvey, Jr. 1989. *Taming the Prince: The Ambivalence of Modern Executive Power.* New York: Free Press.

Marcuse, Herbert. 1968. *Negations.* Boston: Beacon Press.

Mashaw, Jerry. 1985. *Due Process in the Administrative State.* New Haven, CT: Yale University Press.

McCraw, Thomas, ed. 1981. *Regulation in Perspective: Historical Essays.* Cambridge, MA: Harvard University Press.

McDowell, G. 1988. *Curbing the Courts: The Constitution and the Limits of Judicial Power.* Baton Rouge: Louisiana State University Press.

McManus, Edgar. 1993. *Law and Liberty in Early New England: Criminal Justice and Due Process, 1620–1692.* Amherst: University of Massachusetts Press.

Mechanic, David. 1989. *Mental Health and Social Policy.* 3rd ed. Englewood Cliffs, NJ: Prentice-Hall.

Melnick, R. Shep. 1983. *Regulation and the Courts: The Case of the Clean Air Act.* Washington, DC: Brookings Institution.

Melnick, R. Shep. 1989. "The Courts, Congress, and Programmatic Rights." In Richard Harris and Sidney Milkis, eds., *Remaking American Politics.* Boulder, CO: Westview Press, pp. 188–212.

Melnick, R. Shep. 1994. *Between the Lines: Interpreting Welfare Rights.* Washington, DC: Brookings Institution.

Methvin, Eugene. 1992. "Highest Court Cost." *National Review,* March 16, pp. 36–38.

Milkis, Sidney, and Michael Nelson. 1994. *The American Presidency: Origins and Development, 1776–1993.* 2nd ed. Washington, DC: Congressional Quarterly Press.

Miller, Mark. 1993. "Courts, Agencies, and Congressional Committees: A Neo-Institutional Perspective." *Review of Politics,* 55 (Summer):471–89.

Mishler, William, and Reginald Sheehan. 1993. "The Supreme Court as a Countermajoritarian Institution? The Impact of Public Opinion on Supreme Court Decisions." *American Political Science Review,* 87, no. 1 (March):87–101.

Mitchell, V., E.S. Russell, and C.S. Benson. 1989. *Exemplary Urban Career-oriented Secondary School Programs.* Berkeley: National Center for Research in Vocational Education.

Morgan, Richard. 1984. *Disabling America: The Rights Industry in Our Time.* New York: Basic Books.

Morgan, Ruth. 1970. *The President and Civil Rights: Policy-making by Executive Order.* New York: St. Martin's Press.

Morris, Norval, and David J. Rothman, eds. 1995. *The Oxford History of the Prison: The Practice of Punishment in Western Society.* New York: Oxford University Press.

Morrissey, Joseph. 1989. "The Changing Role of the Public Mental Hospital." In David Rochefort, ed., *Handbook on Mental Health Policy in the United States.* Westport, CT: Greenwood Press, pp. 311–38.

Moskos, Charles. 1995. "Affirmative Action: The Army Experience." *New Democrat,* (May/June):22–23.

Nacoste, R.W. 1994. "Policy Schemas for Affirmative Action." In L. Heath et al., eds., *Applications of Heuristics and Biases to Social Issues*, vol. 3. New York: Plenum Press, pp. 205–21.

Nagel, S.S. 1965. "Testing the Effects of Excluding Illegally Seized Evidence." *Wisconsin Law Review*, pp. 275–310.

Nalbandian, John. 1989. "The U.S. Supreme Court's 'Consensus' on Affirmative Action." *Public Administration Review,* (January/February):38–45.

NAPO (National Association of Police Organizations). 2000. "NAPO Is Disappointed by Supreme Court's Decision in *Dickerson v. United States*, Ruling That Evidence Is to Be Automatically Excluded under Miranda." June 26. http://www.napo.org/dickersonvsus.htm (September 24, 2001).

Nappi, Chiara R. 1999. "Local Illusions." *Wilson Quarterly*, 23, no. 4 (Autumn):44–51.

National Center for Educational Statistics. 1995. "Disparities in Public School District Spending, 1989–90." U.S. Department of Education, Office of Educational Research and Improvement. Washington, DC: U.S. Government Printing Office, NCES 95-300.

National Center for Policy Analysis, Idea House. 1995a. "NCPA Policy: Economic Growth v. Affirmative Action." Source: Ralph Reiland (Robert Morris College), "Economic Force of Upward Mobility," *Washington Times*, October 4, 1995. http://www.ncpa.org/pd/affirm/pdaa/pdaa19.html (September 27, 2001).

National Center for Policy Analysis, Idea House. 1995b. "NCPA Policy: How Much Racism Is There?" Source: George Gilder, "The Roots of Black Poverty," *Wall Street Journal*, October 30, 1995. http://www.ncpa.org/pd/affirm/pdaa/pdaa20.html (September 27, 2001).

National Center for Policy Analysis, Idea House. 1996. "NCPA Policy: Black Entrepreneurs." Source: Laura M. Litvan, "The Changing Face of Ownership," *Investor's Business Daily*, June 25, 1996. http://www.ncpa.org/pd/affirm/pdaa/pdaa21.html (September 27, 2001).

National Center for Policy Analysis, Idea House. 1997a. "Affirmative Action: Black America's Economic Progress." Source: John J. DiIulio, "State of Grace," *National Review*, December 22, 1997. http://www.ncpa.org/pd/affirm/pdaa/pdaa36.html (September 27, 2001).

National Center for Policy Analysis, Idea House. 1997b. "Affirmative Action: Black Progress Slower Since 1970." Source: Abigail Thernstrom and Stephan Thernstrom,

"The Real Story of Black Progress," *Wall Street Journal*, September 3, 1997. http://www.ncpa.org/pd/affirm/pdaa/pdaa26.html (September 27, 2001).

National Center for Policy Analysis, Idea House. 1997c. "A Critique of Affirmative-Action Study on Doctors." Source: Gail Heriot, "Doctored Affirmative-Action Data," *Wall Street Journal*, October 15, 1997. http://www.ncpa.org/pd/affirm/pdaa/pdaa29.html (September 19, 2001).

National Center for Policy Analysis, Idea House. 1998a. "Education: Affirmative Action Disadvantages Some Groups over Others." Source: Ron K. Unz, "Some Minorities Are More Minor than Others," *Wall Street Journal*, November 16, 1998. http://www.ncpa.org/pi/edu/pd111698c.html (September 27, 2001).

National Center for Policy Analysis, Idea House. 1998b. "Education: Ending Racial Preferences Should Increase Graduation Rates." Source: Stephan Thernstrom and Abigail Thernstrom, "The Consequences of Colorblindness," *Wall Street Journal*, April 7, 1998. http://www.ncpa.org/pi/edu/april98f.html (September 27, 2001).

National Institute of Justice. 1983. *"The Effects of the Exclusionary Rule: A Study in California."* U.S. Department of Justice, J28.2: Ex 2.

Nieli, Russell, ed. 1991. *Racial Preference and Racial Justice: The New Affirmative Action Controversy.* Washington, DC: Ethics and Public Policy Center.

Northcraft, G.B., and J. Martin. 1982. "Double Jeopardy: Resistance to Affirmative Action from Potential Beneficiaries." In B. Gutek, ed., *Sex Role Stereotyping and Affirmative Action Policy.* Los Angeles: Institute of Industrial Relations, University of California.

Northwest Region Educational Laboratory. 1999. "Lessons from the Cities, Part Four: Recruiting Strong Leaders." *Northwest Education Magazine* (Winter). http://www.nwrel.org/nwedu/winter99/lessons4.html (May 24, 2002).

Oaks, D.H. 1970. "Studying the Exclusionary Rule in Search and Seizure." *University of Chicago Law Review*, 37:665–757.

O'Brien, David. 1986. *Storm Center: The Supreme Court in American Politics.* New York: W.W. Norton and Company.

O'Brien, David. 1999. "Institutional Norms and Supreme Court Opinions: On Reconsidering the Rise of Individual Opinions." In Cornell W. Clayton and Howard Gillman, eds., *Supreme Court Decision-Making: New Institutionalist Approaches.* Chicago: University of Chicago Press, pp. 91–114.

O'Connor, Karen, and Lee Epstein. 1985. "Bridging the Gap between Congress and the Supreme Court: Interest Groups and the Erosion of the American Rule Governing Awards of Attorneys' Fees." *Western Political Quarterly,* 38 (June):238–49.

"Off the Buses." 1994. *Economist,* January 29, pp. 30, 33.

Olson, Walter. 1991. *The Litigation Explosion: What Happened When America Unleashed the Lawsuit.* New York: Truman Talley Books.

Olzak, Susan, Suzanne Shanahan, and Elizabeth West. 1994. "School Desegregation, Interracial Exposure, and Antibusing Activity in Contemporary Urban America." *American Journal of Sociology*, 100, no. 1 (July):196–241.

O'Neill, Dave, and June O'Neill. 1992. "Affirmative Action in the Labor Market." *Annals of the American Academy of Political and Social Science,* 523 (September):88–103.

Orfield, Gary. 1983. *Public School Desegregation in the United States, 1968–1980.* Washington, DC: Joint Center for Political Studies.

Orfield, Gary, and John Yun. 1999. *Resegregation in American Schools*. Cambridge, MA: Civil Rights Project, Harvard University. http://www.law.harvard.edu/civilrights/publications/resegregation99.html (September 19, 2001).

Orfield, Gary, and Susan Eaton, eds. 1996. *Dismantling Desegregation: The Quiet Reversal of Brown v. Board of Education*. New York: New Press.

Peele, Roger, et al. 1984. "The Legal System and the Homeless." In Richard Lamb, ed., *The Homeless Mentally Ill: A Task Force Report of the American Psychiatric Association*. Washington, DC: American Psychiatric Association, pp. 261–78.

Perlin, M.L. 1994. "Law and the Delivery of Mental Health Services in the Community." *American Journal of Orthopsychiatry*, 64, no. 2:194–208.

Peterson, Iver. 1994. "Where Money Is Not Issue but Administration Is Seen as a Problem." *New York Times*, July 23, p. 24.

Peterson, Paul, ed. 1995. *Classifying by Race*. Princeton, NJ: Princeton University Press.

Pildes, Richard. 1996. "Racial Redistricting Redux." *American Prospect*, 24 (Winter):15–16.

Pillsbury, Samuel. 1989. "Understanding Penal Reform: The Dynamics of Change." *Journal of Criminal Law and Criminology*, 80:726–80.

Pocock, J.G.A. 1975. *The Machiavellian Moment: Florentine Political Thought and the Atlantic Republican Tradition*. Princeton, NJ: Princeton University Press.

Pollot, Mark. 1993. *Grand Theft and Petit Larceny: Property Rights in America*. San Francisco: Pacific Research Institute for Public Policy.

Polsby, Nelson, ed. 1971. *Reapportionment in the 1970s*. Berkeley: University of California Press.

Powe, Lucas A., Jr. 2000. *The Warren Court and American Politics*. Cambridge, MA: Belknap Press of Harvard University Press.

Powers, Stephen, David J. Rothman, and Stanley Rothman. 1990. "The Myth of Black Low Self-Esteem." *World and I*, (March):563–81.

Pratt, Robert. 1992. *The Color of Their Skin: Education and Race in Richmond, Virginia, 1954–89*. Charlottesville: University Press of Virginia.

Pride, Richard, and J. David Woodard. 1985. *The Burden of Busing: The Politics of Desegregation in Nashville, Tennessee*. Knoxville: University of Tennessee Press.

Prison Litigation Reform Act. 1996. "PLRA Summary." October 15. http://www.prisonwall.org/stop3.htm (September 24, 2001).

Prout, Curtis, and Robert Ross. 1988. *Care and Punishment: The Dilemmas of Prison Medicine*. Pittsburgh: University of Pittsburgh Press.

Rabkin, Jeremy. 1989. *Judicial Compulsions: How Public Law Distorts Public Policy*. New York: Basic Books.

Raffel, Jeffrey. 1985. "The Impact of Metropolitan School Desegregation on Public Opinion: A Longitudinal Analysis." *Urban Affairs Quarterly*, 21, no. 2 (December):245–65.

Raskin, Jamin B. 1996. "Bad History, Bad Politics." *American Prospect*, 24 (Winter):16–18.

Reagan, Michael. 1987. *Regulation: The Politics of Policy*. Boston: Little, Brown.

Reiland, Ralph. 1995. "Economic Force of Upward Mobility." *Washington Times*, October 4.

Reuters. 1999. "*Miranda* Rights under Assault: Clinton Administration Defends 1966 Decision." Washington, DC, November 1. http://www.google.com/search?q=cache-:FeE-FTWt8k0:abcnews.go.com/sections/us/DailyNews/miranda991101.html+Mira

nda+Rights+Under+Assault:+Clinton+Administration+Defends+1966+Deci-
sion&hl=en (Google Cache, September 21, 2001).

Riddlesperger, James W., Jr., and Donald W. Jackson, eds. 1995. *Presidential Leadership and Civil Rights Policy.* Westport, CT: Greenwood Press.

Rist, Ray, ed. 1979. *Desegregated Schools: Appraisals of an American Experiment.* New York: Academic Press.

Rosen, Jeffrey. 1995. "The Color-Blind Court." *New Republic,* July 31, pp. 19–25.

Rosen, Jeffrey. 1997. "Originalist Sin: The Achievement of Antonin Scalia and Its Intellectual Incoherence.*" New Republic,* May 5, pp. 26–36.

Rossell, Christine. 1990. *The Carrot or the Stick for School Desegregation Policy: Magnet Schools or Forced Busing.* Philadelphia: Temple University Press.

Rossell, Christine. 1995. "Controlled-Choice Desegregation Plans: Not Enough Choice, Too Much Control?" *Urban Affairs Review,* 31, no. 1 (September):43–76.

Rossell, Christine, and David Armor. 1996. "The Effectiveness of School Desegregation Plans, 1968–1991." *American Politics Quarterly,* 24, no. 3 (July):267–302.

Rossell, Christine, and Willis Hawley, eds. 1983. *The Consequences of School Desegregation.* Philadelphia: Temple University Press.

Rothman, David J. 1971. *The Discovery of the Asylum; Social Order and Disorder in the New Republic.* Boston: Little, Brown.

Rotman, Edgardo. 1995. "Failure of Reform: United States, 1865–1965." In Norval Morris and David J. Rothman, eds., *The Oxford History of the Prison: The Practice of Punishment in Western Society.* New York: Oxford University Press, pp. 169–97.

Rubin, Eva. 1986. *The Supreme Court and the American Family: Ideology and Issues.* Westport, CT: Greenwood Press.

Rubin, Jeffrey. 1978. *Economics, Mental Health, and the Law.* Lexington, MA: D.C. Heath and Company.

Rubin, Paul, and Raymond Atkins. 1999. "Effects of Criminal Procedure on Crime Rates: Mapping Out the Consequences of the Exclusionary Rule." Independent Institute, Working Paper 9, October. http://www.papers.ssrn.com/so13/papers.cfm?abstract_id=140992.

Sales, Bruce, and Daniel Shuman. 1994. "Mental Health Law and Mental Health Care: Introduction." *American Journal of Orthopsychiatry,* 64 (April):172–79.

Sanders, W., and J. Rivers. 1996. *Cumulative and Residual Effects of Teachers on Future Student Academic Achievement.* Knoxville: University of Tennessee Value-Added Research and Assessment Center.

Sandler, Ross, and David Schoenbrod. 1996. "How to Put Law Makers, Not Courts, Back in Charge." *City Journal,* (Autumn):61–67.

Scalia, Antonin. 1987. "Economic Affairs as Human Affairs." In James Dorn and Henry Manne, eds., *Economic Liberties and the Judiciary.* Fairfax, VA: George Mason University Press, pp. 31–37.

Scarrow, Howard. 1994. "Vote Dilution, Political Party Dilution, and the Voting Rights Act." Paper presented at the 90th Annual Political Science Association Meeting, New York: September 1–4.

Schlegel, John. 1995. *American Legal Realism and Empirical Social Science.* Chapel Hill: University of North Carolina Press.

Schlesinger, S.R. 1979. "The Exclusionary Rule: Have Proponents Proven That It Is a Deterrent to Police?" *Judicature,* 62, no. 8:404–9.

Schuerman, Leo, and Solomon Kobrin. 1984. "Exposure of Community Mental Health Clients to the Criminal Justice System: Client/Criminal or Patient/Prisoner?" In Linda Teplin, ed., *Mental Health and Criminal Justice*. Beverly Hills, CA: Sage Publications, pp. 87–118.

Schulhofer, Stephen J. 1996. *"Miranda*'s Practical Effect: Substantial Benefits and Vanishingly Small Social Costs." *Northwestern University Law Review*, 90 (Winter): 500.

Schulhofer, Stephen J. 1997. "Bashing *Miranda* Is Unjustified—and Harmful." *Harvard Journal of Law and Public Policy*, 20 (Winter):347–73.

Schwartz, Bernard. 1986. *Swann's Way: The School Busing Case and the Supreme Court.* New York: Oxford University Press.

Schwartz, Bernard. 1993. *A History of the Supreme Court.* New York: Oxford University Press.

Scott, W. Richard, and Bruce Black, eds. 1986. *The Organization of Mental Health Services: Societal and Community Systems.* Beverly Hills, CA: Sage Publications.

Sears, David, Carl Hensler, and Leslie Speer. 1979. "Whites' Opposition to 'Busing': Self-Interest or Symbolic Politics?" *American Political Science Review*, 73:369–84.

Seeburger, Richard H., and R. Stanton Wettick, Jr. 1967. *"Miranda* in Pittsburgh—A Statistical Study." *University of Pittsburgh Law Review*, 29, no. 1:1–26.

Shafer, Byron, ed. 1991. *The End of Realignment? Interpreting American Electoral Eras.* Madison: University of Wisconsin Press.

Shapiro, Martin. 1978. "The Supreme Court: From Warren to Burger." In Anthony King, ed., *The New American Political System.* Washington, DC: American Enterprise Institute, pp. 47–85.

Shils, E. 1962. "The Theory of Mass Society." *Diogenes,* 39:45–66.

Shull, Steven. 1993. *A Kinder, Gentler Racism? The Reagan-Bush Civil Rights Legacy.* Armonk, NY: M.E. Sharpe.

Shulman, Steven, and William Darity, Jr., eds. 1989. *The Question of Discrimination: Racial Inequality in the U.S. Labor Market.* Middletown, CT: Wesleyan University Press.

Siegel, Fred. 1999. "Comeback Kid: Fair Philly." *New Republic*, October 1. http://www.the-newrepublic.com/magazines/tnr/current/siegel100199.html (September 24, 2001).

Skrentny, John David. 1996. *The Ironies of Affirmative Action: Politics, Culture, and Justice in America.* Chicago: University of Chicago Press.

Smith, Christopher. 1988. "United States Magistrates and the Processing of Prisoner Litigation." *Federal Probation,* (December):13–18.

Smith, Christopher. 1993a. "Black Muslims and the Development of Prisoners' Rights." *Journal of Black Studies,* 24, no. 2:131–46.

Smith, Christopher. 1993b. *Courts and Public Policy.* Chicago: Nelson-Hall.

Smith, James P., and Finis R. Welch. 1986. *Closing the Gap: Forty Years of Economic Progress for Blacks.* Prepared for the U.S. Department of Labor. Santa Monica, CA: RAND Corporation.

Smith, James P., and Finis R. Welch. 1991. "Closing the Gap: Forty Years of Economic Progress for Blacks." In Russell Nieli, ed., *Racial Preference and Racial Justice: The New Affirmative Action Controversy.* Washington, DC: Ethics and Public Policy Center, pp. 499–510.

Smith, James P., and Finis R. Welch. 1994. "Black Economic Progress after Myrdal." In
    Paul Burstein, ed., *Equal Employment Opportunity: Labor Market Discrimination
    and Public Policy*. New York: Aldine De Gruyter, pp. 155–82.
Smith, Wesley. 1994. "Don't Stand So Close to Me: Judges Are Giving Neighborhoods a
    Bum Rap." *Policy Review*, (Fall):48–54.
Sniderman, P., and T. Piazza. 1993. *The Scar of Race*. Cambridge, MA: Belknap Press of
    Harvard University Press.
Sowell, Thomas. 1984. *Civil Rights: Rhetoric or Reality?* New York: William Morrow and
    Company.
Sowell, Thomas. 1990. *Preferential Policies: An International Perspective*. New York:
    William Morrow and Company.
Spiotto, J.E. 1972. "Search and Seizure: An Empirical Study of the Exclusionary Rule and
    Its Alternatives." *Journal of Legal Studies*, 1:243–78.
Stastny, Charles, and Gabrielle Tyrnauer. 1982. *Who Rules the Joint? The Changing Politi-
    cal Culture of Maximum Security Prisons in America*. Lexington, MA: Lexington
    Books.
Stedman, J.H., S.M. Morris, and D.L. Dennis. 1995. "The Diversion of Mentally Ill Persons
    from Jails to Community-Based Services: A Profile of Programs." *American Jour-
    nal of Public Health*, 85, no. 12:1643.
Stedman, J.H., et al. 1984. "Identifying and Treating the Mentally Disordered Prison In-
    mate." In Linda Teplin, ed., *Mental Health and Criminal Justice*. Beverly Hills, CA:
    Sage Publications, pp. 279–96.
Steeh, Charlotte, and Maria Krysan. 1996. "Affirmative Action and the Public,
    1970–1995." *Public Opinion Quarterly*, 60:128–58.
Stephens, Otis H., Jr. 1973. *The Supreme Court and Confessions of Guilt*. Knoxville: Uni-
    versity of Tennessee Press.
Stephens, Otis H., Jr., Robert L. Flanders, and J. Lewis Cannon. 1972. "Law Enforcement
    and the Supreme Court: Police Perceptions of Miranda Requirements." *Tennessee
    Law Review*, 39 (Spring):407. Lexis-Nexis Academic Universe.
Stimson, Shannon C. 1990. *The American Revolution in the Law: Anglo-American Juris-
    prudence before John Marshall*. Princeton, NJ: Princeton University Press.
"A Strong Prejudice: Affirmative Action." 1995. *Economist*, June 17, pp. 69–70.
Sullivan, Larry. 1990. *The Prison Reform Movement: Forlorn Hope*. Boston: Twayne Pub-
    lishers.
"Supreme Court Increases Inmates' Burden in Correctional Lawsuits." 1991. *Corrections
    Today*, (August):187.
Surber, Robert, Martha Shumway, Richard Shadoan, and William A. Hargreaves. 1986.
    "Effects of Fiscal Retrenchment on Public Mental Health Services for the Chronic
    Mentally Ill." *Community Mental Health Journal*, 22, no. 3 (Fall):215–28.
Sutherland, Daniel. 1998. "Affirmative Action after Adarand: The Supreme Court v. the
    Clinton Administration." Center for Equal Opportunity. http://www.ceo-
    usa.org/html/afterad.html (March 22, 1998, 1–12).
Swain, Carol. 1993. *Black Faces, Black Interests: The Representation of African Americans
    in Congress*. Cambridge, MA: Harvard University Press.
Swain, Carol. 1995. "The Future of Black Representation." *American Prospect*, 23
    (Fall):78–84.
Swain, Carol. 1996. "Carol M. Swain Responds." *American Prospect*, 24 (Winter):18.
Szasz, Thomas. 1970. *The Manufacture of Madness*. New York: Harper and Row.

Taggart, William. 1989. "Redefining the Power of the Federal Judiciary: The Impact of Court-Ordered Prison Reform on State Expenditures for Corrections." *Law and Society Review,* 23:241–71.

Taylor, Jared. 1992. *Paved with Good Intentions: The Failure of Race Relations in Contemporary America.* New York: Carroll and Graf.

Teplin, Linda, ed. 1984. *Mental Health and Criminal Justice.* Beverly Hills, CA: Sage Publications.

Thernstrom, Abigail. 1987. *Whose Votes Count? Affirmative Action and Minority Voting Rights.* Cambridge, MA: Harvard University Press.

Thernstrom, Abigail. 1999. "Courting Disorder in the Schools." *Public Interest,* 136 (Summer):18.

Thernstrom, Stephan, and Abigail Thernstrom. 1997. *America in Black and White: One Nation, Indivisible.* New York: Simon and Schuster.

Thernstrom, Stephan, and Abigail Thernstrom. 1999. "Racial Preferences: What We Now Know—In a Much-Lauded Effort, the Former Presidents of Harvard and Princeton Attempt to Justify a Disastrous Policy; They Fail." *Commentary,* 107, no. 2:44–50.

The Third Branch. 1996. "New Law Brings Broad Reforms to Prisoner Litigation." June 1. http://www.uscourts.gov/ttb/jun96ttb/litigate.htm (September 24, 2001).

The Third Branch. 1999. "Changing Trends in Prisoner Petition Filing." http://www.uscourts.gov/ttb/d*ec99ttb/prisoner.html (October 2, 2001).

Thomas, Charles. 1991. "Prisoners' Rights and Correctional Privatization: A Legal and Ethical Analysis." *Business and Professional Ethics Journal,* 10 (Spring):3–45.

Thomas, George C., III. 1996. "Is *Miranda* a Real-World Failure? A Plea for More (and Better) Empirical Evidence." *UCLA Law Review,* 43:821–37.

"3. Empirical Research on Affirmative Action and Anti-Discrimination." http://www.clinton-2.nara.gov/WH/EOP/OP/html/aa/aa03.html (May 17, 2002).

Tocqueville, Alexis de. 1974 ed. *Democracy in America.* New York: Schocken Books.

Torrey, E. Fuller. 1988. *Nowhere to Go: The Tragic Odyssey of the Homeless Mentally Ill.* New York: Harper and Row.

Torrey, E. Fuller. 1995. "Editorial: Jails and Prisons—America's New Mental Hospitals." *American Journal of Public Health,* 85, no. 12:1611–12.

Tushnet, Mark, ed. 1993. *The Warren Court in Historical and Political Perspective.* Charlottesville: University Press of Virginia.

"2. Affirmative Action: History and Rationale." http://www.clinton2.nara.gov/WH-/EOP/OP/html/aa/aa02.html (May 2, 2002).

U.S. Commission on Civil Rights. 1976. *Fulfilling the Letter and Spirit of the Law.* Washington, DC: U.S. Government Printing Office.

U.S. Department of Justice. 1995. "Memorandum to General Counsels." June 28. http://www.clinton2.nara.gov/WH/EOP/OP/html/aa/ap-b.html (September 21, 2001).

U.S. Department of Justice, Bureau of Justice Statistics. 1997. http://www.soci.ni-u.edu/~critcrim/prisons/pris.pop (September 27, 2001).

U.S. Department of Justice, Bureau of Justice Statistics. January 16, 2001. http://www.ojp.usdoj.gov/bjs/correct.htm.

University of Chicago Law Review. 1971. "The Role of the Eighth Amendment in Prison Reform." *University of Chicago Law Review,* 38, no. 3 (Spring):647–64.

Veroff, Joseph, Richard A. Kulka, and Elizabeth Douvan. 1981. *Mental Health in America: Patterns of Help-Seeking from 1957 to 1976.* New York: Basic Books.

Wainscott, Stephan, and J. David Woodard. 1986. "School Finance and School Desegregation: Ten-Year Effects in Southern School Districts." *Social Science Quarterly,* 67 (September):587–95.

Walker, Samuel. 1990. *In Defense of American Liberties: A History of the ACLU.* New York: Oxford University Press.

Wallace, Donald. 1992. "*Ruffin v. Virginia* and Slaves of the State: A Nonexistent Baseline of Prisoners' Rights Jurisprudence." *Journal of Criminal Justice,* 20:333–42.

Ward, Mary Jean. 1946. *The Snake Pit.* New York: Random House.

Wardle, Lynne D. 1987. "Judicial Appointments to the Lower Federal Courts: The Ultimate Arbiters of the Abortion Doctrine." In Dennis Horan, Edward R. Grant, and Paige C. Cunningham, eds., *Abortion and the Constitution: Reversing Roe V. Wade through the Courts.* Washington, DC: Georgetown University Press, pp. 215–41.

Wasby, Stephen. 1995. "A Transformed Triangle: Court, Congress, and Presidency in Civil Rights." In James Riddlesperger, Jr., and Donald Jackson, eds., *Presidential Leadership and Civil Rights Policy.* Westport, CT: Greenwood Press, pp. 71–85.

Watts, Lewis, Howard E. Freeman, Helen M. Hughes, Robert Morris, and Thomas F. Pettigrew. 1964. *The Middle-Income Negro Family Faces Urban Renewal.* Waltham, MA: Florence Heller Graduate School for Advanced Studies in Social Welfare, Brandeis University, for the Department of Commerce and Development, Commonwealth of Massachusetts.

Welch, Finis. 1989. "Affirmative Action and Discrimination." In Steven Shulman and William Darity, Jr., eds., *The Question of Discrimination: Racial Inequality in the U.S. Labor Market.* Middletown, CT: Wesleyan University Press, pp. 153–89.

Welsh, Wayne. 1992. "The Dynamics of Jail Reform Litigation: A Comparative Analysis of Litigation in California Counties." *Law and Society Review,* 26:591–625.

Welsh, Wayne, and Henry Pontell. 1991. "Counties in Court: Interorganizational Adaptations to Jail Litigation in California." *Law and Society Review,* 25:73–101.

Whitby, Kenny. 1997. *The Color of Representation: Congressional Behavior and Black Interests.* Ann Arbor: University of Michigan Press.

Wightman, Linda F. 1998. "Are Other Things Essentially Equal? An Empirical Investigation of the Consequences of Including Race as a Factor in Law School Admission." *Southwestern University Law Review,* 28. Lexis-Nexis Academic Universe.

Wilkey, M.R. 1978. "The Exclusionary Rule: Why Suppress Valid Evidence?" *Judicature,* 62, no. 5:214–32.

Willie, Charles, and Susan Greenblatt. 1981. *Community Politics and Educational Change: Ten School Systems under Court Order.* New York: Longman.

Wilson, James Q. 1989. *Bureaucracy: What Government Agencies Do and Why They Do It.* New York: Basic Books.

Wilson, James Q., and George L. Kelling. 1982. "Broken Windows." *Atlantic Monthly,* March, pp. 29ff.

Wilson, William J. 1987. *The Truly Disadvantaged: The Inner City, The Underclass, and Public Policy.* Chicago: University of Chicago Press.

Witt, James W. 1973. "Non-Coercive Interrogation and the Administration of Criminal Justice: The Impact of *Miranda* on Police Effectuality." *Journal of Criminal Law and Criminology,* 64:320.

Wolf, Eleanor. 1981. *Trial and Error: The Detroit School Segregation Case.* Detroit: Wayne University Press.

Wolfe, Christopher. 1986. *The Rise of Modern Judicial Review.* New York: Basic Books.

Wolfstone, Gary L. 1971. *"Miranda*—A Survey of Its Impact." *Prosecutor*, 7:26–27.
Yackle, Larry. 1989. *Reform and Regret: The Story of Federal Judicial Involvement in the Alabama Prison System.* New York: Oxford University Press.
Yale Law Journal. 1963. "Beyond the Ken of the Courts: A Critique of Judicial Refusal to Review the Complaints of Convicts." *Yale Law Journal*, 72, no. 3 (January):506–58.
Yarbrough, Tinsley. 1985. "The Political World of Federal Judges as Managers." *Public Administration Review*, (November):660–66.
Yeazell, Stephen. 1987. *From Medieval Group Litigation to the Modern Class Action.* New Haven, CT: Yale University Press.
Zelnick, Bob. 1996. *Backfire: A Reporter's Look at Affirmative Action.* Washington, DC: Regnery Publishing.

Index

About the Authors

STEPHEN P. POWERS is a Research Associate at the Center for the Study of Social and Political Change, Smith College. He is coauthor, with Stanley Rothman, of a number of articles as well as *Hollywood's America: Social and Political Themes in Motion Pictures.*

STANLEY ROTHMAN is Mary Huggins Gamble Professor Emeritus of Government and Director of the Center for the Study of Social and Political Change, Smith College. He has authored, coauthored, or edited more than 15 books and 150 articles and reviews. His books range in topics from *Environmental Cancer: A Political Disease?* to *Prime Time: How TV Portrays American Culture.*